SHE'S IN CTRL

www.penguin.co.uk

SHE'S IN CTRL

HOW WOMEN CAN TAKE BACK TECH

ANNE-MARIE IMAFIDON

bantam

TRANSWORLD PUBLISHERS
Penguin Random House, One Embassy Gardens, 8 Viaduct Gardens, London SW11 7BW
www.penguin.co.uk

Transworld is part of the Penguin Random House group of companies
whose addresses can be found at global.penguinrandomhouse.com

Penguin
Random House
UK

First published in Great Britain in 2022 by Bantam
an imprint of Transworld Publishers

A CIP catalogue record for this book
is available from the British Library.

ISBN 9781787635029

Typeset in 12/16.5pt TT Commons Classic by Jouve (UK), Milton Keynes
Printed and bound in Great Britain by Clays Ltd, Elcograf S.p.A.

The authorized representative in the EEA is Penguin Random House Ireland,
Morrison Chambers, 32 Nassau Street, Dublin D02 YH68.

Penguin Random House is committed to a sustainable
future for our business, our readers and our planet. This book
is made from Forest Stewardship Council® certified paper.

Contents

Introduction

I was born in June 1989, just a few months after Sir Tim Berners-Lee invented the World Wide Web. So, although it's barely a memory, I do recall a time before the world went fully digital. You might too. Back in the analogue world, you memorized the phone numbers of your closest family and friends, or jotted them down in a book that lived next to the landline in the hallway. Every time you wanted to make a call, you had to dial those numbers, digit by digit. If you'd arranged to meet a friend at a certain time, you had to stick to your plans – you couldn't fire off a quick text to say you were running late, held up or taken ill. If you were the one who was waiting, you had to just sit tight until your mate arrived.

As a child, I was fascinated by how the things around me worked. Just like my peers, I was fond of asking why machines work the way they do, but perhaps less like other children, I would also try to take these machines apart. I was keen to find out exactly *how* the gadgets at home were put together, and my parents, to their credit, indulged my curiosity.

One thing led to another and I live my life today in the realms of technology and education. Because I've always been fascinated by technology – and curious enough to investigate it, experiment with it and take control of it – I sometimes forget that not everyone's like me. Rest assured that if you don't feel like you're good with tech, or if you're not really engaging with the tech that's becoming ever more important in our lives but are still curious, then this is a book for you.

Taking CTRL and understanding the benefits of the myriad digital elements of so many different parts of our lives, and their implications, can be extremely empowering – from the ways in which we organize our love lives and social lives, to how we manage our work, entertainment, healthcare and personal admin. Speed is an obvious advantage – the click of a button versus a lengthy phone call or, worse, snail mail – but there's also the range and depth of information we can access by using our digital skills. The quality of our work is enhanced by our understanding of the digital world. If you have technical literacy in a world that is becoming increasingly technical, your understanding will give you agency in certain scenarios, and will allow you to take CTRL of them. I lean towards using the process and motivation of curiosity to build literacy and then put your skills into action.

Curiosity has led me to all manner of boardroom tables, important meetings and exciting events. Within these pages I hope you'll discover just how significant a healthy dose of inquisitiveness can be. It inspires the work I do every day with Stemettes – the social enterprise I run, which encourages girls and non-binary young people, from the age of five and up, to pursue careers in science, technology, engineering and maths (STEM) – and it's led me to have amazing conversations with awesome technical women on my *Women Tech Charge* podcast. I've visited companies where I've tried to pull apart terrible workplace cultures and build them back in a better way. While my curiosity is no longer purely technical, it's certainly allowed me to take CTRL in a wide range of circumstances.

The world of tech is not without gatekeepers, however. There are many individuals out there who would like to say that tech isn't something that women are capable of engaging with. If we look back to the 1960s, a time when women couldn't secure their own mortgages or open their own bank accounts without involving their fathers or husbands to sign off on them, we can imagine how stymied our lives were. It wasn't just about women having control over their decisions, though – it was about how other people and *their* decisions had a direct impact on what we now consider to be a basic function of modern life. In the same way that you should be able to open your own bank account, you should be able to explore technology freely, make informed decisions about it, and also enjoy a basic literacy in it.

The scale of gatekeeping is deep rooted, spanning decades, and it remains a factor today. There are those who still believe that boys are naturally better at maths, science and computing than girls, even though the earliest computer programmers were predominantly women. From a very young age, girls assume that maths isn't one of their strengths and capabilities, and that logical tasks are performed better by boys.

Personal anecdotes from the Everyday Sexism Project high-light girls' experiences in technology spaces at school, where their teachers have dismissed their interest in STEM subjects and girls aren't expected to survive the computer science term. You might have first-hand experience of being viewed as strange for wanting to explore technology, of people suspecting you of being incapable of genuine or meaningful engagement. On top of that, popular imagery of STEM subjects can portray them as joyless spaces, so it's no wonder that girls can be inclined to reject them.

My ambition is to turn all this on its head. It's not just *my* ambition; I'm one of many voices from the industry and wider society that are urging women to engage with technology. We aim to support you by creating spaces for tech learning, and by sharing resources, our journeys and the joys of tech, while being honest about the tough times, the lowlights and the challenges. Despite those challenges, the world of tech is a powerful place to be. It can be fulfilling, it can be creative and, ultimately, it can be altruistic. The reasons for wanting more women to enter the tech world vary, but for me, it's about using technology 'properly' to better solve the problems of society. We can't leave it to the usual suspects. Let's face it – they haven't done technology proud. I know things can and will be done better when there are different voices in the room – including those of women.

●

When it comes to engaging with technology, the overall journey is one of comfort, competence and understanding – in that order. Initially, we are comfortable with what we have at our disposal – we embrace the improvements it brings to our lives. We move on to becoming competent enough to explore, challenge and question our tech. At this point, we're not experts – we know enough to feed our curiosity and take advantage of tech to make our lives easier. After this comes understanding. We are no longer scared and there is a corner of the digital world in which we fully embrace how, why and where it works, its applications, and what it means for our lives. The journey will continue as tech itself evolves and there becomes more for us to explore. At the end, we will have the tools to become comfortable, competent and understanding of new developments.

Understanding technology is crucial because it puts us in a good position to take CTRL. CTRL will be evident in the actions we are able to take as a direct consequence of the technical journey we have embarked on. At each step of this journey our capacity to take CTRL will increase.

Within these pages I'll show you why the tech journey is one worth taking, especially for women. We'll look at the challenges you might encounter along the way and highlight the kind of role you might take on as someone who is in CTRL. I'll provide thought experiments, support and guidance in the Getting Started sections at the end of each chapter for when you begin to exercise your taking CTRL muscle. The future is coming, whether women take a greater role in shaping it or not, but wouldn't it be better to be a part of the future, to ensure that the tech we make reflects our needs, enhances our skills and aids our learning? The world needs more women to take CTRL in the workplace, and by the end of this book you'll begin to imagine what the world could look like if that were to happen.

Dipping our toes into the world of tech is not as daunting as we might imagine. I'll hold your hand on the journey, inspire your curiosity and give you the tools to take CTRL of your future. By showing you how large a role tech currently plays in our lives, I'll demonstrate that our engagement and our pro-active choices will not only create tech that serves our individual and specific needs, but will also empower us to use our voices in ways we might not have imagined possible.

The premise of this book is that if you have technical literacy in a world that is becoming increasingly technical, your understanding will give you agency in certain scenarios, allowing you control of them.

As you begin this journey – and it's a lifelong journey – remember that it's not about learning everything at once. Curiosity is your foundation. Asking questions is key. Having the self-awareness to say, 'I won't ever know it all, but I want to know a little bit more,' will launch you on your way. And knowing a little bit more is better than knowing what you currently know.

So let's get started.

1

BE
CURIOUS

My questions as a child were endless. *How does that bus know which route to take? Why do we add those numbers together? Was it always going to be that answer when you added those two numbers together?* For me, maths was a way of exploring. Now, as an adult, my curiosity is just as strong. *Why are those people doing that? Why is that person homeless? And why do people not know how that works?* I'm still always asking questions, listening to answers, and processing everything I hear in order to tie elements together and look for patterns. It's natural to classify things so that we can try to understand what's going on around us.

You too might have been curious once upon a time, keen to explore ideas in the digital world, but you might have become more cautious as you've grown older. Perhaps because you were told off for asking too many questions, or because the repercussions of your tech mistakes were blown out of proportion. You might be worried about a big refund cost, about damaging something that can't be repaired or repeated, or about deleting something you can't recover. These scenarios can lead to a fear of making mistakes in the future, or seeing mistakes as something you might be punished for.

Sadly, it's not irrational to worry about being punished for slipping up. Various studies have found that women who make mistakes are more heavily penalized than their male counterparts. Male brokers at US bank Wells Fargo were five times as likely as their female colleagues to be investigated for misconduct, but 69 per cent of the women resigned or were fired as a result, compared with 41 per cent of the men.[1] Doctors referring their patients for surgery are far less likely to refer to a female surgeon who has had one bad patient outcome, but the same doesn't apply to male surgeons.[2]

It won't always be like this. The more women take CTRL, the less likely it is that we'll be punished for being curious. We've always been curious, so don't let anyone tell you otherwise.

My mother taught linguistics and English at a college close to where our family lived in East London, and my father was an ophthalmic researcher who spent all his time studying the eye and how it works. One of my earliest memories is being allowed to use his computer to type out the story of Little Red Riding Hood. I couldn't have been more than four years old, but I remember doing my best to reproduce the fairy tale on screen, using the keyboard to make the corresponding letters and words appear, and also adding my own personal touch – my lead character's hood was purple rather than red.

When I'd finished 'typing', I went off to do something else, but my dad saved the document. The next day, I was incredibly proud to learn that my version of 'Little Purple Riding Hood' hadn't just disappeared when the computer was switched off. My creation – probably gobbledygook – was still there, living inside the computer (as it seemed to me), and that was fascinating. What I find even more exciting is that if you were to find that computer today, plug it in and wait a long while, you'd probably still see a bit of four-year-old Anne-Marie in that file.

I was hooked. My curiosity led to a greater exploration of the electronic devices around the house, and a few years later I became fixated with our VCR (video cassette recorder). For much of my childhood, we had two TVs in the middle of one wall of our living room, one stacked one on top of the other and connected to the VCR. We'd use one to record TV programmes and the other to watch those recordings. Next to the TVs were piles of black rectangular video cassettes, each with a label detailing its contents. Cartoons and animated films were my favourites, especially Disney's *The Lion King*.

I'd watch very carefully as one of my parents would insert a cassette into the front of the VCR and then press 'play'. A family gathering that someone had recorded might appear on the screen, or perhaps Simba, Nala, Timon and Pumbaa would show up. I developed a fierce desire to know how the VCR knew what to play. And how was there enough space for the cast of *The Lion King* inside the machine? Were the characters inside the cassette?

One day, when I was on my own, I dismantled one of the tapes in the hope of finding the cartoon characters who, of course, never materialized. So I tried to put the video cassette back together again, which, of course, I couldn't.

I then went for the VCR itself.

Prying open the front flap of the machine didn't get me very far. Given how dark it was in there, I couldn't see much. Maybe I could answer all of my questions if I could actually get inside, I reasoned, so I popped the player onto the floor so that I could get a good grip on it; the plug came out of the wall fairly easily. Turning the machine on its side, I tucked my fingers inside the flap and held the top part firmly. My other hand went into the same opening and pushed down on the heavier part of the player. With a lot of pressure and an almighty *crack*, the top came away. I was in!

Lots of pieces of metal, little wheels, stiff ribbons of wire and small green boards lay before me. Still no sign of Pumbaa, though. What an anti-climax. I was planning my next move when I heard behind me a loud '*Anne-Marie?!*'

I'm thankful my dad didn't kill me.

The VCR never worked again. I might not have been able to put it back together, but I'd discovered its inner workings, and that brought me so much joy and entertainment. Trying and failing had taught me a lot, and now that the itch had been scratched, I set my sights on understanding the other tech in our house.

I ended up spending more and more time on the family's desktop computer, and one of the applications I discovered was PowerPoint. I'd use the mouse to click around the software and familiarize myself with its various functions. I'd fill in the heading field on a slide with a word or phrase from my school homework and list the rest of my homework as bullet points below. I'd then animate each bullet point, change its colour, make the heading bold, and generally play around.

I wondered whether the software might be a useful tool for my dad's work presentations. His job involved a lot of technology, to make it possible for him to look inside the human eye without having to cut it open. He'd often travel to give talks about his research; occasionally, the entire family would go with him to a conference and it was fun to feel like part of his entourage. He had a rack of slides to practise with at home – diagrams, statistics and text, all related to everything that can go wrong with our eyes. These slides were made from images that my dad had taken in the lab and sent away to be put onto film. They'd come back as little cartridge frames, a few centimetres square, and he'd have to pack them up to take with him for his presentation, careful not to get his fingers on the translucent film. Once at the conference he'd insert the slides into a carousel and project them onto a screen for the delegates.

Dad's presentations were the perfect opportunity for me to try out my new PowerPoint skills. So, using one of the numerous templates on offer, I converted his slides into a PowerPoint file. Still not having reached double digits, I didn't understand the ophthalmic language I was typing out, but the end result was the same, and everyone at the conference was impressed by Dad's 'futuristic' display.

These days, of course, It's par for the course to turn up to a conference with your slides on a USB stick, or even your own laptop, then plug in to present them. Back in 1998, Dad's contemporaries were curious about how he'd done it. Given how much easier a floppy disk was to carry, and that you didn't have to fly with those fragile little cartridges, they wanted to be able to present in that way too. So, at the end of one of his talks, my dad left some time for me to meet with his colleagues, and I ended up running a workshop for them. Nine-year-old me teaching a group of ophthalmologists how to use PowerPoint! It felt like a game – I was just a child who wasn't afraid to learn by trying and failing – but it was clear to me that tech was something these medical professionals feared. All the same, it was also something they wanted.

●

My childhood curiosity enriched the way I picked up other skills and increased my knowledge of all things technical and mathematical. My presentations at school always looked better than everyone else's thanks to my PowerPoint skills, and I was less afraid to try new things because I had the technical skills to resolve anything that did go wrong. At school I was known as the IT expert – always on hand to help with troubleshooting. If a teacher's presentation ran into problems, they knew who to call. And as my experience grew, so did my confidence.

The first time you clicked or tapped around your smartphone or computer, you probably used a step-by-step guide, which asked you to make choices for various settings, or showed you around the different features on screen. Building on my successes with PowerPoint, I'd click on every menu on the computer and navigate for hours. What's in the Control Panel? What's in Settings? Taking the time to click, read, scroll, click, read, go back, scroll – this was how I set about getting technical. What's behind that icon? What happens if I'm playing with the software and then click *this* or *that*?

Self-guided exploration of tech is a fun thing to do. Giving things a go in software and trying stuff out allows you to be as creative as someone who is learning to draw for the first time, and it was in this way that I got into databases. As a kid they were my favourite thing to play with. Using a workbook, I'd imagine an entire school. I'd create data tables of made-up classes, teachers, students, subjects and grades. In one data table were two Reception classes, which I labelled 'Blue' and 'Purple' and assigned a teacher to each; in another table were the Year 1 classes, and so on. I would then name all the students and place them within a class, and drill down even further by allocating homework to the students and awarding them grades. At the end of the exercise it was possible to see which student belonged to which class, who their teacher was and how well they were doing at their studies. The database came into its own when I held an imaginary parents' evening!

It was my equivalent of 'playing school' with dolls and stuffed animals for teachers and students, or playing restaurant with plasticine food and soft-toy customers. I also had a fictional company that sold trainers, with projects and a logo that I could use across all kinds of software. Exploring this way on make-believe projects meant that when it came to more 'serious' ones, such as coursework or homework, I felt better prepared.

Data is information and a database is simply somewhere to store that information, much like a bag that contains whatever you throw inside, but one which also organizes those items in a way that makes it easy to find what you need when you need it. What appealed to me about databases was that how you set up and structure them has an impact on how well you can retrieve information later on.

For my school database to give me the information I needed, I had to logically map out the full extent of the data that might be collected. I also had to do that right at the beginning because once there were ten thousand elements to juggle, I couldn't start making serious structural adjustments – it would have fundamentally changed with the information I removed. Databases: what's not to love?

My self-guided curiosity ran out of steam when there were no more grades to check at my pretend school and no new applications to explore. I'd built all the databases I could from my imagination and my dad was now creating his own Power-Point slides. What next?

The early World Wide Web became my step up. We'd recently got dial-up internet at home, and my newfound knowledge of how to navigate the internet meant that I could track down past exam papers for some extra practice, or could improve my French by looking up the context and etymology of new French vocabulary I was learning. The tech allowed me to do more than just rely on my own imagination, and because my curiosity and these skills are so deeply rooted, I still apply them to any situation I find myself in. That might be a board meeting that someone wants to join virtually and unexpectedly, or a visit to the supermarket when I want to get my shopping done as efficiently and economically as possible.

Around this time, and between AOL, Internet Explorer and Notepad, I started creating my own webpages from scratch. I taught myself using online tutorials. The brilliant thing about some technologies is that their very logical make-up means that you can look at their source and 'see behind the curtain'. Try it with your favourite website. Depending on how you normally access the web, you'll be able to find an option to View Page Source or Inspect Element, which allows you to see in all its glory the code that displays the webpage. If you do this enough times with different websites, you'll begin to spot some patterns.

Most of the time, the code will start with a series of tags, which look like this: <html> or <head>. You can search through the code for bits of the page you recognize, such as a heading, or words from a button. As I did this over and over again, I figured out how to interpret the code others had used to build their webpages, then I started to compile a scrapbook of lines of code I liked and wanted to use in the future.

For example, there used to be a really popular tag called <marquee>, which made text fly across the screen like a ticker. The first time I saw the words 'Get free ice cream' scrolling across a webpage, I chose the option to View Page Source, then did a search for the words 'Get free ice cream' in the code. I saw that the code actually read <marquee>Get free ice cream</marquee>, so I tried it out myself to see if I'd get the same results: <marquee>Anne-Marie loves East London</marquee>.

Just like that, my love for East London was soaring across my screen in a ticker I'd made. BINGO.

It wasn't too dissimilar to taking apart a VCR.

I'd use these tags to write code for my own webpages as part of my imagination-based projects. Some snippets would work for me, others wouldn't. I'd try to figure out why and, over time, I got much better at creating. As my confidence grew, I continued to look for more examples online and started to build even more complex webpages.

On the web, we use HTML (Hypertext Markup Language) to represent and display content, such as chunks of text, headings and images. As I went along, I would ask myself what else might I add to the webpage to make it look cooler, or how might I modify the elements already there. I'd make rainbow-coloured headings, for example, shift the images around and play with the layout. To inspire me, I started to look behind the source code of the pages I admired the most. It was then that I noticed they had extra styling added in, in a different language from the HTML I recognized.

This styling was in extra lines of code written in CSS (Cascading Style Sheet), which is a bit like make-up layered into the HTML-defined layout. All HTML pages are separated into two big chunks – one is the 'head', where much of the CSS is stored, and the other is the 'body', which performs the heavy lifting, such as displaying the text or images or showing the video. This CSS can be used to style a whole page, or many pages, and reduces the need to design each individual page manually. Let's say you want to ensure every main heading on your page is blue, for example. You could add the code for indigo whenever a large heading appears in your HTML, but with CSS you can condense instructions, so that a single line of code carries out complex commands.

Magpieing other people's code gave me knowledge of CSS to make my pages look better, before I moved on to JavaScript, an even more complex language that allowed me to animate and feature interactive webpages. Subsequently, the fearlessness I cultivated during my teenage years led me to the adult world of tech. Even though the stakes were higher, my fearlessness didn't abate, in no small part thanks to those skills and principles I learned through pulling apart tech and making databases and websites.

Even if things went wrong, I knew enough to sort them out. My capacity to save the day, solve issues, and create something new and better exists because of the time I have spent in the world of tech and the experience I have gained there. My life has continued to be a series of 'What can I take apart and try to rebuild?' scenarios, as I try and fail and learn along the way.

Seeing what happens when things break also helped me to develop resilience. Making mistakes is vital to making progress. Nothing is too complicated.

That being said, I'm always very conscious that I don't know everything, and I never will.

There are things I don't know about technology, or even about maths, which I studied at a really high level. That's because the beauty of technology is that it keeps changing, and it keeps moving forwards. There's a nice kind of tingle you get when you explore something new or hear a different perspective. You'll sometimes hear it in my voice, when I'm talking to a guest on my podcast, and I say, 'What? You're using it *that* way?'

Embrace that instinct to be curious.

Getting Started

At the end of each chapter you'll find some suggestions for how to get started on your technical journey beyond these pages. All of them are no (or very low) cost and have been put together to help get you thinking. You can do them in whatever time you're able to allocate.

Our individual circumstances vary wildly, so some of the suggestions will be easier to take up than others. You'll be able to multi-task with some of them, you might have to set aside a weekly 'CTRL hour' to try out others. There will be some you might spend ages on, and others you'll do super quickly. None of them are meant to stress you out or add to your workload without giving you some sort of CTRL reward in return. The more you're able to do, the greater the benefits you'll reap.

Fortunately, tech is a 'big thing', so there are many options when it comes to developing your curiosity on this journey. Cast your net far and wide. Give yourself an introduction to current tech trends and buzz. As with most types of knowledge and learning, there are so many avenues for exploring new 'techie' things. Experiment with them, try a few and then settle into your own rhythm of discovery.

○ Explore the myriad sources you might consult in order to fuel your imagination and learn. Do you read a newspaper regularly, or subscribe to a particular magazine? Does it have a technology section? Browse the magazine aisle in your local supermarket or newsagent more widely – does it stock any technology publications? Is there a

technology section in your local library? How about radio
shows and the TV you watch? Have you spotted any
programmes on technology? *The Gadget Show* is
available in the UK, and BBC's *Click* is broadcast
worldwide, with an accompanying podcast. Listen, watch
and absorb anything new you hear about.

- When I'm in ideas mode I love to keep a record of those
  ideas. I send my thoughts to myself, which is a habit I've
  had since I was little. There are lots of different tools that
  you can use to store your thoughts and knit them
  together, and I've used many of them over the years –
  from the Notes app on my phone/main device to sending
  myself quick memos via email, messaging apps or texts.
  You might also want to experiment with a special app that
  syncs notes across devices, such as Evernote, Google
  Keep, Notion or Trello. If you want to keep things
  analogue, start with paper and ease yourself into it.

- Use a variety of search engines. The main one folks
  recognize is Google, but there is also Ecosia, DuckDuckGo
  and Bing, all of which give you differing results lists as you
  search to find. Search is fantastic for discovering – as you
  build curiosity and go discovering, new terms will come
  up all the time. What should you search for to begin with?
  Try 'tech trends'. I love using Ecosia because the results it
  shows you are slightly different from other search
  engines, and with every search a tree is planted. So it's a
  positive-reinforcement habit – as you indulge your
  curiosity, trees are planted, which is always a good thing.

- Subscribe to technology-related newsletters. *Springwise* is one I recommend, and *Femstreet Insider* is another. Clicking around these news round-ups is a great use of your time. Carve out ten minutes a week just to sit and read and learn things as you go. It will become easier to navigate and understand what you've been told.

- Podcasts are great to listen to while you're doing something else. Search for 'tech podcast' online, or search in the podcast app on your phone or other mobile device. Pick an episode of any of the options that come up, and see if it works for you. One of my favourite podcasts is *Techish*, and I host one called *Women Tech Charge*.

- Videos. In addition to the well-known video platform YouTube, also check out Vimeo.

- Return to books, if you want to read and understand. Whatever the format, note down what you're reading in them. Do a bit of a deep dive on the subject.

There's no one right way to start exploring. We all learn differently, we all have different perspectives. You might well know that feeling of ending up down a Wikipedia rabbit hole – when you go to the site for one thing, and end up clicking through to a completely different entry. Take advantage of that time to exercise your curiosity and learn something that takes you beyond where you are now. There is so much to learn that you'll never get to the end of the clicks – you'll never see it all and learn it all. But that's exciting. There will always be something new on the horizon.

CHOOSE
TO
ENGAGE

As a family, the Imafidons normally spend New Year's Eve at a pentecostal church. It's a loud affair with gospel music playing, and everyone perfumed and in their brightest Sunday best, catching up with one another's news. Those who have known me and my siblings since we were children see us in church at least once every couple of years.

One particular year – I must have been twenty-two or twenty-three – an auntie came over to me just after the service had finished and said, 'Hey, Anne-Marie – how are you? Still doing all your little techie things?'

'Hi. Nice to see you again,' I said, hugging her. 'Yes, I'm doing my little techie things.'

I was being polite, but also thinking, *Oh, my goodness, my 'little techie things'? You know it's the twenty-first century, right?*

Everything we do these days is touched by technology in some way, whether that's the 'little techie thing' that allows us to get on the bus and knows automatically what fare to charge us for the journey, or the 'little techie thing' we keep in a wallet that means we no longer have to carry cash. There's also email, which saves us from having to post letters across the world and wait weeks for a response. You *can* send a letter, if you wish, but if you ping someone an email, in three seconds it's already half-way round the world.

By the time I had that conversation with my auntie, technology was already transforming grocery shopping in a major way. In the UK, we've had the option of grocery home delivery or click and collect at the four biggest supermarkets since the nineties. In 2009, 15 per cent of grocery shopping in the UK was done online, and by 2019, it was 30 per cent.

As well as your food, consider your utilities. How do you choose your gas or electricity provider? How do you decide upon the best deal, find out what this year's tariff is, or monitor your energy usage? Maybe you still get all that information in the post, but switching to a digital or smart meter means that you can get your reading to the nearest minute, and you may even receive a discount. You can track your usage for the week and see it displayed on a little device you're given. Paperless communication and a direct debit system operate in the back-ground, so if you've got that set up it means you don't even need to remember to pay that bill.

Or take job hunting: Job Centres now teach digital skills for finding jobs online – how to apply, where to see adverts, even how to use the database they use to search local jobs. Every-thing is done digitally – it's no longer about printing out your CV and sending it off, or taking it to different shops and busi-nesses like we used to. These days you prepare your CV digitally using a Word template, and upload it to one of the numerous job sites. Then you've got your profile and the job comes and finds you.

Looking for a new place to live? Of course, you can walk

into an estate agent's office, but you can also subscribe to an email newsletter. Select your preferences – the area you're interested in, your budget, how many bedrooms you're looking for – and whittle down their listings to those that suit you. You no longer need to take printed handouts, because the estate agents deliver all that information digitally. You can even search the sales history of properties on a particular street or in a particular postcode. These days, 95 per cent of home buyers use the internet to search for their next home.

I could go on, of course. We could talk about technology in the fields of insurance, banking, healthcare, self-care, entertainment . . . It's become the way we live our lives. Transactions, decisions, necessities and nice-to-haves – these considerations affect everyone across the whole of society.

I'm always excited about the practical applications of tech and choosing to opt in. Doing tech the right way means we can apply it to areas of our lives to make things slightly easier, more efficient, or more broadly usable. We'll touch on lots of examples in this book, but you might want to consider: What difference does technology make to my life? What does this progress mean and how can I get involved?

It's one thing to use technology, but given that tech is a tool, by its very nature we're also able to *make* it ourselves and actively participate. Hopefully this book will inspire you to get started on an active path, having made the most of your passive involvement. The full extent of taking CTRL involves getting active, creating, shaping and influencing technology.

When you start out, it can be hard to make and create. Sometimes you'll experience a mental block. But the more tech spaces you visit, the more events you get involved with, the more tutorials you do, the more you'll get into the habit of flexing your creative muscle.

Trying something out, taking something apart, looking behind it or lifting the lid on it is a really important part of practising with your tech voice. It's the same kind of vibe as songwriting. You don't just have to sing other people's songs, sometimes you can write your own material. Make and create: for your industry, for your pain point, for your mother, your sister, your aunt.

There will be different platforms for you to experiment with – depending on the type of technology you're exploring. Coding is a language like any other – made up of words, which are made up of letters. To communicate your meaning in any language, you type words letter by letter to make up sentences, bearing in mind the syntax, grammar and spelling as you go.

The computer Stephen Hawking used to communicate required him to spell out the words he wanted synthesizing into his 'voice', but certain frequently used words required only the touch of a single button, words such as 'hello' and 'goodbye' and probably 'quantum'. Coding is not so different – there are certain common instructions you will use time and time again. On a typical coding platform for non-beginners, you type the letters by hand every single time you want to issue a certain command, but a low-code platform, which you might want to experiment with at first, is one where you might click certain blocks of commands or a visual representation of what you are trying to achieve. A popular visual programming language we use at Stemettes, aimed at 8–16-year-olds, is Scratch. Its drag-and-drop interface that uses colourful blocks makes it one of the most intuitive programming languages to learn.

Low-code platforms require an entry-level knowledge of

coding (often visual, just like Scratch). If you're building an app for Android (non-Apple phones), then the MIT App Inventor is a cool low-code platform to explore. If you need to give coding a go at some point (why not, if that's where your curiosity has led you?), then you'll get making in a piece of software called an IDE (integrated development environment). This software will help highlight your code and check it for errors.

A no-code platform requires no knowledge of coding whatsoever. You simply decide what you want your website to look like, then select predetermined elements, detailed in plain English, from a drop-down menu in order to apply them to the text and any images. All the coding happens in the background. Website-building app Squarespace is an example of such a platform, and there are other no- and low-code platforms for all manner of technical creations, from games to virtual reality to mobile apps.

So whether it's the IDEs, low-code or no-code solutions that you use for making and creating, the more you try out, the more versed you'll become in user interfaces, how things might fit together and how software might work.

Essentially, computer code is a set of instructions for the computer to follow, written in a language very close to the computer's native language. For example, when you want to make a cup of tea, there is a set of instructions you have to follow – boil the kettle, put the teabag in the mug, pour in the hot water, wait, take out the teabag, add milk if you like milk, and so on. The same principle applies to computers. Instructions are entered and the computer will follow them, enact them, and repeat them again and again, without much further input from you (unlike a cup of tea).

There are many languages that computers understand, and which perform differing functions. Some process mostly numbers, others give you graphics or visualizations, and there are those that focus on interpreting music. These programming languages all have particular strengths and patterns of being written. A lot of precision and care is needed to write lines of these languages – lines of code – correctly, as each line performs a specific function in the grander scheme of what the code is trying to achieve. Each phrase can be looked upon as a building block – much like in our own human, spoken languages. It's a way for us to communicate with a computer to get it to do what we want it to do, in a repeatable way, and in a way that any computer with the same setup can repeat and enact when we're not there.

As with learning any language, over time you'll start to recognize some of the grammar, or some of the quirks in the way the language is written – from the use of capital letters to how spaces and indents may or may not matter. You acquire this kind of learning if you persevere with trying to make and create and play and use different platforms.

Technological improvement doesn't happen overnight. We might not fully understand some of the technologies in existence today, and we might feel apprehensive about their use. Being a technologist means taking your time, ironing out a way to apply it, or seeing more about how that technology works, and then working with it until it becomes part of what we have and what we can use in our daily lives. This message is something I hope you're able to take on and use as motivation as you opt in and choose to get involved. It's almost like getting on to the property ladder – the earlier you do it, the better. You'll be able to benefit from being engaged with it and understanding it for a longer period of time. And you'll only be able to resist it for so long before it starts to limit the way you live your life.

Let me give you an example.

Recently I found some coins lying around the house. I like living a completely cashless life, so I decided to take them to my local bank to cash them in. At the branch, I found myself in the queue behind a lady and her elderly mother. They were talking to the cashier and, because it was very quiet, I overheard the conversation.

The cashier was trying to help the ladies to set up an online account so that next time they could save themselves a trip to the bank and carry out the transaction themselves from home. As part of a series of questions, the cashier asked, 'Do you have an email address?' Both women replied, 'No, we don't.'

I remember being struck by the same thoughts I had when my auntie asked me about my 'little techie things': What are the implications for people who don't engage with technology, who don't have an email address, and who aren't able to communicate in that way?

There's no getting away from it. Technology's importance is increasing by the day. Have a think – on a daily basis, how often do you touch not just your phone, but other technology systems? When you call a customer service line, are you asked to key in a number to select an option? Or do you just say the number out loud and voice-recognition software tries to interpret what you're saying? Think again – is there any part of your life that technology has *not* been able to touch?

It's there in the small as well as the big. Technology isn't just influencing the personal elements of our daily lives, it's embedded in the way that bigger decisions about them are being made. In one dramatic example from 2018, Hawaiians were alarmed to receive a text message telling them to seek immediate shelter from incoming ballistic missiles.[1] Some ran for shelter, and some gathered their children into their most secure room and said their prayers. Others called their loved ones to say what they thought might be their last words.

Luckily, it was a false alarm. Someone at the state's Emergency Management Agency had hit the wrong button during a shift changeover. A correction was emailed out within twenty minutes, and a follow-up text message telling everyone not to panic was issued within the hour, but consider how quickly that information was disseminated in the first instance, and then pulled back using digital technology. Compare it to the way Boris Johnson wrote to every household in the country at the beginning of the Covid-19 pandemic – how long that took, how much it cost, and the effort required to post each envelope through front doors up and down the land.

Given all that technology makes possible – for us personally, for our locales, and for the world at large – and that its importance is increasing by the day, we're in the enviable position of being able to apply it to even more problems and situations. There's never been a better time to start being in CTRL.

In the 1950s, technology was used mostly by companies and governments. They were using computers and international communications networks for projects that entailed everything from sharing university research to processing data collected by spies. Back then, it was still possible for an ordinary person to live a completely analogue life, without the need for a computer or a telephone.

We're no longer in the 1950s and technology is no longer a

niche interest. It's become baked into how we live. (When you first read the title of this book, did you see the world 'CTRL' and spell out the letters in your head? Or did you read the word as 'control'?) A certain level of digital literacy is necessary to get along in life.

Some context for those digital skills: the basics of language literacy are listening, speaking, reading and writing skills. In maths, basic literacy comprises the ability to add, subtract, multiply and divide. In the UK, a good set of basics in digital literacy has also been agreed: an Essential Digital Skills Framework outlines what people should know ideally, in order to use technology effectively in their everyday lives.* Of course, the definition of digital basics is always expanding and evolving. What 'basic' meant five years ago is different from what it means today, and will be exponentially different in five years' time.

This digital skills framework was developed by Baroness Martha Lane Fox, who started the first online travel company Lastminute.com in 1998 with her business partner Brent Hoberman. In creating the framework, she took her mission – to get everyone online and digitally literate – into the House of Lords. Her plan for the skills everyone needs consists of five pillars:

1. Communicating
2. Handling information and content
3. Transacting
4. Problem-solving
5. Being safe and legal online

---

* Originally called Basic Digital Skills and drafted for the UK Government in 2015 by the digital charity Go On.

These pillars are underpinned by the digital foundation skills of knowing how to turn on your devices, your phone or computer; being able to connect to the internet using Wi-Fi; and knowing what kind of information and services you can find online. Some of that knowledge comes from a little exploration and practice, such as being able to use different controls, a mouse or a touch screen, and the ability to find websites. Some of it is to protect you as you explore, such as understanding why passwords are important and why you should keep them private and not write them on a Post-It note stuck to your computer screen.

You've clicked around your phone and your laptop, you've looked more curiously at the ATM, you've explored the different listening devices, such as Alexa, that you might have in the house. You understand how that device works as a piece of hardware, the logic of switching on and switching off again, you know what needs to be plugged in (or what doesn't) to connect to the internet. You know that you need some kind of infra-structure to be able to connect to the internet, whether that's a router or a data connection on your phone. You have your foundation skills.

So now let's look at the five pillars, one by one.

The first is communicating: how do you use digital to com-municate effectively with others? How do you use technology to communicate on a wider, societal level? So many of the benefits of technology come from the way it facilitates commu-nication and connections between people. As well as allowing you to stay in touch with family and friends, email and messag-ing services can enable you to interact with companies and institutions. Using email and communication software at work might involve learning new skills and new habits, such as creating and sharing documents or hosting online meetings. This pillar also includes the use of social media.

The second pillar covers handling information and content, which is essentially being able to find out what you need to know and being able to retrieve it at will. What we're talking about here is partly the use of devices and software, but also information: where do you get information from? How do you know it's the right kind of information? Can you trust it? Everything from learning how to store photos in the cloud, to accessing entertainment online and organizing files into folders forms part of this pillar too.

Being able to manage your money online is an essential digital skill, which is why the third pillar is transacting. Making purchases, paying bills, finding cheaper utility suppliers, or even applying for jobs all assume some basic digital skills, such as filling in online forms or checking whether a website is secure before typing in your bank details.

That being said, it's not all about performing routine administrative jobs using your devices. The fourth pillar is problem-solving. All the information that is online, all the human skills and knowledge, all the organizations that exist to help you, are accessible if you have the essential skills to find them and ask for what you need. That might mean looking up a YouTube video where somebody shows you how to fix your washing machine, or planning your work using a spreadsheet rather than doing it on paper.

Just as important is the ability to spot the gaps: the problems we can't solve using the digital tools that we have at the moment, or the problems created by the existing digital tools. Solving problems is also about working out the tech we don't currently have but need, and what tech is making things worse and therefore needs to be changed, or used differently, or replaced.

The final pillar is all about being safe and legal online. Learning good habits and skills protects you and your family or colleagues from being hacked or scammed, or from viruses infecting your devices. Although it's important to know your way around the tech, it's also important that your human or instinctive skills (sometimes referred to as 'soft skills') kick in and make you think twice when you get a weird message from a friend who suddenly needs to borrow money, or from HMRC informing you that you have to pay a penalty. As the second part of this pillar, we should all be making a habit of thinking of the legal implications before posting photos of children on social media, or taking an image somebody else created and using it on a website without asking them for permission first.

All five pillars are about agency, about being able to do things for yourself. You can communicate, you can find information and handle content, you can transact, you can solve problems, and you can keep yourself safe.

Most of this feels as if it should be well within the capabilities of most people, but according to the Lloyds Bank Consumer Digital Index in 2021, 21 per cent of 4,000 people surveyed in the UK lacked the full set of basic digital skills. Seven per cent of working adults were without basic digital skills and 8 per cent of people had no basic digital skills at all. Look closely at the Essential Digital Skills Framework.[2] What skills are familiar to you? Is there anything on it that's *un*familiar? Do you or anyone you know fall into any of these groups who are lacking in digital skills? Or do you perhaps have digital skills that you didn't realize you had?

Tech companies are household names. In 2019, according to 41 million consumers across fifty-one countries, the world's three most valuable brands were Amazon, Apple and Google.[3] You'd be hard-pressed to find someone who's part of society and hasn't heard of them. The highest-ranking non-tech brand, McDonald's, came in ninth place.

We've also reached the point where there is plenty of (even if not completely universal) access to technology. In 1995, 16 million folks were connected to the internet. Now, almost 5 billion of us (out of a global population of nearly 8 billion) can access the internet in some way. Users spend an average of six hours and forty-two minutes online each day. More than 5 billion people in the world own mobile devices.[4] Not everyone has access, even though everyone's lives are affected by this technology.

The pervasiveness of technology also means that the stereotype of who 'does technology' no longer makes sense. It's no longer purely about the maths genius in a shiny lab, or the kid in a hoodie sitting in the dark, tapping away on a laptop. Research from the Geena Davis Institute shows that the media representations we have aren't as diverse as they could be, or as life is.[5] The stereotype of a lone nerdy scientist in a lab coat, a mad scientist, a socially awkward white man, or even a dead white man, reinforces this idea that science, that technology, is a male pursuit and it's not for everyone. Those images don't just come from the media, though, they also come from our retelling of history. The thing is, tech is for everyone to engage with – people doing their grocery shopping online, banking online, moving their insurance policies and their utilities accounts to new providers, and texting their children. All kinds of folk are having to engage with technology.

Thankfully, in recent times the portrayal of the genius figure has being undergoing something of a makeover. Consider Rihanna's character in *Ocean's Eight* – Nine Ball – who is a computer hacker. Or even Shuri from *Black Panther*, who has a really good sense of humour as well as being responsible for running the technology for the entire fictional and futuristically innovative country of Wakanda. Those of us who are non-dead, non-white or non-men need to be, and have a right to be, a part of the technology picture. Opting out is no longer an option. And technology is not just for nerds.

No Option to Opt Out

The benefits of opting in to what technology has to offer are myriad. One example is the way in which we are moving towards cashless societies. In Japan, Spain and France, between 60 and 67 per cent of people prefer cashless payments.[6] I'm not saying you have to invest in bitcoin right away, but you probably already use digital banking, and you can send money around the world instantly, which means being able to travel, transfer money to overseas relatives, or trade with people in other countries.

Across East Africa, a banking app called M-Pesa allows people to send and receive money from their mobile phones. In leapfrogging the stage where you have to queue up in a building to pay in and take out cash, arrange loans, collect your salary or pay bills, M-Pesa makes all those services as easy as topping up your phone data or sending a text using 3G.

It's been really cool to see the growth of that kind of service across East Africa. By the end of M-Pesa's second year, 10 per cent of Kenya's GDP was being transferred via the app. Its success proves that you don't have to suffer some of the pains of innovation – you can learn from others, see those examples and build something better. Also, in the right environment it *will* be adopted – ten years in and there are 30 million users across ten countries and counting . . .

Let's return to the thought experiment from earlier, when we considered what areas of your life are untouched by technology. Think about the progress that's been made in them. Think about how satisfied you are with those areas of your life. Is there anything (perhaps efficiency) that you could gain by opting in to technology in those areas?

An understanding of technology can lead to things happening for people, whether it's starting up side hustles or businesses, being able to fix a car or sort out eyelash extensions. Technology continues to march on. Why wouldn't you want to be a part of shaping that, of informing progress and trying to make sure that it's better? Not just for the present you, but for the future you, for the people you care about, and for those who are to come.

When we were at school, it might have felt possible to opt out of technology completely. Especially if it wasn't on the curriculum. If it was an option at GCSE, you might have been forced to choose between technology and arts subjects. You might have felt that you either *got* science, or you didn't. You either *got* maths, or you were an arts person. They're all false choices. You can probably see now that all subjects overlap and blend into our understanding of life. Not getting maths at school doesn't mean that you don't understand the subject – it just means that the way it was taught, or the person who taught it, didn't work for you.

Regardless of your experience at school – if you didn't get on with your maths teacher, for example – you will still need maths in your adult life. Has a terrible relationship with a music teacher ever stopped anyone enjoying music as an adult? Part of my motivation for starting Stemettes was to provide a space for young people to have positive STEM experiences because they might not have had enough of them at school.

Stemettes works with girls and non-binary young people to broaden their understanding of technical fields and show them all the options that can result from an appreciation of technology. Since 2013, through programmes, events and online content, we've shown thousands of young people that even though science and maths are taught as separate subjects at school, in the real world they are interdependent. We also show our young people that technology can be applied creatively to solve problems outside of those subjects.

Take history, for example – we once held a Remembrance Day-themed coding event where a young woman built a poignant app that commemorated each life lost. Or home economics – we once ran a 'Food, Coding, Weekend' event where young women built apps to combat food waste. Or music? In collaboration with O2 and Abbey Road Studios we run AIGirlRhythm events that focus on the music industry's relationship with technology.

A lot of people talk about STEM, but in Stemettes we talk a lot about STEAM – that's science, technology, engineering, *arts* and maths. You need that breadth of subjects brushing up against each other to explore the richness of life, and the joy of being alive. The skills across all areas are transferable and additive, and go beyond what's defined in the curriculum – collaboration, creativity and the power of expression.

You don't need to be the 'best' at all of these subjects, but having a basic understanding or appreciation of them means that you're able to make better decisions. You're able to understand more about what's going on around you, you're able to do more and create more. Restricting yourself to saying I'm either *this* or *that* isn't really how life works. You're not a student of English *or* maths – you need to understand bits of both for a rounded perspective. Design and technology is basically engineering, but much of it is taught alongside the arts. And we're already beginning to see artists using technology such as Tilt Brush to paint in 3D and then print their creations in 3D too.

Let's choose to opt in. Let's choose to be curious about technology and understanding at least bits of it. Doing so in an open way will allow you to take it on as a new literacy. Understanding the world is contingent not just on the language you speak and having some kind of idea that one is less than ten, but also having some idea of a system, a technology, a science application that's gone practical. So use it as another means to understand, and to create new things.

So much of technology operates on a rule-based system. You'll learn or figure out what the rules are, and then you'll see how it works. After that, you can decide how you might take advantage of it, or how it can be operated fairly. The more you understand, the less the wool can be pulled over your eyes.

Imagine it's time for your car to get its annual MOT. When you're presented with the invoice, you're being charged for knowledge and experience you don't have – you're not a mechanic and so you have to take the word of the garage and accept that your car might need some work. You might be charged for unnecessary work, but you have no way of knowing that, because you're not an expert and the mechanic is, so you pay your bill.

The same thing can happen with tech, but the barriers to entry and learning are much lower and literacy is much more transferable. In this instance your poor digital literacy is being preyed upon. You might receive an email or a text out of the blue, asking you to click on a link. If you don't know that first-directbank.com isn't the legitimate domain name for First Direct (which *is* a bank), you might click through and find yourself being scammed. Or you might be paying for something online, but because you don't know that there has to be a padlock symbol in the domain bar while you're entering your credit card details, you might end up giving them away to a thief.

Some kids at my school (not me!) took advantage of their MS Word skills and forged their (bad) school reports to show higher grades. They were able to match the fonts on the original reports, which meant it wasn't that hard to recreate authentic-looking documents. The same trickery can be done with online phishing scams. It really isn't so difficult to create a legitimate-looking page that will pull the wool over our unsuspecting eyes. You'd have to access the Royal Mint's methodology to replicate a £50 note, but building a replica of Amazon's webpage is a much simpler task.

The other side of the coin is that the internet has changed the way we can now verify information. And if we make the effort we can become more aware and improve our digital literacy. If we think back to the 1990s, our reach was limited and time-consuming, often involving phone calls and visits to libraries. Today, if we wanted to check the correct domain name of First Direct, we have multiple sources we can refer to online.

For any domain, you can do a WHOIS lookup to see who owns it, when they acquired it, and from whom. In most countries you can also pull up the contact details of the person who registered the domain.

Knowledge is power. Technology gives us control, a higher form of agency, which comes from understanding what's going on. We're able to identify that fake website, do that research, sign that petition, check out Tripadvisor and choose a better hotel. Agency also allows us to discover, discuss, organize and challenge, and technology has ushered in a time when we have more agency than ever. We've seen the effect of a good understanding of technology in movements such as Black Lives Matter and MeToo, and for women experiencing domestic violence.

The hashtag #BlackLivesMatter has been used billions of times across social media, but it started with one person, Alicia Garza, writing a heartfelt response to the murder of Black teenager Trayvon Martin. When his killer was acquitted in July 2013, Alicia poured out her feelings on Facebook in a 'love letter to Black people', ending with the words, 'Black people. I love you. I love us. Our lives matter.' Fellow activist Patrisse Cullors turned her words into a pithy hashtag and, with Ayọ Tometi, they created a website and social media presence.

It was another tragic death in 2014 that sent #BlackLivesMatter viral, when a police officer in Ferguson, Missouri, shot and killed another Black teenager, Michael Brown. Hundreds of protestors took to the streets, and the social media message rippled out across America. By the end of 2014, Hillary Clinton used the phrase in a speech on human rights, and it became inseparable from growing protests against police violence.

Fast forward to 2020, and millions of people glued to social media during the pandemic viewed footage of the murder of George Floyd as he was held forcibly on the ground by police. On this occasion, the ripples were international. As well as physical protests, between 26 May and 7 June that year the hashtag was used 48 million times. TikTok reported 12 billion views for #BlackLivesMatter. What happened in the digital sphere led to offline public support and there were real changes that will have long-term impacts.

In the campaign to end violence against women, coding events have been held to build technology that can be used to either help victims and survivors or raise awareness. Take, for example, the day of the 2021 European Cup Final, when a clear link was established between the tournament and increased levels of domestic abuse. Instances of violence against women were estimated to have risen by around 38 per cent on the night England lost to Italy at Wembley Stadium. A good under-standing of technology enabled those involved in campaigning to mobilize and use social media to share such desperate data, raising funds and amplifying outrage as a result.

Breaking this type of news on the same social media plat-forms where football is being discussed, using the same hashtags as the Championship, means you are able to reach further, shout louder and be heard. It's a highly effective way of talking to a very wide audience.

Whether it's Black Lives Matter, MeToo, or any other way of folks being able to say, 'I have had this harrowing experience', and being able to share it, technology means you don't have to use existing structures. An understanding of technology allows you to go a step further and create a different structure yourself – to make something new, to build something or solve a problem.

With curiosity as your motivation and your process, along with the basics outlined in the Essential Digital Skills Framework, you'll be engaging with technology in a way that will open up new elements of agency and new elements of CTRL in a world that's increasingly technical. Regardless of what your experience of school was, taking CTRL *now* cannot be anything but an enriching experience.

Getting Started

Here are a few suggestions to help you start building your literacy, and never forget that practice makes progress. If you've never done anything technical before, these tasks will suit you down to the ground. You'll find some of them easier than others, and some will work better for you than others. Remember, different people learn in different ways from different platforms. If you try something and it doesn't stick, don't fret; try another task. The suggestions that follow have multiple options within them, you just have to find the option that suits you. Get practising and get literate.

- You could start, like I did, with the technology around you. Consider the devices you already own or have access to. Your phone. Your TV. Your car. Your dishwasher. Your TV services box. Don't have any devices? What about a computer at your local library? A friend's tablet? A (trusting and close) friend's phone? Do you have any old devices you're about to recycle or donate? Can you find a settings menu? Explore the different options in it. What does each one mean? Which settings can you control? If you have a phone, what apps came pre-loaded? Read online reviews of each of the apps, search for tips and tricks and guides on how to use them. As you do this, you'll notice that there are similarities between lots of things that you have access to – from the legal notice that always appears in 'Settings > About' to the Privacy and Data settings available on anything that connects to the internet. Do the same thing with websites you access regularly. Click around them – are there any sections you've never seen or looked at before? What's in them?

- On one particular day, be sure to explore the technical side of the everyday things you're doing. Does a particular service you use – your transport provider, or where you buy your food or clothes – have a website? Does that website look different when viewed on a mobile device? Does the service in question also have a dedicated mobile app? What are the differences between each platform? What is available on each one? Do they require any other aspects of tech? Like a headset? Or a camera? What permissions and parts of your phone does the mobile app require access to?

- Refer back to the Essential Digital Skills Framework discussed in this chapter, or look it up yourself. How many foundation skills do you already have? As much as you might not see yourself as a technical whizz, it's possible you're already much more literate than you realize, by virtue of being alive in the twenty-first century.

- Digital inclusion became a hot topic during the pandemic but has been widely identified as an issue and worked on by governments around the world for some time. Check to see what resources are available for those in your local community who aren't literate or who don't have digital access. Libraries, banks and schools/colleges are all places that may offer some basic help and a space for you to explore the full range of digital skills for free. Big tech companies have also got in on the act, so don't be afraid to access local resources and make the most of free sessions and classes. Basic digital skills are a foundation for higher and more advanced digital skills, and when you know you have them, it'll be easy for you to pass them on and support others.

○ Have a go at the following exercise, to see how you handle information: try to find the nutritional benefits of the last meal you ate. How many conflicting opinions can you find?

3

WHOSE GATE IS IT ANYWAY?

Another reason you might have felt like opting out is the fact that tech, like many things that give you power, has a lot of gatekeepers. And no, it's not just in your mind. There are lots of folks out there who would like to say that tech isn't something that we, as women, are capable of engaging with.

Hedy Lamarr, the Hollywood actor and inventor, was often told this. She had great ideas, to which she brought her technical literacy and creativity, but was consistently told by producers (and her first husband) just to sit there, look pretty and read her lines. Like me, Hedy Lamarr liked to learn how things worked by taking them apart – when she was five she took her music box to pieces. She also had a father who encouraged her to be curious. Her mother was a concert pianist, though, so – unlike me – Hedy had ballet and piano lessons and went into the performing arts. Austrian film director Max Reinhardt discovered her at the age of sixteen and, after moving to the US, she became a Hollywood star.

Her curiosity and technical ingenuity never left her. She even invented between takes, in her trailer on set. Working with inventor George Antheil, one game-changing invention was improved torpedo-guidance systems that used frequency-hopping.' Together they co-invented 'spread-spectrum frequency-hopping'. During the Second World War, the Americans were trying to communicate over long distances with their teams in Europe, but their methods were unsophisticated; if the channel they were using was intercepted, the whole message was revealed. Imagine a long cardboard tube; if you were to roll a marble from one end of the tube to the other, it would flow through very smoothly. If the tube were cut along any part of its length, the marble would fall out.

Hedy Lamarr figured out that while changing radio stations, and flicking between different frequencies, she could pick up the odd word. She imagined a spy system whereby the receiver might flip from specific channel to specific channel, catching a single word from each, which would eventually, when put together, form a complete sentence, like cutting the tube at various points so the marble, so the words of the message, might drop. She invented a system in which part of the message intended for communication was on one channel, a little on another, and so on; all the receiver had to do was hop between frequencies to hear the whole message. It would thus be much harder for communications to be intercepted, because listening to only one channel would reveal only part of the message.

Sadly, her technology wasn't used immediately – it took a long time to secure the patent and for the technology to be adopted. Today, however, this is how wireless communication works. In fact, Lamarr is sometimes called 'the Mother of Wi-Fi', and it's a great shame that you might not have heard of her. We use this kind of communication for Bluetooth, for GPS, and for across distances – it's a very solid principle for wireless digital communications.

It's sad to think that Hedy died bitter and frustrated because her curiosity was quashed throughout her life. Every time we connect to Wi-Fi, we should thank her for her invention that makes it possible.

Like Hedy, you might have experienced gatekeeping, but in the form of unhelpful maths or science teachers, unhelpful remarks from parents or peers, or unhelpful comments in the media. It's why we've ended up with so many individuals thinking they're not technical. After all, it's hard to ignore all the subliminal messages telling us that tech is this distant land for magical people who are overwhelmingly white and male. It's a problem to the point that, when asked, 78 per cent of students couldn't name a woman working in technology. Only 16 per cent of the female students surveyed had had a career in technology suggested to them, compared to 33 per cent of the male students. And only 3 per cent of those girls said that technology was their first choice as a career, versus 15 per cent of the boys.[2] The fact she *isn't* in CTRL is an intentional issue we'll come back to later on. Gatekeeping is when others control access to resources, power and opportunities. Technical gatekeeping is when folks restrict access to technical spaces and try to take control of you and your destiny, including your technical capabilities, in a way that they're not entitled to.

A huge amount of gatekeeping happens across the technology industry, and certain people with power or agency try to make newcomers, or others who might have taken a different route into the industry, doubt their abilities or the value of their contribution to decisions being made in the technical space. These gatekeepers try to embed the idea that they were 'born' with coding or technical gifts that can never be attained by those they deem unworthy. This is wildly frustrating to someone like me, who learned to code, and I'll tell you why. Let's start with storytelling as an analogy for writing code.

Imagine that every time you write a story, you go, as a starting point, to a certain book that contains all the answers on how to write a good story. You're looking for, say, how to write an archetypal villain. Inside this book, you find, in all its descriptive detail, a readymade villain. You pull that – the bare bones of the character – into what you're writing, and start your creative process from there. As you go on to write your story, every time you get stuck for ideas, need to work out what the talking cat does next, or figure out how to make the characters live happily ever after, you can return to that book for help.

In the same way, an alarming amount of tech code is put together using material that already exists in a forum called Stack Overflow, where coders seek help from one another and give suggestions on how to solve coding problems. As it's a forum, the advice stays up there and is searchable. The chances are that if a coder searches for their issue on Stack Overflow, someone else has already asked the same question there and had a workable solution proposed involving some lines of code written by someone else, and which might work to achieve the results they'd like for their code project.

The great thing is that Stack Overflow isn't just for a few beginners. Research by the Fraunhofer Institute for Applied and Integrated Security showed that in a particular year, 15 per cent of all Android apps contained security-related code snippets from Stack Overflow.[3] One study found that when coders get stuck on a coding problem, 90 per cent of them visit Stack Overflow. Fifty-four per cent will do other work first, then come back to the problem later. Forty-nine per cent will call a co-worker or friends. Fifteen per cent, funnily enough, play games. But the key point is that 90 per cent of them end up visiting Stack Overflow at some point in their workflow. So you've got to think: they're all looking at this one resource for answers, and it's accessible to anyone. It's not just for the 'coding geniuses' to reference.

The thing is, Stack Overflow isn't something that many individuals working in the technology industry want you to know exists, especially if you're going to go into development as a newbie. They won't want you to know about the place they go to find a lot of answers and to stash a lot of their thoughts. They want you to think their coding knowledge is something innate! And – here's the key point – not innate to women.

Gatekeeping is a power play. It's more than saying, 'I've spent a little bit of time doing this, I don't want just anyone to be able to walk in and be a part of it, so I'm going to hoard it and keep it for myself.' It's not only about proactively hoarding but also the assumption that gender is related to technical competence, even when women have jumped through all the necessary hoops to become technologists. It's gone on for so long that generations of individuals still genuinely believe women aren't technical.

One example of the prevalence of this belief is GitHub, an online development platform where people can store and share their code snippets – almost like an online library. You have your own profile with your own scrapbook of code, which you can share with others and use to work on bigger projects together, collaboratively. Research says that women's contributions have a higher acceptance rate than men's; however, when you can tell by a person's username that they're a woman, that rate drops noticeably.[4]

A developer friend of mine has had first-hand experience of this sexist bias, at work. In one job, every time she submitted a piece of code to their workplace equivalent of GitHub (a process known as 'committing'), one of her male colleagues went in, rejected her code and rewrote everything she'd done, in his own way. Imagine what that must feel like. It happened to her on a daily basis. This kind of intervention doesn't even happen in secret, but out in the open – there is an audited trail of someone undermining you. The sad consequence of this behaviour is that we don't have as many lines of code written by women, from women's perspectives, embedded with their assumptions or their approach to coding.

There's a definite smoke-and-mirrors element to it all. For something that should be all about logic and objectivity, there's a lot of psychology at play, and a lot of expectations and assumptions being imposed on other people. None of it was inevitable, though. The shift was intentional.

If you're fortunate enough to find yourself in a room with individuals who are old enough to remember the beginning of the technology revolution, when computer programs were written – physically written – on punch cards, they'll tell you things were different back then. Punch-card work was very female focused. When the US census was first tallied by punch cards in 1890, the machines were originally operated by a day shift of women and a night shift of men. When it turned out that the women on the day shift were 50 per cent faster than the men, the night shift was dropped and the workforce became predominantly female.

It's just one of many examples of how social constructs affect women. Did you know that after the introduction of gender-neutral children's clothing (to help with home economics and reusing clothes for newborns), the colour blue used to be popular for girls, and pink/red for boys, until marketing departments determined after the Second World War that pink was more feminine and blue was for baby boys.[5] It's led us to believe that girls liking pink is somehow an innate preference. To illustrate this point in the technology sphere, we might go back in time to the 1990s when it was decided that games consoles should be marketed towards boys and men, who, it was also decided, had more expendable income for 'boys' toys'.

These decisions inadvertently created the male-dominated gaming subculture in tech that still persists today. To follow the logic: If you were playing with games consoles at home, you would know how, for example, to solve glitching during a game. Boys were spending a lot of their spare time playing with technology and were therefore more likely to be hired for their tech skills by tech companies.

Gaming became such a significant part of the tech subculture that anyone who wasn't a big gamer was also considered not to be a real techie, and therefore not entitled to enter tech spaces. These environments became intolerant, aggressive, and generally exclusionary towards girls and women. If a woman did make it into tech *and* was a big gamer, she was generally assumed to be thick-skinned enough to put up with the bullying and harassment she almost inevitably encountered there.

The gaming industry is big business. Revenue there is higher than in film, TV and music combined, it's grown, and yet, if you're not playing a particular type of game, you're not considered to be a gamer. The gatekeeping implications are vast, and partly because marketing departments on tight budgets had to decide what boys do and girls don't do. It's no longer sustainable.

Consider the 5G mobile network, or some of the newer experimental technologies that will soon become fully industrialized and fixtures in our infrastructure. There simply aren't enough individuals coming through the current training schemes, such as apprenticeships or chartered degrees, to actually fill the workforce gaps and service these products. We're going to have to break out of gender stereotypes to keep these industries safe, ticking over, innovating, or even being built, because there's a bar of outdated criteria excluding not just women but other underrepresented groups from taking up space in the field.

The more central to our lives that technology becomes, the more important it is that lots of different people – not just different genders – are keeping an eye on what's going on and who's building what. The future is coming, and what the current gatekeepers, who don't adequately reflect society, are building is affecting all parts of our lives in all sorts of ways. It's therefore crucial that we take a seat at the table. It matters if we're to make progress with politics, it matters if we're to make progress with healthcare, it matters if we're to make progress with education. And it matters if we're to make progress with technology.

I've become a bit obsessed with the future. Not only because it's what I'm preparing Stemettes for, but also because so much of what happens next is, as yet, undecided. Whenever I speak to audiences, I always talk about the future because I want us to keep our eyes on the prize. We're building what happens next, we're solving problems. And we're taking steps with every line of code we write – with every new launch and every solution proposed, we're taking a step in a specific direction.

You can contribute to that direction, and you can shape the future. What impact do you want to have? What future would you like to see? What does 'better' look like? What are we aiming for? When you think about five, ten, twenty years into the future, what do you imagine? What problems have been solved? What's new? What role is technology going to play in that?

I'm not saying you have to become a developer – in the same way that you don't learn English to become Shakespeare or Jane Austen. You learn English so that you can read signs, navigate, get yourself around and set your own narrative. What I am saying is that failing to engage with technology is detrimental to you because your perspectives, the things that matter to you and the things that keep you safe aren't necessarily being built into that technology. You are not an island – there are many like you, who share your needs. So many others, as well as future generations, will be let down if your views aren't taken into account. There are only downsides to non-engagement.

Let's take seat belts, for example. They were designed to save a man's life, with his stature, weight and generally bulkier proportions taken into account. If we further extrapolate this approach to product development, we might consider driverless cars, where the entire vehicle is technology-based. We must ask, in what ways might women's lives be affected if we are left out of the equations used to design driverless cars? Maybe you won't be recognized as a human being and be struck by a driverless car? Maybe the buggy you're pushing won't register as an object to avoid if there's an imminent crash? If driverless cars aren't being built to recognize that a human being with a buggy is actually two human beings, the impact on many women's lives – you and other people like you – would be catastrophic. The implications of poor technical decision-making are far-reaching.

We can also consider technology used to measure your performance in the workplace, and if it takes into account that, as a woman, you visit the loo more often when you're on your period. If frequent use of the toilet is one of the variables the technology is measuring for performance, you might be penalized. If the person setting up this system didn't take menstruation into account it will impact you, others who are also on their period, and the people who are yet to work at your company who have periods. It will also affect the male manager who doesn't consider women on their periods. How will he manage and motivate the workforce if he is inadvertently penalizing the women in his team? Loo breaks come up time and again. Whether it's Uber or Amazon, you can pee in a bottle if you're a man, but what are female delivery drivers doing?

It's Exciting to Create Tech

When we talk about the importance of technology, it's not just about using it – as great as tinkering with gadgets may be – it's also about how creative we can be with it.

I'm still excited to know how any of the websites, or anything I've created over the years, live on, almost as though they're my children. (I'm saying this as someone who hasn't had children.) My creations are living on without me. People are continuing to access tools that I've created. Their technology, structure and logic mean that users will always see the same version of the website – I don't need to be there to hold it up.

You dream up something, you make it, and it exists. Whether it's a digital product that gives you recipes to use up the leftover produce at the bottom of your fridge, or a physical product to measure your blood oxygen levels, the buzz that comes with creating tech and seeing other people benefit from it is immensely satisfying. That being said, I also think there's a secondary excitement that comes with the act of creation – solving problems and finding solutions . . .

I have a vivid memory of being ten years old, sitting my maths GCSE in the exam hall at a local boys' school. There were two papers – one to do with a calculator, one to do without. I remember the silence, turning each page, working through the problems, really enjoying knowing what I was doing. What will they ask me next? OK, cool. I can do this. I also saw certain problems (looking at you, Circle Theory) and remember thinking, 'I don't like those but I'll just keep going.'

The excitement I felt came from solving those problems and getting an answer – not necessarily knowing whether it was right or not, but getting an answer all the same. Being able to follow a process, and seeing what came out at the other end, not having known what the problem was going to be when I woke up that morning.

A few months later came the delight of hearing I'd passed. I wasn't cocky enough to assume I had it in the bag. It was a surprise, because even though the examiner didn't know a ten-year-old had written those answers, they had still found them good enough. That day the surprises kept on coming: finding out I didn't have to do the washing-up for a week was amazing (as the eldest of five, I had to do a lot of chores at home, because for a long time the others were too young to help out) and then my dad treated me to a McDonald's.

Tech creation gives me the same problem-solving buzz. For me, it has always been about turning the page to discover the next challenge and working out how to solve it. It's all about the creation and not knowing what will happen next.

Given the chance, would you want to create and shape the future? Imagine a world where you have the skills to take CTRL, to improve your life, to make things slightly easier or fairer for whoever's coming after you. Imagine having tech skills as a tool to achieve this.

Whether it's the mobile phone, the ebook, systems that allow you to make global transactions or send an email across the world, tech gives each of us the ability to create, to make a mark, to leave a legacy. That being said, as much as we talk about the future, making and creating tech can also have an effect on the present.

Imagine you're on a bus and you see a fellow passenger wearing a beautiful necklace or an amazing skirt. You ask them, 'Where did you get that from? That's really cool.' And they reply, 'I bought it in Italy five years ago, so I don't know if you'll be able to get it.' Jenny Griffiths, software engineer turned entrepreneur, solved the problem of tracking down items that grab your attention with her visual search engine Snap Vision.

Jenny's journey started in childhood, with her curiosity and creativity encouraged by her parents.

'The first toy that I remember was a little plastic car,' she told me. 'It had an aerofoil at the back, which you pulled off, and inside was a screwdriver. You could then take the wheels off the car and open up the bonnet. I think my parents were really conscious that they didn't just want me having "girl toys". My dad's an engineer, my mum's a teacher specializing in maths. So I grew up going to all of these museums, seeing what people have invented.'

What Jenny saw on her family outings inspired her own

dreams. She grew up wanting to be an inventor and wrote to companies with her ideas – to Birds Eye, for example, about dog-shaped waffles called 'woofles'. However, as she got older, she started to revise her career plans. Teenage Jenny didn't believe that being an inventor was a real job: 'I didn't think you could just invent products for a living.' The idea of being able to create your passion every day seemed too good to be true. She set her sights on becoming a scientist or an engineer instead.

The seed of an idea took hold when she was studying computer science at university. As a fashion-conscious student on a budget, Jenny identified the perfect problem for her computer science skills to solve. Her lecturers were talking about computers of the future that would be controlled with gestures. A shrug would mean one thing and a double shrug would mean another. It all sounded cool and futuristic, but the near-term tech was going to be cameras. Computer vision and the ways in which you could use that technology got her particularly excited.

> I had that pull back to my childhood of suddenly thinking, 'This is an idea that I've completely fallen in love with.' I think, for me, that was my personal eureka moment of seeing that everyone's going to have a camera in their pocket. With fashion, you can read fashion magazines, but it's inherently your vision that's telling you whether you like something or not. So tapping into an inherent human behaviour is where I got really interested in applying this field of science that I loved to an industry that I loved.

The idea was snap and search, where you take a photo of an item of clothing you like and use it to find something similar online. Inspired by her fellow students' limited budgets, the idea was basically to get the look for less. Read *Vogue*, manage to buy it in Topshop. Her final eureka moment was when she started talking to all her friends, especially the women, who told her, 'Oh my God, I need this in my life.'

From that student project, Snap Vision emerged with Jenny as the CEO. She has since been awarded an MBE and won the Royal Academy of Engineering silver medal in 2019. Like me, she thinks it's important that more women get involved in creating tech as well as using it: 'If you're going to change massive problems in tech, like bias in AI [artificial intelligence] – the one that I'm obsessed with – women have to be there from the beginning, inputting as much as men, rather than just being really adept at using it on the other side.'

Making decisions involves understanding an input, such as music, images or another type of data, processing it, and then coming to a conclusion each time. Where traditional coding means laying down a precise set of instructions to be followed, many substrands of the wider artificial intelligence field aim to be less precise in instructions, and let the computer 'figure things out' on its own.

For Jenny, the fact that something like Snap Vision hadn't been invented until she created it is a symptom of women's absence from creating and inventing technology. She went on to explain that even though online fashion is a huge industry, worth £8 billion a year to the UK economy, she still took a lot of flak for creating a visual search for fashion. *Ah, you're a woman, you just love shoes!* She assured me that she's relatively thick-skinned: 'Shoes or handbags, I don't care – this is a huge bit of society that wants a product. And it's a huge economic problem that needs to be solved. If people can't find what they're looking for, they can't buy it.'

Jenny had clearly recognized a gap in the market for something that not only benefits customers (predominantly female consumers at that) but also has a more general economic function. She believes that there are certain areas of computer science where it takes quite a bold person to move into them, because they know that there's stigma around doing engineering for women. In her mind, if women had been there from the beginning of e-commerce, we wouldn't have the problems that we have with it now. The experiences would be nicer, the technology would be better. Instead, in the tech world, a £4,000 handbag is sold in the same way that Amazon tries to sell a cheap toothpaste.

'I don't think that we'd be in that situation at all if women had been in on the ground,' she told me. 'In real life, £4,000 handbags wouldn't even be sold in the same shop as cheap toothpaste. The experience around the purchasing and the way you make your decision for either product is very different.' However, the person who built the website selling both has probably never bought a luxury handbag in a real shop and doesn't know that consumers might have a problem with a simple drop-down menu with click-to-select colour options. It's fine to sell expensive bags online, but if the developer had had the real-life experience or at least talked to someone who had, they might have tried to replicate a similar, more high-end experience online.

When we train our algorithms, we have to look at what makes this dress *this* dress. I have to explain to my team – who are brilliant – what the difference is between a cropped pair of trousers and ankle grazers. We have these weird, hour-long conversations around how women shop and how women look at clothing, and why an ankle grazer's different to a pedal pusher.

Training Jenny's algorithm involved feeding in lots of images. Imagine you're studying to be a chess master, or a memory master or an athlete; you repeat the moves, the tests, the exercises, over and over again, and then examine your results. How does your chess game pan out when you move your queen early compared with when you don't strike out with it? How well do you run your races when you drink a glass of orange juice beforehand versus when you don't? Over the hours and different iterations, you start to learn more and more about what works and what doesn't. An algorithm is trained in the same way, but rather than it being about learning over time, you train it on images – dresses, for example. Does the algorithm recognize polka dots or not; does it recognize a peplum? It's trained by being shown lots of images of a peplum, and then presented with another dress and asked if it has a peplum. Over time it will figure out exactly what a 'peplum' is.

Because Jenny grew up reading fashion magazines and talking to her mates, this kind of knowledge was inherent. However, because there just aren't that many women in tech, she found herself needing to step into the role of representing women a little bit more. 'And I'm in one tiny niche – fashion – but if you think about that multiplied across a load of different niches that men won't have been as absorbed in, there's a huge knowledge gap in the inherent learning of being a woman, or being a girl growing into a woman.'

Jenny's technical innovation has proved useful in fields

beyond fashion. 'The secret sauce behind fashion is being able to do shape recognition really well,' she told me. 'What makes this jumper *this* jumper? Is it the neckline, is it the cut, is it the sleeves?' But shape-matching is important in other industries too.

Jenny made a 'proof of concept' with Innovate UK, the government's funding body for innovative research, around the question: Can you find prohibited items in X-ray images? A proof of concept is not strictly a technical term, more of a business term. If you are innovating, you first make a smaller, less complex version of your product with far fewer resources, to show how it would work, before you go ahead and make the full-scale system or product. Jenny showed that her technology, when used at airport security, could distinguish a trigger from a gun, and the pin from a hand grenade. It was a far more sophisticated tool than those trained to identify entire AK-47s shoved into bags.

One day, your bag might be scanned at an airport and Jenny's shape-recognition technology will be checking it for suspicious items. It's so exciting that technology that was created to explore fashion could soon also be used to save lives.

Beyond fashion and security, Jenny's invention is also having an impact on healthcare. In a trial Jenny was involved with for diabetes medicine in the US, she and her team were trying to combat the illegal sale of blood sugar monitors online. Patients who were prescribed these monitors were selling them for revenue, which meant that these people weren't getting the treatment they needed. Jenny was able to work with eBay, or any online site where there are images, and look at all of that imagery.

If Jenny's snap-and-search program recognizes a box of medication for sale illegally, the company can act to get the listing taken down. This helps the pharmaceutical companies and the insurance companies, and the patient is encouraged to take their meds rather than sell them on.

Jenny's innovation illustrates perfectly how tech is in the big and the small. You can make a big difference by solving a small problem for a lot of people. Maybe it's not about finding the perfect skirt, or looking for desperate people reselling their medication online. It might be about being able to make something that allows you to fish more sustainably, or something that helps you make the perfect cup of tea. Your digital literacy can help you to enjoy the 'now' a little bit more, despite the gatekeepers. We can be inspired, right now, as women, to get stuck into making and creating through the myriad ways in which tech is shaping our world, which we will explore in the following chapter.

Getting Started

When you experience or witness anything that looks like gatekeeping, bear in mind that 90 per cent of the time the gatekeeper is preying on your ignorance. This shouldn't make you feel inferior – they don't have all the answers. They can't keep all technical knowledge and technical environments for themselves. This is your space. This is for your agency, and for others around you. Let that motivate you and keep going.

- Develop the habit of carving out ten minutes each week to watch something technology-related on YouTube, or a platform of your choosing. (A little tip to make more efficient use of your time if you're watching a video or listening to a podcast is to play it back at a faster speed. I'll play at 1.25x or 1.5x normal speed, because people often pause a lot when they're speaking.) As you take in what you're watching, think about how it applies to what you're doing at home, at work, with friends. Be infectious with your newfound knowledge and share it with others – what you're learning and what you've been curious about, and what you've been thinking. It's not nerding out, it's skilling up.

- Reflect on the gatekeeping you've experienced so far in your life. Now do the same for your tech life to this point. Who has made you feel inferior? What environments have you experienced where you've been made to feel less than? What language has been used to exclude you?

Looking at those spaces now, how many of the same people are doing the same gatekeeping? How much of that language and those assumptions are still being employed now? Where is your [insert STEM subject] teacher now? What was the crux of their argument and approach?

Whether this gatekeeping was intentional or not, it won't stop you for much longer, not with all the curiosity you've been able to indulge, and the fact that you're reading this book. Next time you feel like you're being pushed away, turn away/leave/exit the resource of your own volition and actively find another. Then resolve to include and bring others in on the spaces and resources that do work for you. As you travel on this CTRL journey, keep an anti-gatekeeping stance in mind. As much as others have pushed you out, being in CTRL is about bringing others in, no matter what level of technical knowledge you possess.

- Flex your creative muscles. What's the tech equivalent of writing a poem? Maybe it's creating a new logo for your favourite product, or making a really simple app to help you solve a problem you've been experiencing at home or at work, or inventing a basic website to promote your dream business idea with a view to showing it to potential investors. You'll find tutorials online for pretty much everything. From Udemy to LinkedIn Learning, there are lots of resources to help you upskill.

- Tutorials are the most flexible way to learn something technical. Either as an intro to creating something, or as an extra boost while you're working through a creation. I regularly start on a new piece of software by myself, using the intuition I've built from just clicking around, then search for tutorials as I get stuck on things. Try it yourself. Search for beginner tutorials on the software you already use at work. How much of the information being shared are you familiar with? What new knowledge can you apply when it comes to using your favourite app? Or your email system?

o Create a project. This might not be the digital equivalent of playing teacher, where you create a database of students and grades as I did as a child. But what problem can you try to solve using the tech you've seen and the interests you have? Write down the parts of the problem you understand, then map that to the types of technology you've been hearing about. Try a tutorial to build a mini project.

o As with writing an essay or a report, your project needs a plan. What needs to be built? Who is it for? How might it work? What does that look like? We start Stemettes hackathons by asking our young delegates to draw what they want to create – the app screens, the logo, the buttons. They visualize it all. At first, your technical knowledge might fall short of what you've drawn, but having that vision will guide you. You'll fail to make all of it happen all at once – but that's fine. This is about exploring in order to develop literacy. Keep track of what works and what doesn't. What about a version 2.0?

Remember, you can also make 'fun' things. As much as
I love solving problems, there's much to be learned in
game-building, design work or playing with hardware kits, all
of which is transferable across tech and useful for your
overall literacy.

THE TECH THAT'S SHAPING OUR WORLD

It's undeniable that tech is becoming an integral part of our world – from your experience at work, to how you learn about a job, how you're hired, how you're managed, how decisions are made about your pay and your promotion and your shifts. We use technology to pay for children's school lunches, view their grades, apply to university or higher education courses.

Technology might even deliver course content and put students in touch with their lecturers. The lifelines it affords us were even more apparent during the first lockdown of the Covid-19 pandemic when we used video conferencing platforms such as Zoom to stay connected in almost every aspect of our lives – work; education; health; leisure; weddings, birthdays and other celebrations.

I'm going to introduce you to some of the other exciting tech trends that are already shaping our world, and that will likely shape the future. I've chosen them because upon first hearing each of them, I found them particularly fascinating and they are, I believe, genuinely reshaping the way we understand our lives and enhancing our perspective on what's possible. They're also trends we can look to and consider the problems they might solve for us as women. Down the line, knowing about this tech may have a positive impact on your sense of agency, and your knowledge of it will give you the power and ability to take CTRL.

3D Printing

We're used to the idea of printing in two dimensions – 2D. Most of us are familiar with the process of printing a document. The words and images you see on your screen are transformed from a digital file into markings on a flat piece of paper, which you can hold in your hands. You can fold the sheet to post it or file it away. Printing in 3D is similar but, instead of words or images being printed, a solid object in three dimensions is created: a new cap for your favourite water bottle, a unique piece of jewellery, or maybe a replacement machine part for the one you broke when you dismantled that VCR (sorry again, Dad). Anything from toys to cutlery to clothes can be printed in this way – the possibilities are endless.

You can buy a 3D printer from £100, and print anything you'd like using modelling software (what we call CAD – computer aided design – software), which is downloadable.

To create a 3D version of any item of your choosing, you draw the 3D object in the same way you would use a pencil to make a 2D object, but then also add depth, height and width, and use any colours and repeating patterns that take your fancy. This data is then exported as an STL (stereo lithograph) file, which is used by the 3D printer to make the object using printing 'ink'.

Layer upon layer of plastic, vinyl, metal, ceramic powders, proteins or even chocolate is printed onto the 2D surface, to build up your item in the third dimension – height. I love food, so some of my favourite examples are 3D-printed pancakes, or even whole meals made by building up layers of ingredients in paste form to produce a plateful of food that looks like a normal meal.

A more serious application is achieved by the fantastic Sammy Payne and her team at Open Bionics, who 3D print prosthetic limbs. Being able to print a limb that fits a child precisely as they grow over time, and which features the latest fashions, is a superb use of the technology. The limb could match the child's exact skin tone instead of being the generic peach coloured plastic, or be designed to look like that of their favourite superhero or character – from *Frozen*'s Elsa to Iron Man. Even living tissue can be printed in 3D, using 'ink' that is living cells from a human being. One day, patients who need an organ transplant will be able to have a heart or liver printed to order from their own cells.

The technology can even bring back precious historical artefacts that were seemingly lost for ever. When ISIS occupied the Syrian city of Palmyra, they made a point of destroying buildings and monuments that were thousands of years old. However, using hundreds of photographs, the Oxford Institute for Digital Archaeology was able to build a digital model of the Palmyra Arch of Triumph, and then use that to 3D print a physical replica, which has been displayed in cities around the world. It's no replacement for the original, but a poignant way to remember how the UNESCO World Heritage site was, learn lessons from it, and celebrate the lives, art and architecture of the city.

Artificial Intelligence (AI)

Perhaps the biggest technology story right now is that of artificial intelligence (AI). The goal of AI is computers being able to make decisions in the way a human would, and the hopeful end point is that in some cases they will be able to do so *better* than a human. Useful instances would be situations in which there are many data points to consider, such as medical diagnoses or airport security scanning. (It's interesting to note that concerns in the medical AI arena are less to do with the absence of a human's sixth sense and more to do with the issue of culpability in cases of medical negligence. Who is responsible if the AI makes a mistake? Is it the software maker, or the person who provided the reference data, or the doctor who used the input from the algorithm without double-checking it? What parameters should we set?)

AI is very good at making connections between things. Whether that's discovering new antibiotics, appealing parking tickets, or composing new music based on historical information that tells us what combination of notes sounds good, there's lots that we've been able to do with the technology.

Let's look at one example of AI in greater detail: computer vision. If I were to draw an image of a stick man, you'd recognize it as such by using your eyes to identify a representation you are familiar with. Much of AI boils down to the simple idea that information, such as sounds, images or words, must be converted into a language the computer can process or understand. This often involves turning the information into numbers, thereby creating a computerized version of that sound or image or word. The stick figure would thus become a series of numbers and the computer would store it in a matrix. Each pixel of the image is codified and then the computer does its own maths to interpret what's going on in those pixels, such as figuring out the predominant colour.

Every time you train the AI with a new image, it will learn, through a series of calculations – often billions by the second – to correctly ID the image, whether it's a plant or a skirt or a drawing of a stick man. Over time it will refine these calculations into something it thinks is good enough for you as a human being, or is good enough for a medical diagnosis or scanning a bag in the airport. The AI is making a decision about what it is looking at based on its *artificial intelligence*; the AI is not 'looking' at the image as we human beings might.

Because the AI's calculations are so different to how we assess images or information, sometimes it will make connections that human beings might not. For example, in security scanning, there might be things we humans miss because we're looking with our eyes and using our perception skills and interpretation, whereas the AI is focused solely on its numbers and calculations.

It's a broad church – not all applications work the same way or use the same principles, and not all of them make connections in the same way. Some toothpastes don't just clean your teeth, for example – they focus on whitening, maybe, or protecting sensitive teeth – but we still call them toothpaste.

Blockchain and Bitcoins

Blockchain is a database that is tamper-proof and secure, whilst being openly accessible. Records in the blockchain are stored across a collective – computers owned by a wide community of people with spare processing or computing power and storage. Storing the information in this way is a large part of what keeps it secure. The word 'blockchain' comes from the concept of blocks of information being chained together, and by design this distributed ledger is currently unbreakable. Once information is fixed to the chain it cannot be edited or deleted – an individual cannot change their version of the transaction because it wouldn't then match up with the other copies of the same transaction stored across the collective. A block explorer is used to view the information stored in each block.

Whether it's a supply chain, so you know how a particular T-shirt has got to you and whether the people who made it got paid, or being able to know medicine is genuine, you're able to chain a series of events and blocks of information together in a way that's not editable. You can be sure it's not been tampered with and that's why it's used for money applications. There's a lot of hype around the technology and people are excited about its potential uses.

If you haven't heard of blockchain you might have heard of bitcoin or other cryptocurrencies. Bitcoin is a type of digital currency whose transaction records are stored on the blockchain. You can get bitcoin by mining, or by exchanging them for items of value with someone else who has mined them. Their value fluctuates based on supply and demand. Importantly, bitcoin is not backed by one institution or government, like a normal currency. The trust in the cryptocurrency comes from trust in the blockchain technology.

Consider gold or oil, both of which have to be physically mined. When it comes to mining precious metals, you are extracting something that has taken millions of years to form. As much as we might claim that gold reserves won't last for ever, this isn't strictly true. If we mine more slowly, then more gold will have a chance to form and we can carry on, probably indefinitely. The same goes for oil, in that it's formed of layers and layers of sedimentary rock – if we slowed down, we could carry on. Bitcoin is also mined, but it involves numbers rather than raw materials.

Think of prime numbers – the first few are quite close together, but as we start to calculate, the distance between each prime number and the next grows. To find a prime number it must be indivisible by every number that came before it, and so for the very big prime numbers it takes a lot of computing time to complete this process.

Rather than finding prime numbers, there were a series of puzzles for the members of the collective to find, defined by bitcoin's creator, Satoshi Nakamoto. Unlike gold or oil, there is, without question, a finite number of bitcoins that can be mined – roughly 21 million. It's been estimated that it will take a long time to mine the final few, but once we get there we'll have found them all. At that point supply will be fixed, but the value of bitcoin will be defined by demand.

The cryptocurrency was built on the fact there is this finite set of bitcoins to be found. If your computer does the calculation and finds one, then you own that bitcoin; it has a certain value based on supply and demand. You can then break your bitcoin down into hundreds and sell these units. As with stocks and shares, their value will fluctuate as demand goes up or down. Every time a bitcoin or a part of a bitcoin is sold, that transaction is stored on the blockchain. If you have access to the blockchain, it's then easy to trace its transaction history, back to the very beginning and the original person who decided to split it up and sell it.

There are lots of types of cryptocurrencies out there. Not all of them work in the same way, however, and while most work on the principle of supply and demand, not all of them are mined. Each currency is based on a set of rules or a methodology determined by its creator. Anyone can make their own crypto-currency, so however they define it needs to be repeatable and understandable to others.

A powerful example of the real-world use of bitcoin came in 2020 during the demonstrations against police corruption and brutality in Nigeria. Using bitcoin, folks around the world were able to fund medical supplies and other support for people who were protesting. Rather than sending the money to Nigeria via the traditional banking system, where the government had control over what happened to it, you could send bitcoin to a group who would then be transparent about how they were using that funding. For example, UNICEF has been able to use bitcoin to get money into environments where children need support but other structures have failed them. The charity also uses blockchain to track how it spends donations.

I believe that the existence of a tamper-proof ledger will pro-vide security, safety and transparency in many more spheres than those above. Although blockchain and bitcoin have drawn criticism and controversy because of the high carbon footprint involved in processing currency, it's still early days and these concerns need not be a feature of the way we interact with this technology.

Having a basic understanding of blockchain will allow you to take CTRL by exploring opportunities that will solve problems for you and others. You might feel uncertain about approach-ing a subject as complicated as cryptocurrency, but the worst that could happen is that you don't understand and might need to check another resource.* The more you know, the more you can share your knowledge with others and go on the journey of understanding together, which in itself makes it a less intimidating enterprise.

The Internet of Things

Long, long ago, in the early 1990s, human beings only used the internet to send email, communicate and store information. Then someone figured out how to allow devices such as heaters, light bulbs and fridges to use the internet too. These were *things* on the internet.

An example application for this development is tracking parcel deliveries on your phone. You see a live feed from the delivery vehicle, updating you on the route and the proximity of the courier to your home. No live person is inputting this data, the vehicle is beaming out its location, and a server is receiving that information as the vehicle moves ever closer, pinpointing its position on a map. Your house or flat is on the map, and when the courier arrives, a notification is triggered to alert you that your package has been delivered.

Many bus networks operate in much the same way – every bus in service is constantly sending messages about its location to a server so that individual bus-stop displays can calculate how far away the bus is and how soon it will arrive. The stop that the vehicle has just left also knows when the bus is moving *away*, and so removes it from the digital display.

---

* We've covered it a number of times on my *Women Tech Charge* podcast.

This process works via a system of triggers. Again, no human being is actively sharing this information – *things* on the internet are communicating – sensors, buildings, vehicles. From this type of tech we end up with 'smart cities', such as London, where the entire bus and tube network is in communication with its servers and can be viewed online. Copenhagen is another such place where sensors across the city help people find parking spaces, tackle air pollution, and even make rat traps more efficient.[1]

On a smaller scale, in a smart home, your toaster, washing machine, fridge, heating system and lighting might be connected to the internet and controlled via internet-enabled devices. You can even check on the health of your grandma by giving her a pendant that will send you a message if she hasn't moved for a while, prompting you to see if she's OK.

My friend Andy lives in a smart house that uses Twitter. His front door, porch lights and heating are all smart. The last time I spoke to him he was planning to make his dustbin smart too – by getting it to scan the packaging of what he's throwing away and add the items to his shopping list for his next trip to the supermarket. When people in Andy's house take a bath, because his water tank is smart, the water usage is tracked. Even his mouse traps in the attic are connected to the internet – when a mouse is caught, the trap sends a 'trigger' message to Twitter, and a tweet is posted from his house's Twitter account: 'Mouse caught in the east attic.' Andy did a TEDx talk at the University of Warwick on his house, which is a hilarious watch.[2]

There are, of course, security implications when it comes to posting something like this to Twitter, even though Andy's accounts for his house are set to 'private'. There are two sides to any tool; you can use a knife to chop vegetables or you could use it to harm another person. With all these technologies we have to consider both sides of the coin. Naturally, posting security-sensitive information to the internet opens us up to safety and privacy threats, as well as perhaps having our house hacked, but this possibility spurs us on to build good technology where we try to build in a way that mitigates such risks.

Essentially, 'smart' means being able to have devices on the internet that talk to each other without necessarily needing human interaction or input, but in a way that then serves a human purpose. One example that leaps to mind when thinking about the vulnerabilities of cyber security concerns the 'smart' car that had its controls hacked while it was on the road, in order to expose to the manufacturer the vulnerabilities within the system.[3] The flip side is your smart washing machine, which you can turn on remotely, rather than setting a timer. When the cycle has finished, the machine can let you know with a message that says something like, 'Hey, come hang out the washing.' The next stage might be for the washing to hang itself out!

There are vulnerabilities as well as opportunities and benefits across all forms of technology, and it is part of your digital literacy to always consider both sides of the cyber coin. As there are quite a few devices we can now connect to the internet, the possibilities with this technology are endless. Always be wary of where the security issues might lie, but the convenience of being able to remotely control the devices you interact with, and the freedom that comes with that, is an obvious advantage. You have the agency to embrace this technology and use it well, *and* if you find yourself at the mercy of one of these systems, your knowledge of the Internet of Things will allow you to surmount or counteract the problem.

Virtual Reality (VR)

When I was younger, the animated TV show *The Magic School Bus* was huge. In each episode the teacher would take her students on a school trip to somewhere impossible, such as inside someone's bloodstream or (becoming less impossible with every day that passes) outer space.

Virtual reality is like going on the magic school bus, but not in cartoon form. Popping on a headset and headphones with software transports you to somewhere you aren't. It could be a concert by your favourite artist, a prehistoric forest or a roller-coaster. As you move your head while wearing the headset, the image you see also adjusts. If you look left, the image pans left. When you look right, it pans right. It's as if you're really in the place you can see, in real time. The image moves at the same speed as you do, so the experience is incredibly visceral.

We set up a VR demo for the girls at the very first Stemettes hackathon event in 2013. A hackathon is a little like a music-jamming session in your front room, where you get together with your friends to make music just for the fun of it. It's similar in that it's a 'no strings attached' coding weekend. You bring your laptop and code together with the other people there, usually for twenty-four or forty-eight hours. You sleep over and there's always food and drink on tap. There's usually a theme for the event, such as sustainability, ending violence against women, helping the NHS, or a particular technology – webpages, apps, or a proof-of-concept exercise, perhaps. Over the course of the weekend, as a team, you'll build something quick and simple and small. You test the tech, take it through various iterations, and then, at the end of the hack, a demo day is held where you present your product to judges or a panel. Prizes are often awarded, such as funding to take the idea further.

Anyway, at this particular VR demo, although the girls were seated, several of them fell off their chairs as a result of how realistic the rollercoaster VR was. A few screamed . . . very loudly. Restricting the senses by using a headset that allows you to see just the VR images only adds to the verisimilitude. The technology has also been used at Davos to help world leaders build empathy with refugees. It's been used by firefighters to learn how to put out fires without the need to set buildings on fire, and it's even allowed children to go on school trips under the sea without getting their packed lunches wet, or the teacher having to fill in the most terrifying risk assessment forms. With virtual reality, anyone can feel transported to somewhere else.

Wearables (aka Wearable Tech)

This relates simply to technology you can wear upon your person. You might have this already in a watch or fitness tracker. There are also smart glasses that will add information alongside what you can see. Eventually retired due to privacy concerns, Google Glass were a product that looked a bit like Snap Spectacles, which record video for Snapchat, and had a little projector and speaker built into them. As you walked around, they'd overlay directions or information relevant to what you were doing. Think of those characters in films or games that have 'futuristic specs' that allow them to identify the bad guy in the room, or analyse what they can see, thanks to overlaid stats from a database or computer.

In 2010 Katy Perry famously wore a smart, digitally connected dress to the Met Gala. Designed by CuteCircuit and covered in 3,000 micro-LED lights, the LED colours were programmed by the team.[4] Then, in 2012, the same team created a Twitter dress for Nicole Scherzinger to wear to a party celebrating the new 4G network in the UK. Fans were able to send tweets with the hashtag #tweetthedress that then showed up on the fabric of the dress. The bigger idea is that there's no need to own more than one skirt because you can download different designs each time you wear it, to match other elements of your outfit. It might vastly reduce the need to consume clothes at the rate at which so many people currently do.

Another trend that has been made possible by wearables is 'quantified tech', which includes Fitbits, Apple Watches, and other devices that can measure your blood oxygen levels, give you an ECG reading, track your workouts and calorie intake, or monitor sleep patterns. All the functions can be used to make better decisions about your health and fitness.

This kind of tech can also help make people's lives infinitely easier and more accessible. Let's look at the example of a surgeon wearing Google Glass. She might ask the glasses to pull up some information there and then on the procedure she is performing, which would do away with the need for her to step out of the operating theatre, remove her gloves, wash her hands and then physically look up what she needs to know. A wheelchair-bound nature rambler might use Google Glass to find accessible paths, check the weather or call for help, all without ever having to use their hands, which would give them more autonomy and independence. Although it might sound like something from the distant future, these kinds of products are already here.

Tech Is Shaping the Future, and Much More Than That

If the present or the future aren't your thing, how about the idea of preserving the past?

The tech trends in this chapter have made me excited about what could come next. As with the Palmyra example earlier, technology isn't just about the future, or even the present. It's a tool that can also help us better understand the past.

Through Stemettes, I've been really fortunate to meet lots of young people. Someone who stays in my mind, and who is one of our fantastic ambassadors, is a young woman called Savinay. Sav has been a Stemette since the age of thirteen, and went on to study archaeology and ancient history at Wadham College, Oxford.

She explained to me how technology has been used to analyse organic seabed material, which has revealed how people have been using the sea in the Mediterranean for 13,000 years – to travel and for natural resources. Researchers identified that a particular rock came from a volcano on Milos, a Greek island in the Aegean, which had never been connected to its present location by land.[5] 'So it means people must have got that [rock] from the sea,' she told me.

Savinay believes that science and technology have the power to fill in a lot of gaps in our knowledge of the past: 'You get a better, more well-grounded view into the past if you go down the scientific archaeology route when you're looking for answers.' Archaeology has been a field of study for hundreds of years, but of late, it's been able to do more, and understand the past better, because of its use of tech.

Savinay sees technology as key to widening access to her subject, and not just because it enables her to tutor overseas students remotely, from Ireland to Pakistan, in Classics and Ancient Greek. Using virtual reconstructions, researchers like Sav can visit sites thousands of miles away. It also offers up a non-invasive way to create archaeological reconstructions without disturbing the site. There are also online archives of documents and texts in Old English, Ancient Greek and Latin, and in online communities you can gather with other ancient historians and ask questions of top professors in your field.

It's amazing to consider the ways in which we apply technology to archaeology. In a similar way, Miranda Lowe, a curator at the Natural History Museum, analyses the science of history. Tech allows you to explore a museum virtually or, if you're there in person, hold up your phone camera to learn more about the exhibit in front of you, information that goes beyond the content the curators are able to fit on the little display plaques, or beyond what a tour guide could tell you in the time they have available.* There's a lot of technology in history: being able to form an approximation of a Neanderthal face based on a skull, being able to 3D print things so that people can touch and hold an artefact without destroying the artefact itself. It's exciting to be a part of all this.

---

* As an aside, I have a portrait of me by oil painter and printmaker Susannah Nathanson. It has augmented reality built into it, and if you hover over areas of the portrait with your phone camera it will play a video of me.

•

It's not just one Big Bang of innovation and, ta-da, here it all is. It has taken years, sometimes decades, of work to bring technologies to a point where they can function in society and are adopted. What's more, as we build the future, these developments won't be used in isolation, they'll be connected. You might, for example, combine 3D printing and virtual reality to create an experience where you can hold the objects you see in the virtual universe, or craft something in the virtual universe and then manufacture it in the real world. Bringing together 3D printing with VR might mean you print your own specialized VR headset, or one for someone who has a need for an adapted headset. You might create a virtual world for people to explore in virtual reality and then 3D print parts of that world, so that when they come across it, it feels more real, and augments the experience.

Or you might take the Internet of Things and blockchain and put them together. You could have a very reliable (and tamper-proof) record of all the times your fridge texted you to remind you to buy milk because you'd run out. Or perhaps all the times your fridge ordered milk from the supermarket. It might help with arguments that centre on there being no milk left in the fridge!

The different elements of tech are like ingredients you can mix together, allowing us to build on what's come before. It's creative problem-solving, and that has huge potential. It's also why anyone can be a tech creator. Everyone has their own perspective. Everyone has their problems that they're particularly aware of. Everyone has their own process in their head for how we get from A to B. Being able to create is exciting because while it might be likely that you create something similar to what others have done in the past, the real point of difference could be in terms of the way your idea is applied.

Getting Started

The technology mentioned in this chapter won't even be 'new' by the time you read this, as the tech world is ever evolving and morphing. That being said, take some time to reflect on the technology. Can you see any uses for any of it in your life? Do a deeper dive — can you see how any of the technologies could be used to solve some of the bigger problems in society that you're aware of?

- What hobbies or interests do you have? Do a search (in your preferred format) for 'the future of hobby'. Do any of the results resonate with you? Are they solving or touching on the most important aspects of your particular interest? Are there any glaring omissions in the 'view of the future' and applications of technology for it?

- Do a quick search of 'top tech trends' in your preferred format. What comes up? How does it relate to the future of your hobby? Note any similarities or areas of overlap. Note if any themes arise. It might all sound like jargon to start with, but that's par for the course. There will always be something new to learn, so develop this particular curiosity muscle early on.

- As you try to move your learning on, consider looking at the technically creative actions of others. Attend a couple of demos of things that other folks have created, or watch back showcases, pitch days and demo days.

and analyse what's been done or created. You might even decide to get involved in a showcase of some sort yourself.

○ At the time you are reading this, what are the latest tech trends? There's always something around the corner. Tech ethics, NFTs, the metaverse, Web3 – each month brings with it new things with new names. Deciding upon your trusted source for developing your curiosity, and knowing how to use it to get the information you want, in a format you understand, is a big part of taking CTRL.

5

A
WOMAN'S
WORK

I'm a young Black woman, and that fact has made my curiosity about tech even more important. All the things that make me 'different' from the 'norm' have made my questioning and my perspective all the more valuable. My difference is a positive rather than a negative. For all the times we've been told as women that maths isn't for us, or that technical things are beyond us, it's imperative that we remain boldly and loudly curious. Technologies are life-changing, so why shouldn't we probe and ensure our perspectives and experiences are considered in their creation?

You could argue that I'm not a typical woman, whatever 'typical' might mean. I certainly know that not all women are the same. We're not a homogeneous group, and that's why we *all* need to be in the room when we talk about getting curious, getting involved, taking CTRL. Although we have that commonality of being women, we're still very different from one another. If it reads like I'm making an overarching generalization, it should be interpreted as a statistic, as I'm referring to a majority or a large proportion as referenced in some research or a study. So, a disclaimer about the use of the word 'we'. This is all big-picture stuff, not every single element is fully applicable to all.

Many women don't consider themselves 'technical', but

women are problem-solvers and technology is nothing more than a tool. Previous generations of women were particularly good at using tools such as typewriters, telephone exchange panels and punch cards from the early days of computers. The logic was that we were better at this work because we were more dexterous thanks to our smaller fingers, but these jobs were also seen as clerical rather than technical.

So often women are the hardest hit by problems – from poverty to violence – because our role in society is a really specific one. It varies from culture to culture but, largely, we've been given or have inherited a position based on a sociological model that has been around since the 1950s. Some people call it the four Cs, some call it the seven Cs.

Women are most likely to be in charge of **caring** and **childcare**. We're most likely to be the ones doing **cashiering**, working retail jobs. We're most likely to be working in **catering**, most likely to be **cleaning**. We're most likely to be doing **clerical** work (which is why we started off as the ones in charge of technology when it was seen as low-grade clerical work). And, of course, we're the ones most likely to be working in the **casual** and informal economy. All this means that we have less economic security and are less resilient financially, because we're over-represented in low-wage sectors.

If there's a crisis, such as a pandemic, we'll most likely lose our jobs first. Lower-paid ethnic-minority women were at especially high risk of exposure to Covid during the pandemic, because of their presence in social care, nursing and pharmacy jobs.[1] We're the ones who have to shoulder the greater load of domestic chores, we're the ones who do the most unpaid labour.

When governments started measuring GDP, they decided

for simplicity that they weren't going to include working in the home and unpaid jobs. They knew it was valuable to the economy, but it was just too complex for them to measure, or not the highest priority. It reflects the fact that a lot of the problems that women face are undocumented, or seen as too complex to be included in models.

We're overwhelmingly the ones who have to endure periods, and the ones who go through menopause, both of which bring their own problems. If there's anyone who knows about problems that need to be solved with tools, it's women.

When we look at ways to mitigate the issues that come with our role in society, there is another C – **control**. Specifically, taking technological **CTRL**.

When we consider the well-documented disadvantages of being female, intersecting with other factors such as age, literacy levels, health or ethnicity, there are all kinds of things working against us. Technology is one of the best tools to tackle those problems, and that's why it's so important for women to get technical, to get digitally literate, to choose to engage.

It's also one of the core reasons I run Stemettes – for the sake of future generations of women. We don't have to be doing those seven Cs, we don't have to be confined to those roles in society. We can also look at philanthropy, personal development and education to break out of the moulds we're often shaped into by society, but choosing to engage with technology is one of the most powerful ways to be able to move forward.

●

During the pandemic, we saw this: when restrictions first started to ease, you were able to go for a haircut appointment for at least five weeks before you were allowed to book a massage or a nail appointment. We've been made to feel that certain beauty treatments are non-essential, frilly. (Is it a coincidence which appointments are more commonly booked by men?) However, think about the kinds of individuals who are employed in the beauty industry, and consider the opportunities and the agency they have, or don't have, because of the way the industry is run. When you then add in certain policy assumptions, you end up with an entire industry of a quarter of a million people being left behind, being told they're non-essential. And nine out of ten of those people are women.

WAH Nails was founded in 2009 by entrepreneur Sharmadean Reid, and operated concessions in Topshop and Harvey Nichols. The salon spawned a whole industry of nail design, turning it into an art form, featuring contemporary and culturally relevant designs. In 2017, Sharmadean closed the store to focus fully on her new tech startup, Beautystack, which runs a platform for people to book beauty treatments based on visuals.

Sharmadean has been using technology to say, 'Here's how we women are going to empower ourselves, here's how we're going to continue to earn, learn, move forward and have progress.' Beautystack gives people the tools they need for accounting, marketing and booking within the beauty industry, but for Sharmadean, it's also been an opportunity to show women that they don't have to be tied to a salon and at the mercy of a manager. Her message is that you can use a technology platform to deliver the same beauty treatments, in the same industry, but you have a lot more agency and control. She's since pivoted to the Stack World – a technology-based media platform that connects women to take advantage of their collective knowledge and experiences for empowerment.

It's one way to counter what we've often seen happen over the course of history, where female-dominated areas have been undervalued, under-served, and under-researched. Sharmadean has been thinking about the needs of other women, and the need to take control begs the question: What have you been thinking about, and what can you imagine you might want to take control of?

Ultimately, imagination is about new and unreal things; technology is about making the unreal real. Taking control of technology doesn't always mean creating the new from scratch – it can also mean adding something new to what already exists. Ideas can be planted in the imagination from all kinds of sources, but your experiences are a key component of what you imagine – your upbringing, your formative experiences and your day-to-day reality combine with your values and priorities. The existing social constructs around being a woman also feed into what goes on in your imagination. The same is true of any gender.

It's also important to consider the effect science fiction has on the imagination. So many of the folks that are super excited to be technologists credit sci-fi, games, and films and TV shows they enjoyed during their formative years with influencing how they see the world and what they think should happen in it next.

Do you remember *Knight Rider*, the 1980s TV series? Michael Knight would fight crime with his car, KITT. He talked to his vehicle, it would understand what he was saying, and sometimes it would talk back. It's quite funny to think the premise was so futuristic, so novel and exciting back then, but these days we talk to inanimate objects all the time. We talk to our phones, and they answer us. We ask a robot to turn off the lights, or tell us the weather forecast. Science fiction becoming science reality is something we've seen time and time again.

Just as someone dreamed up *Knight Rider*, it's possible to dream up all kinds of scenarios that could become a reality. You're probably already imagining things that could make your life easier, or solve problems. You might also already be dreaming about alternate universes and what 200 years into the future might look like. What do you see? What is life like for the equivalent you in 2222? Take some time to daydream. Don't do any research, just imagine. Maybe a drawing will help. Maybe a poem.

Is it dystopian? Is it like any of the sci-fi movies you've seen? Are there aliens? We make a lot of TV shows like *Black Mirror* and films such as *The Terminator* that point to a fearful future and showcase the dark side of science fiction. However, for every Terminator there should be a saviour, an enabler, a creator – we just have to imagine them. Read widely and think differently to take in the picture of humanity around you. Ask yourself: What do people need? How can I help them? What problems can we solve?

Some years ago I was excited to be a part of an 'alternate' sci-fi project by the organization/responsible-technology think tank Doteveryone. They asked: How many times have we heard about the female perspective in science fiction – a woman's experience of being an astronaut or how a woman would find living on Mars? What would it mean if babies could gestate outside a woman's body? Or if you had to choose between bearing children and exploring deep space? What if it turns out that women's bodies are more suited to space travel than men's?

So many of the stories of our history are male-centred. What if we had a positive, female-centred view of the future? Why does it need to be the terrifying *Handmaid's Tale*? We should explore more positive outcomes, and use them as motivation for why women should be engaging with tech, and aiming to be in the room.

We are part of the future too, yet so much of the current forecasting doesn't include us. This is in spite of the fact that there are times when only we, as women, with the journeys we've had, can be the ones to suggest an idea, or dare to dream. It's a negative that we can turn into a positive. Much bad tech is the result of a lack of perspective or experience, which limits the imagination of the person creating the tech. Often, whichever of the dreamers secured the most funding at the time becomes the person most likely to turn those dreams into something tangible. We recognize these innovators as mainly men, who can speak to only a narrow interpretation of progress.

Take, for example, Elon Musk. As well as running his own space programme, he founded The Boring Company. Imagine being rich enough to realize your dreams, and deciding that boring into the Earth is a good use of your money? I can think of many more worthwhile and life-enhancing projects!

Science fiction has inspired so much of Musk's work that it makes us wonder what our world might look like if he'd read different books when he was younger. What if he'd read sci-fi about a post-cancer world? Or if he'd read more about legions of people affected by endometriosis? Or even sci-fi based around a cohort of exclusively female astronauts?

Tech should be about serving the needs of the many, not just the few dreamers who have enough money to turn their visions into machines. I appreciate that it can sometimes feel as if there are too many choices to make, so it's also important to choose your problem – like a billionaire philanthropist trying to decide which good cause their money should go towards. How about the eradication of a terrible disease, like the Gates Foundation aiming to get rid of polio by funding vaccinations worldwide? Or funding the development of a new vaccine, in the way that Dolly Parton did by donating $1 million towards Moderna Covid-19 vaccine research?

You might prefer to fund the school or university that you went to, or the arts, or a museum. Between 2007 and 2017, British millionaires gave nearly £5 billion to higher education (mostly Oxford and Cambridge universities), £1 billion to the arts, but just over £2 million to alleviating poverty. Similarly, in the US, barely one dollar in five donated by philanthropists goes to the poor. No wonder philanthropy doesn't improve inequality.

Maybe you'd be inspired to make choices more along the lines of those of Julian Richer, who owns home entertainment chain Richer Sounds. He gave his employees 60 per cent of shares in the company, through a trust,[2] and handed them a total of £3.5 million – £1,000 each for every year of service. Rather than keeping their wages down and then donating his wealth to help the poor, he decided to pay his employees properly and gave them some control over the company too.

If we're talking about power and money, and the role those things play in the tech that's built, it becomes clear that we're not very good at choosing the right kind of problems to solve, let alone solving them very well. Lots of projects have been funded that probably shouldn't have. It's an issue that plays out in a big way for tech. However, rather than feel downhearted, as a woman trying to take CTRL, I'd argue that it's an exciting prospect to consider. The types of problems that you see and want to solve, and the types of choices you want to make in how you solve those problems, can be a great tool for holding yourself accountable, as well as holding others accountable.

Consider Dame Stephanie Shirley. Exasperated by the sexism she was confronted by in her workplace during the fifties and sixties, she built and staffed her tech empire with an all-woman, work-from-home staff. She and her employees at Xansa pioneered the idea of women re-entering the workforce after a career break to have and raise their children. They promoted job-sharing, profit-sharing and company co-ownership. When our imaginations are held in check, we replicate the injustice and unfairness around us. Stephanie Shirley dared to dream differently. When she eventually sold her company she became extremely wealthy, as did her employees. She went on to become the first person ever to fall off the *Sunday Times* Rich List as a result of giving.

A playful example of the importance of imagination is *Dr Who* and the decades-old absence of a female Doctor. The show is a fictional series, set in a made-up world, so what stopped the show's creators from imagining a woman in the role for so long? The limitations we put on the imaginations of others by not telling a breadth of stories has an impact on the tech in our lives. There is an incredibly rich herstory of tech to tell.

Do not restrict your imagination, do not put a cap on your dreams. It only limits the dreams and creations of others, and fails to serve the needs of the underprivileged and excluded.

I'm a firm believer that if more people of all genders were aware of the rich heritage women have enjoyed in the technical space, the limits on our imaginations would disappear and the caps on our technical dreams would no longer exist. I'm excited to share with you the herstory of tech in the following chapter.

Getting Started

You're engaging with all kinds of tech and being curious in many ways, following on from previous chapters. As you come across new forms and applications of technology, how many of them touch on what is seen as 'women's work'? How many of them ignore women's work?

Here's a thought experiment framework that you may want to use as you hear and see new things, or review what you've seen already:

- What does this mean for me?
- What does this mean for her?
- What does this mean for us?
- What does this mean for the future?

Anything that you watch, or anything that you read, ask yourself what the applications and implications may be. Keep being curious! Have you dipped back into any of the feeds or resources you discovered while doing the exercises at the end of Chapter 1?

THE
HERSTORY
OF TECH

On International Women's Day 2020, I found myself at 10 Downing Street, sitting next to UK Prime Minister Boris Johnson and Olympic gold medallist Dame Kelly Holmes, in front of a group of secondary school students. One of the girls asked the PM, 'Do you still believe that patriarchy is prevalent in today's society, and if so, what challenges could we face as young women?'

'If you mean by patriarchy,' replied the prime minister, 'a system that insists on male dominance, just as some societies were matriarchies in the ancient world, I don't think we have exactly that. I think it has changed a huge amount, but I do think that there is still implicit unspoken discrimination. And we need to tackle it, because it's so stupid, because it means that we are not releasing the potential, and not allowing so many people in the country to develop their talents in the way that they could. And it's not just dumb, it's wrong. So, it's not strictly a patriarchy, but we're not there yet.'[1]

My face must have given away what I was thinking, because the host came to me next.

Yes, I said that the patriarchy is alive and kicking – kicking us.

Women are curious. We should be motivated to choose to

develop that curiosity and choose to engage as a woman, but we also need to understand the obstacles that have stood in our way.

Because of all the unpaid labour that you probably do, your time to indulge your curiosity is more limited than that of any male counterparts you might have. A Stanford University study found that one in five male academics has a stay-at-home partner, versus only one in twenty female academics.[2] During the Covid-19 pandemic, when schools remained closed, the weight of extra childcare fell far more heavily on women: twice as many mothers as fathers spent more time on housework, and one in five was doing an extra five hours of work every day.[3] That being said, this culture of inequality extends beyond the pandemic to a system that is afraid of women being curious, learning and taking CTRL.

Your natural curiosity might be something for which you've been scolded. There's even a Bible verse that says women shouldn't ask questions in church, that they must be silent. If they want to ask anything, they should ask their husband when they get home. That's St Paul, writing in Corinthians.

For centuries, women's education has been deprioritized, and this is still the case in many countries. It's been a vicious circle: because women were denied education, there was a lot they didn't know. Because they were ignorant, they weren't seen as worth educating. However, not only were women denied education, they also weren't allowed to educate them-selves by asking questions in public. Only those people who already had an education could ask the questions.

Generations of patriarchy have meant that our curiosity has been quashed, and this domination and discrimination has continued into the tech world of today. There's a rich *his-tory* of tech that you may even be able to recount. But what of the *her*story of tech? It's something I talk about a lot: all the women who were involved, right from the start of the techno-logical revolution – like the women who worked on punch cards.

There are countless other women too, beyond the limited stories we're told of Marie Curie, Rosalind Franklin and Florence Nightingale. Consider how the tech side of Florence Nightin-gale's life has been obscured. She's heralded as an inspirational nurse, but she was also a statistician who pioneered the way we represent data. In 1859 she was elected the first female member of the Royal Statistical Society.

There are the hundreds of women who worked at Bletchley Park, cracking codes and programming early computers along-side Alan Turing. There are also the women who *were* computers at NASA, calculating the trajectories of spacecraft that took men to the Moon, as we saw in the film *Hidden Figures*. We've been there the whole time. We don't hear these women's stor-ies very often, but they happened.

I wept seeing myself reflected on screen for the first time, as a young Katherine Johnson stood at a blackboard solving a quadratic equation in front of a class of gobsmacked people almost twice her age. The camaraderie she shared with Dorothy Vaughan also meant a lot to me. Someone in the 1950s had lived an experience that so closely resembled elements of my child-hood in the 1990s and which are still heralded as unique. I'd always known that it couldn't have been just me who 'got' maths at a young age. Seeing such a parallel on screen meant a lot.

Whenever I look into the sky on a cloudless night I'm reminded of Williamina Fleming, an astronomer from Dundee who was one of the founding members of the Harvard Computers, an all-women body of human computers hired to compute mathematical classifications at the Harvard Observatory. She went on to discover hundreds of stars, and in 1888, she identified the Horsehead Nebula, part of the Orion constellation. A great advocate for women in science, Fleming was vocal in her assertion that the inequality between the sexes in the world of science was cultural rather than biological, which was a progressive idea at the time.

Whenever you use GPS, you should thank mathematician Gladys West, who saw studying and exploring her curiosity as a way to get away from the farm where she grew up in West Virginia. For her, an education was a way not to have to do manual labour all day, either in the fields or at the nearby tobacco factory, so she worked hard at school to be awarded a university scholarship.

She figured out that geostatic satellites, which are static relative to a point on the surface of the Earth, can be used to find out your location. If you can calculate where you are in relation to at least three of those satellites high above Earth, you can determine your position on the ground, or in the ocean, or even in mid-air. Gladys West is the reason we have a blue dot to follow on our phones or in the car, or know which direction to head in when we're following a route. I like to refer to it as the 'Gladys Positioning System' instead.

Then there's Stephanie Kwolek, a chemist working in the 1960s who one day decided to look at the waste or 'mistake fluids' from the project on which she and her lab mates were working. Kwolek went on to perform further experiments that led to her discovery of Kevlar, the material that makes bulletproof vests bulletproof.

The last woman I'd like to mention here, but that's not to say there aren't a huge number of other great minds worthy of inclusion, is Katharina Paulus, who invented the modern folding parachute. She was a German aerial acrobat, born in 1868, and the first German woman to jump out of a hot-air balloon. You do have to be pretty curious to want to jump out of things from a great height. The NASA Rover *Perseverance* landed on the surface of Mars in 2021 using a parachute that Katharina would have recognized. I think she would have liked the message encoded on it too: 'Dare Mighty Things!'

Our rich herstory has been initially hidden and resulted in innately curious women like yourself being conditioned out of our natural state. Exploring what has been, and imagining what could be, via avenues like sci-fi, is what excites me about a world where she is in CTRL.

Patriarchy Meets *Herstory*

Patriarchy is about power. Men, and power. Modern use of the word describes the society in which we all live, one where men dominate, control or have power that women lack, but the word comes from the ancient Greek for the rule of the father, the patriarch. It's related to the word 'patrilineal', which is the handing down of things through the father's side of the family: names, property, power . . . It's why the things we inherit, from our family or our culture, are sometimes called patrimony. We inherited them from our forefathers.

That being said, our inheritance is more than the patrimony

passed down from our fathers and grandfathers. Our grand-mothers, aunties and non-male ancestors also contributed to the world we live in today, sometimes in spite of all the obstacles they faced, and all the efforts to hamper their curiosity and inventiveness. Even so, when they pushed through that barrier to ask questions, learn, invent and create, their lives and achievements were sidelined. It's why we don't really understand the history, the *her*story, that we have. Women like Gladys West and Stephanie Kwolek should be household names, but they're not.

My message is simple: You don't have to be white and male and dead to do STEM. STEM is for anyone. You can make this knowledge your own. Look at all these other amazing individuals who have achieved incredible things before you, in the face of all kinds of prejudice.

Through Stemettes we run something called tech incubator programmes. Much like an incubator that helps tiny babies thrive, a tech incubator is a project that nourishes and nurtures nascent startups and businesses, and prepares them to be strong enough – financially and in many other ways – to succeed in the real world. They are intensive support programmes where mentoring is given, greatly needed expertise is passed on, and where incubatees form a community with others like them. Dropbox, Airbnb and Reddit all started life in tech incubators, and I was inspired to create a version designed for the young people who come through Stemettes and want to create their own startups.

In 2019, Stemettes and I went to a big investment conference, and ended up having one-on-one meetings with various investors who wanted to talk to me. I sat down with one of them, and as soon as I started to say, 'We have these teenage girls on a tech incubator programme . . .' he jumped in with, 'So it was all startups around beauty, then?'

I hadn't mentioned the word 'beauty', and in fact none of the startups were anything to do with beauty. This was entirely his assumption just because I was working with women. I was so annoyed.

Things are changing, though. Not only are women asking questions in public, women are speaking from the stage. I do lots of public speaking to all kinds of audiences – people who work in the tech industry, and people who are curious about the world – but I still look at the stage sometimes, especially at tech events, and see a white, all-male panel. We've even given a name to a male-only panel: a manel. It's another example of patriarchy, where the power of knowledge, or authority, the technical power, is seated in just one gender, or one type of person.

Some folks justify manels with a line such as, 'There aren't any women performing the important roles in business', as if that's the only way of knowing whether someone can contribute meaningfully to a panel discussion. If women have been shut out of those roles, but are affected by the topic at hand, why keep them away from the stage? We are at least at the point where organizers are now embarrassed to put on an event with a manel.

Restricting technical power and authority to men only ensures a one-sided, lopsided way of creating technology, and if you've got an uneven way of creating a tool, you're never going to create the right product. The result of such a small set of people building technology that has had an impact on all of us is bad tech. The power imbalance has not only obscured the rich herstory that we have, it's also had an effect on the state of our technology right now.

•

Mar Hicks is Professor of History at the Illinois Institute of Technology in Chicago, Illinois. Their book, *Programmed Inequality*, zeroes in on the post-war efforts to use IT to rebuild countries, focusing on the UK's post-war strategy in particular, but the ideas were mirrored around the world.

They describe how, during the Second World War, lots of technology was developed very quickly – not only military but also computing and information technology that had much wider uses. Before the war, women were working in many of these industries, because these jobs were not yet viewed as the exclusive domain of 'men's work'. Once men went off to fight in the armed forces, women had new opportunities to develop their expertise, including in the fields of mechanics, engineering, driving, computing and clerking. However, once the war was over, things changed.

As explored in Mar Hicks's book, the women who held these roles during the war, and who had often done them *before* the war, ended up training new recruits – namely, the men who had returned. The idea was that they would train up these men on the technologies the women had built and the projects they had been working on.

Here's the catch, though – after the training, the women were expected to abandon all their hard work, all their learning, all the competencies that they'd built, and go home and raise babies. Those who stayed became managed by the men. This was especially true in IT, which was going to offer new economic leverage. Tech went from being a clerical job, one of the Cs we spoke about earlier, to being a higher-status technical one for men. The roles were the same, but when men started doing them, the status, and the pay, went up.

By forcing women out of computing, Mar argues, the UK was damaging its own modernization projects and fundamentally hampering its own economic growth in the process. In the 1970s, the British government passed laws to give women equal pay for work of equal value, but it's very easy to get around those laws if men and women are doing different jobs.

Having studied the history of women in tech, and covered all of this in great detail in their book, I wanted to know what Mar thinks should happen now. 'From my perspective, as a historian, it's so tough,' they told me. 'You don't want to rebrand it, swing it back the other way, because it wasn't some wonderful field full of promise for women.' They explained that the incredible work these women were doing was seen as low-level unskilled work. As workers, they were disposable, and there was no career-long commitment to them.

According to Mar, feminization really has nothing to do with the skill level of the work. It's just the perception of the work's importance. In a horrible catch-22, one of the ways in which work becomes perceived as less important is when more women are doing it. Pay levels go down and it results in fewer opportunities and lower pay for everybody who goes into that field, whether they're a woman or whether they're somebody of another gender. Mar believes that unfortunately, that's one of the dangers of trying to get a lot of women into a field, when women's position in the labour market, and economically and politically, is weaker.

This might all sound rather disheartening, but Mar had some words of encouragement: 'From my perspective, I'd say it's a two-pronged approach. All the work that you're doing [at Stemettes] is so important, then on the other side, as a continuation, there has to be a lot of other people pushing on the policy level for things like equal pay, and better treatment of workers of all genders.' They went on to say that this is to make sure we don't get into a situation where companies can take advantage of an influx of really highly skilled women workers to lower the pay, because that happens a lot, and it's a tricky line to walk.

Mar also pointed out that working in technology is also about who holds the power. It's not enough for women to work in tech and have good careers, they must also have the power to change things.

I asked Mar how we'd know when women are finally in CTRL. According to them, one of the hallmarks is going to be when we see women with a technical background in positions influencing policy and legislation.

Mar is optimistic about the long-term prospects for progress, as long as we don't give up. One thing that seems to be a barrier to a lot of folks is a phenomenon known as stereotype threat, where people act unconsciously in line with the negative stereotypes constantly levelled at them, about how their group should act. If women aren't aware that we were once the tech wizards, and continue to be sold the sorry tale that STEM subjects are not for girls or women, it's no wonder that we sometimes feel deflated.

It's why hiding the herstory of tech is so detrimental to progress. It's not just about a few geniuses who beat the odds – you don't have to be a genius to work in tech. Herstory is also made up of ordinary women who programmed computers, who calculated the trajectories of spaceships, who broke codes at Bletchley or soldered circuit boards, whose careers have been forgotten. Tech is something that anyone can do, and it always has been.

I see it as joining a herstorical chorus of women working to change the world.

The story of Marie-Sophie Germain is the classic example I always share. Germain was a French mathematician, physicist and philosopher who wanted to study maths in the late 1700s, when society considered it untoward for a woman to do such things with her brain. Girls weren't allowed to enrol at the prestigious École Polytechnique in France, so Germain had to apply under a male alias and do distance learning. Famous mathematicians such as Joseph-Louis Lagrange and Carl Friedrich Gauss were shocked and astounded to discover that the talented mathematician 'Monsieur Le Blanc' was in fact a woman. Germain continued to collaborate with the best mathematicians of the age, despite being patronized and sidelined.

When the construction of the Eiffel Tower was completed, the names of all the scientists and mathematicians of the day whose work had made this feat of engineering possible were inscribed on the structure. But not Marie-Sophie Germain's. In spite of her work on elasticity that directly contributed to the development of metal structures such as the Eiffel Tower, her name is *still* missing from the roll call.

The issue of the women being sidelined from the history of tech, both in reality and in the telling, happens not just within the tech sector. It's much broader than that. In the media, women make up only 24 per cent of individuals featured as experts on various subjects.[4] In the UK, analysis showed that Covid-19 news coverage included just 19 per cent of expert voices belonging to women versus 74 per cent belonging to men. Women were almost three times less likely to feature as subjects in news headlines than men. This is extraordinary given that 69 per cent of health professionals globally are women.[5] In a 2018 study of 60,000 speakers at private sector events across twenty-three countries, 69 per cent of them were male. We are still not giving women a sufficient platform.[6] What can we do about it?

When you want to find out about tech, or history, perhaps your starting point is Wikipedia. Having said that, the number of women with their own Wikipedia pages is a fraction of that of men, and when it comes to the volunteers who contribute to the website, over 90 per cent stated that they were men.[7] Physicist Dr Jess Wade has made a mission of getting the stories of women scientists told on Wikipedia. Alongside her day job as a research fellow at London's Imperial College, she has researched and written over a thousand Wikipedia entries. Every day she puts up an article on a woman in STEM or someone else underrepresented in STEM.

Wikipedia is open for anyone to edit or add to, but entries must adhere to a specific list of rules. There are rules on who counts as 'notable' enough to justify an article, and there are other rules on what counts as a 'reputable source'. Many of Jess's entries are taken down by the (mainly male) moderators on Wikipedia who repeat the same line: 'This person isn't not-able enough.'

You have to think about *why* that person isn't 'notable', though. If you don't put their name on the Eiffel Tower when their groundbreaking work has been instrumental during its construction, how will we know they're notable? If they're not called on as an expert and quoted in reputable media stories, how will we know they're notable? If you don't credit them or list their name as an author on work they've contributed to, how will we know they're notable?

These aren't just isolated stories; analysis commissioned in 2018, by the Global Institute for Women's Leadership at King's College London, found that 77 per cent of people quoted as experts in online news articles by the main UK news outlets are men.[8] The research looked at the gender balance of expert sources used by a sample of UK media across eight types of news coverage, revealing that women are significantly under-represented.

This is all about power.

Those building technology also like to reinforce the idea that this is not a sector for women, and they don't include them as part of the design process – which is to say we're not part of what they're building, and why they're building it. All of that adds up to generations of poor tech decisions being made, which we'll explore in Chapter 8.

Patriarchy is erasing the story – *our* story – and we all know the power of stories. People want to see and hear and tell them. They're a way to communicate, a way to share ideas. They're a way to make progress and to pass things on. They're also a core part of our culture. Women have been cut out of the tech story for too long, and the technology industry has suffered as a result. I think it's high time that we take our rightful place in the story of tech and that we prioritize adding ourselves back into it. For good tech to succeed we have to be part of the conversation. The story isn't over, so let's change it for future generations.

Getting Started

Given the scale of erasure, this is a tougher chapter to get started from. Jess Wade[9] has been diligently updating Wikipedia with biographies of women in STEM and other underrepresented folks for years now.[10] Search for the women in STEM category on Wikipedia[11] and see if you can spot one that's been authored by her. Then, click through to the 'View History' page. Take a look at the edits and the discussion around the updates and creation of the women's profiles that attract your attention. What sort of comments have been made on the content of the page? You can click on 'oldest' to see the earliest comments.

There's also the wider WikiProject Women in Red, which hosts events around the world where folks can add and improve profiles of women on Wikipedia.[12] Perhaps join the next virtual or physical one. You'll be able to learn Wiki markup language, which is what contributors use to write Wiki articles. If you speak another language, you can also help ensure a global audience for STEM herstory.

○ We at Stemettes have a Stemettes Zine resource (for a younger audience) full of profiles of women who inspire us. It's been a labour of love collating stories of women present and past, and we've got a long way to go. How many of them have aspects of their lives that overlap with yours?

○ There's a list of films you can watch in this space – *Hidden Figures, Bombshell, The Imitation Game.* How many more can you track down and find (about real technical women as opposed to fictional characters)? The film industry has so many more stories to tell.

○ Speaking of which, how are you documenting your own journey? You might not be ready yet, but where are you documenting your own learnings, things that excite you, your thoughts and realizations? A notebook, or other analogue option, is still fine, but perhaps it's time to experiment with something digital – can you create a private digital space where you can store snippets of your learning? Keeping a digital record will mean the content is automatically indexed and easier to search if you need to return to topics that come up time and time again, or if you want to add to information you've gleaned on your CTRL journey.

7

THE
VALUE OF
WOMEN

There will always be problems but, as we know, women are problem-solvers. They are also the missing piece of the puzzle. Think about the last time you added value to a project you were working on. When we talk about 'value' or 'adding value', this means that we're enhancing the narrative or filling the gap. Often our perspective is needed for a solution to take off, and in this chapter we'll talk a little bit about occasions when the absence of women from discussions in society and in technology has limited the scope for innovation or limited the development of the technology itself. Here's why, by virtue of being a woman, you often add value . . .

•

Back in 2000, the UN set the following eight core issues as Millennium Development Goals to be solved by 2015.

1. Eradicate extreme poverty and hunger
2. Achieve universal primary education
3. Promote gender equality and empower women
4. Reduce child mortality
5. Improve maternal health

6. Combat HIV/AIDS, malaria and other diseases
7. Ensure environmental sustainability
8. Develop a global partnership for development

We made some progress, but the target was missed, so the UN came up with a new set of problems, the 17 Sustainable Development Goals – even more ambitious than the original eight. What they learned from failure is that you can't solve problems if you don't include women, not just in the solution, but in the process of solving them. It's a two-pronged consideration.

A 2010 study in Brazil found a child is 20 per cent more likely to survive when the child's mother controls the household income.[1] Women's ownership of the familial assets helps to reduce poverty and inequalities, and improves children's nutrition, health and school attendance, because women tend to spend more of the income on their family members and communities than men do.[2]

As we've discussed, myriad examples exist to illustrate how the exclusion of women results in tech that doesn't work. Or perhaps the tech works only for the people who, coincidentally, are very like the people who created it. Voice recognition is one such case. It's been around for decades, but if you have a thick accent, Siri still can't always understand what you're saying. The same issue might arise when you call your phone company's automated menu and it doesn't quite recognize what you're trying to say.

It happens because the technology has been built with very limited datasets (a collection of information in a form that is easy for a computer or algorithm to understand and process).

It's as if they said, 'Only this type of person exists, so I'm only going to train the product for this kind of voice.' But different people speak very differently. Older people speak slightly slower. Women speak at a slightly different pitch. People with different accents pronounce words slightly differently. All of this is obvious, but apparently remains news to voice-recognition systems.

As frustrating as this is for people, the bigger point is that it's not commercially viable to release a product that works only for a certain set of people. It means the designers end up spending years re-working ye olde Siri, when they could have got to where they need to be quicker, and more efficiently, if they'd just included different types of people represented in broader and more inclusive audio datasets from the start.

Let's consider the world of health tech, and talk about periods in particular. The menstrual cycle is central to a lot of people's health, because it affects so many parts of the body as well as the mind. For health tech companies, completely ignoring menstruation is one thing you do at your peril, as several major ones have discovered. There was a limit to the length of her period a woman could track on her Fitbit: ten days. Anyone who's ever had a period will know that it pretty much does what it wants. You can't say, 'I'm only going to track it for this many days' – that's not how they work. The setting caused anger and frustration amongst women – there's even a Fitbit community page where scores of women implored Fitbit to take the limit off the period tracker.[3]

When you *do* get around to building a tech feature that centres on the menstrual cycle, you might want to talk to some people who menstruate before you go ahead and build it. It's important for women to have agency when it comes to things that are happening to their own bodies, as well as providing data should anything go wrong. It begs the question whether anyone on any of Fitbit's teams had ever *had* a period: the marketing team, the development team, the hardware team or the software team, the design team or the test team. Had no one there, at any point in the process, ever met someone who had ever had a period? Had they considered perimenopausal periods? If they had, they hadn't listened to that person or asked the right questions, which meant that by the time the feature came out, it was essentially useless. The company lost money and sustained damage to its reputation by building something that didn't work.

It's not just about periods – there's lots of this happening in design and product creation. Believe it or not, we only have nylon tights because of space travel. Nylon was a material that was briefly considered for astronauts' suits, but in the end it wasn't deemed suitable. It worked fine back on Earth for women's tights!

By deprioritizing certain people in society, we've ended up with whole areas of biology and medicine completely under-researched and obscured. The pursuit of knowledge is rarely linear. By not understanding female health, we lack a full knowledge of *human* health. If we understood the way women's bodies worked *more*, it's possible we'd have a greater understanding of *everyone*'s bodies. Who knows what will be uncovered when we properly recognize, study and understand the full gamut of women's health? We're here, we're real, some of us gave birth to the people who are using this technology.

Not 'seeing' women limits the scope and the quality of what you're able to do, and the scale at which you're able to grow.

That's the power of the problems that need solving: we are all in this together. The challenge to the patriarchy is that if you seek power in only one place, and you take it from only one perspective, you're not actually going to address all the problems that we face. If you're a company, you're not going to achieve the market penetration that you'd like. Eighty-nine per cent of buying decisions are made by women, which means that if you completely ignore women, you're left with 11 per cent of the market's potential. If you want all the power, it's the wrong way to go about things.[4]

Bringing a woman's perspective to rooms where they've been previously ignored, or been excluded as a result of gatekeeping, adds a lot of value. When you do decide to technically engage, it's important to think about all those generations that you're turning up for. When you do decide to take CTRL, it's not just for yourself.

Sticking with the world of health tech, entrepreneur speaker and women's health advocate Billie Quinlan has created an app called Ferly. It's an app about sexual health, which is a part of the healthcare picture that we don't talk about often enough, and a guide to personal sexual intimacy – what you enjoy and what gives you pleasure, rather than your pleasure being linked purely with the actions of someone else. The idea is that if you find out what *you* like then you are more in control when you're with another person. By the same token, if you know what you like, you will also know what you don't like. You'll have the option to understand and take control of your sexual experiences.

Not enough research has been done into women's sexual health and the importance of the relationship you have with yourself. Mentally, yes, physically, yes, but also sexually. If you know yourself, what you're looking for or what you value, then the relationship you have with others and the agency that you have over your own body will be different.

Billie was working in IT when she was sexually assaulted in the workplace. It was the first time that she was confronted with the notion that our wellness is made up of more than just our physical and mental health. She realized that there's also a third pillar – sexual wellness. Her personal experience motivated her to create Ferly as a way to actively rebuild her relationship with her own body, and her own sexual feelings, through tech.

'It's an area that impacts so many of us,' Billie told me when she was a guest on my podcast. 'So many of us have a very negative relationship with our own bodies, but we don't have the language or the tools to understand it. Instead – especially when it comes to women – we just think that we're having crappy sex because women just don't enjoy sex that much. That's the narrative that we have around it and that's the problem that I wanted to address.'

Ferly is a really great example of how a woman who had a negative experience was able to convert it into something good. The app is providing a solution to a problem that many people would shy away from acknowledging exists in the first place and which, historically, hasn't really been looked into. How exciting is it to be able to create something that does that for the first time, and also use technology to empower people on such a big scale?

The Power of Agency

When we talk about agency, we often mean having financial control. For me, there's certainly a financial aspect when it comes to being in CTRL – but it also goes way beyond that. Traditionally, we measure success financially. Two British economists, James Meade and Richard Stone, devised what we now call GDP as a way to measure the total economic value of a country's output.

In 1941, Stone hired Phyllis Deane to measure the GDP of some African countries that were, at that time, still part of the British Empire. Deane quickly realized that GDP was a useless measure in countries such as Zambia or Malawi, where most of the useful work was unpaid, or paid in cash, and done largely by women.

In her book, *Colonial Social Accounting*, Deane wrote, 'Most of the labour for the basic unit of production, the family, is supplied by the woman. She does most of the recurrent agricultural work, most of the planting, the weeding, the fetching and carrying, the routine harvest work and the preparation of food.'[5]

Fetching water, collecting firewood, preparing food and weaving mats were as essential to the economy of those countries as the coal and chemical industries, farming and textile factories were to the British economy at that time, but the narrow definition of GDP excluded work outside the market system, so it also excluded most of this work being done by women.

Deane pushed for the 'women's work' to be included in official figures, but was ignored. Because of the patriarchy, her request was deprioritized. In 1953, a committee of exclusively male accountants wrote the United Nations handbook on systems of national accounts, which advised national account-ants to exclude household and subsistence labour. The committee that revised the guidelines in 1968 had just one woman on it – Margaret Mód.

Some feminists in the 1970s pushed for housework to be included in economic measures, and the Wages for Housework movement called for it to be salaried work, directly paid. Yet here we are, five decades later. In one report, the independent think tank Autonomy stated, 'There are 3 million people in high exposure (to diseases and infections) jobs in the UK. Seventy-seven per cent of them are women. Of these workers, 1,060,400 are earning "poverty wages". Ninety-eight per cent are women.'[6]

Back in 1981, Canadian campaigner Judith Ramirez, spokeswoman for the Wages for Housework Committee, wrote, 'The failure of the world's economies to recognize the economic worth of women's work has devastating consequences. Women receive only one-tenth of the world's income though we perform two-thirds of the world's work.'[7]

It's worth keeping in mind that success comes in many forms. If we start to look at other measures, beyond economics and GDP, then we're able to see those other types. We can still have CTRL and make an impact in other ways.

When my best friend got married a few years ago, I learned that only her father's occupation was asked to be entered on the marriage register. Given the fact that she doesn't have a relationship with her father – her mother performed both parental roles – she gave her mother's occupation instead. At the time, I remember being taken aback by this inequality.

A couple of years down the line, as I began to plan my own wedding, I was informed by our church that the law was about to change, and that the occupation of the mother would be added to the register too. Delays ensued due to the Covid pandemic, but the law has finally been amended – to much public fanfare. By the time I do get married, there will be a space for both my mother's occupation as well as that of my father, but for anyone in the UK who got married before 4 May 2021, that information will be missing from the historical marriage register. All those mothers' occupations will remain invisible on the public record.

It's this kind of overhang that keeps us used to viewing success in the way it's been framed by the patriarchy, and used to thinking that only particular types of success matter. However, if we look more roundly at the potential for women's success, it's more than just money and financial gain. Over the years, we've adjusted how much we talk about money with young people at Stemettes, and discuss the ways we can add value beyond GDP much more.

It's great to be able to say, 'If you come into tech, or if you get a tech job, you'll be paid really highly.' Even in 2018, a few years after we started Stemettes, there was a statistic that showed women who work in STEM earn 57 per cent more than non-STEM women.[8] If you want to earn well, and have all the control, agency and power that comes with that kind of earning power, that's a very good reason to come into tech. We don't want to diminish that in any way. It's important – so important that many have suggested the fastest way to close the gender pay gap is to increase the number of women entering the STEM workforce. Even so, I think there's also something to be said about the other benefits that come from having agency.

For me, tech is altruistic – it's about solving problems. Whether it's health, education, environmental outcomes, or improving or overcoming poverty. We need to think about all these issues not just in an economic context, but also in the wider context of quality of life.

•

There's a direct line between the problems we need to solve and women having more agency. More economic participation from women translates into improved children's nutrition, school attendance and health. It's why it's so important for us to think about the things we're able to do if we can take control of our work, our education, our lives. And technology has been a really good tool for folks to use to take control in those ways, whether it's online distance learning, working remotely to give more flexibility during your working week, or using technical services to connect with communities for support.

Some of the young women and non-binary folk who come through Stemettes will end up working particular technical roles and being well paid. They'll fulfil their personal potential and will be gainfully employed. They'll also have technical agency and power – which will be a benefit for all of us. However, the impact of Stemettes isn't purely about financial gain. As a social enterprise we operate to a triple bottom line. It's about people, and about the planet, as well as being about profits (or surplus).

When we consider the implications of generations of patriarchy in tech, it's clear that generations of harm have been done. Non-financial issues have been neglected. As a woman, these are pretty solid obstacles to come up against. We've established that we can't build things properly without including women. It's just as important for us to think about what we're striving to achieve. What does good look like? How much of that utopia can we imagine that's not money-related? And how much of it can we influence and do something about by using tech? How do we understand tech so that we can apply it to the issues we've identified, solving our own problems and the problems of others in the process? We can't deny the power of money, but there's also the power of agency. The power of potential. There is an opportunity to use this power to hold tech to account.

Getting Started

What matters? What does success look like? How might tech support that vision? Utopia means all kinds of things to different people, and many of us haven't ever been able to stop and reflect fully on what it might mean. Perhaps it's time to go sci-fi at this stage in your CTRL journey . . .

○ Imagine the equivalent of yourself in the year 2222. What's a typical day in the life of this person? What is tech doing for them? What has tech allowed them to do that you can't do today? How has technology removed barriers for them? Not all sci-fi has to happen on another planet. Not all sci-fi has to be dystopian. Let everything you've learned up until this point unite with your dreams and your frustrations with everyday life, and write something that excites you about what things could be like.

○ Where are you missing out in the technology you use on a daily basis? What could a better-designed bus mean? What could our social lives be like?

○ Billie Quinlan turned a terrible experience into a new chapter when she created Ferly. Without triggering yourself, what terrible experiences do you think might be turned around by 2222?

○ Take a look at the femtech space (add to your 'to search' list). There's so much on offer, and so much more to come. What would be your contribution to that space? Or how might you refine some existing products and services?

8

HOLDING
TECH
ACCOUNTABLE

Many damaging things happen as a result of people's use of technology and the way that technology has been built. As well as gender discrimination, one of the issues that concerns me the most is when tech is used to enable racism or the outcomes of the use of tech are racist.

Let's take a look at Twitter. When you upload a picture, it usually appears in the feed cropped, and you have to click on it to enlarge it and see the whole image. The thing is, Twitter dictates which part of the image is significant in the thumbnail. It's not always about reducing the image size based on dimensions – the AI powering Twitter tries to be smart by focusing on the area it believes will be of most interest to the viewer.

Say you have a photo of three white faces in one row, with a Black face in the row below. Twitter will show you one of the white faces, which might make sense given there are more white faces overall. However, if the situation is reversed (three Black faces in a row and a white face below), Twitter will cut to the white face in the thumbnail. Why is the Black person never the focal point in an image unless only Black faces are shown?[1]

Twitter apologized for not fully testing for racial bias before releasing the algorithm, but it isn't the only platform guilty of such egregious errors. For example, the virtual backgrounds featured in Zoom's video conferencing platform recently removed the head of a Black academic from a session because it has a poor facial-recognition algorithm for detecting Black faces against the virtual background.[2]

Twitter has the power to decide which news stories are displayed the most and what is censored. Royal family scandals tend to be far less visible, but the racism directed towards the Black England football players following the Euro 2021 final was left unchecked. It regularly uses its power to hide news stories, but had to experience severe pressure before deleting just over 1,000 abusive tweets.

Phrenology – the theory that certain mental faculties and character traits are related to the shape of a person's skull – is now, at best, viewed as a pseudo-science. It was originally used by eugenicists to politically justify the colonization of certain countries by theorizing that the inhabitants were less intelligent. The practice has been retired because it's really just white supremacy dressed up as science. However, we continue to see tech utilizing elements of this pseudo-science in their software.

Nature Communications, an open-access journal, published a study suggesting a person's trustworthiness could be determined by their facial features, an idea which stinks of eugenics. When such rubbish gets published on such a highly regarded platform it suggests that the software being used is bona fide, endorsing its uptake in modern technology. Racist science is being codified and used in the systems that help to hire people, and companies are using this bad tech to 'help' humans make decisions about other humans. Abeba Birhane, @abebab on

Twitter, is constantly pointing out examples of this while she completes a cognitive science PhD at University College Dublin.[3]

What's happening here is not OK, and racism itself is illegal in the eyes of equality legislation across the world. It's of paramount importance that, as part of taking control of tech, we're able to hold tech accountable. It's also important to be clear that the technology is racist as a result of the society within which it is operating, as well as old social inequalities that get reflected in datasets and decisions that are made about technology.

A computer science term you'll hear often – and one that's particularly relevant when it comes to bad tech – is 'garbage in, garbage out', or GIGO. If you put in any old rubbish as data, the information or model you get out the other end will also be rubbish. If we allude once more to GIGO, it will make sense in this context – *racist in, racist out.*

Because technology is able to make decisions much faster than human beings, and at scale, it means that if we use older, unchecked data in small ways initially, the implications will be magnified in the future.[4] We must be wary of this happening. If we want these decision-making systems to be anti-racist and anti-sexist, we must give careful consideration to race and sex as we build them.

Systemic racism is defined as: 'discrimination or unequal treatment on the basis of membership of a particular racial or ethnic group (typically one that is a minority or marginalized), arising from systems, structures, or expectations that have become established within society or an institution.'[5]

Dr Joy Buolamwini achieved her childhood dream of attending one of the most respected universities in the world, Massachusetts Institute of Technology (MIT). However, when she tried to build an art project called the 'Aspire Mirror', which projected different inspiring images onto her face every morning, she discovered that the off-the-shelf software she was using wouldn't recognize her. It wasn't just failing to recognize her as Joy, or as Dr Buolamwini. It wasn't recognizing her face as a face.

This prime example of systemic racism was the start of her journey, captured in the documentary *Coded Bias*, that led to the foundation of the Algorithmic Justice League, which campaigns against algorithms that discriminate. The film focuses on facial-recognition software, which is also being used in the UK, and generally works very badly on any faces that aren't white and male – like the ones used to train the software.

Joy's MIT research project, Gender Shades[6], tested three different facial-recognition products, first on her own TED speaker photo, and then on the faces of 1,270 politicians from six African and European countries. All three claimed to classify faces into male and female, but Joy discovered their levels of accuracy varied wildly. Error rates for all three were higher in female faces than male ones, and higher in darker-skinned subjects. All three performed worst on darker-skinned female faces, with two getting it right just two-thirds of the time. Not a good outcome, considering that tossing a coin would give you a 50 per cent chance of getting the right answer.

We've seen that if you don't value women or their point of view when you're building technology and making decisions, how are you ever going to build something that automatically values them? The same holds true for race, and the outcome is racism.

One inventor caught up in such racial injustice was Mary Kenner, who, in the 1920s, tackled a taboo subject by inventing a belt to hold sanitary pads in place.[7] After Mary was finally able to afford the expensive patent-filing process, in 1956, a company contacted her about manufacturing her design. When they met her and discovered she was Black, they pulled out. Other companies also turned her down. Mary never made any money from her design as it wasn't made commercially until her patent had expired.

If Mary were around today, she might have crowdfunded her project, which democratizes the process in one sense and would have helped her to get past fewer gatekeepers. There are some big differences between the period when Mary was innovating and now, when *you* are innovating. The technology is moving forward, things are better and you will be able to take more control. That being said, you need to know about options such as crowdfunding in order to take part.

We see countless examples of racism playing out in daily life, whether it's the media being unable to tell one Black person apart from another, or the police stopping and searching and pulling people over – sometimes because they're driving a good car, or because they fit a 'certain profile' of someone 'more likely' to end up in prison.[8]

Dr Nira Chamberlain is President of the Institute of Mathematics and its Applications, but when he said he wanted to be a mathematician, his school teacher told him somebody of his 'build' was more suited to being a boxer. He became the first Black mathematician to appear in *Who's Who*, the annual reference publication on important and influential people.

Tobi Oredein is a great example of somebody who saw a problem, identified what was missing, and used technology to help fill that gap and meet those needs. She loved women's lifestyle magazines from an early age, and when she was eleven her father took out a subscription to *Cosmo Girl* for her, to stop her from standing in the magazine aisle at the supermarket and reading all the magazines while he did the shopping.

Once she entered the world of work, she ran into trouble trying to find her dream job. She was working as a lifestyle journalist and had held positions at various women's and entertainment publications. In 2012, the year Whitney Houston died, Tobi was interning for a magazine that put out a special tribute issue to the singer, but mistakenly printed a picture of Oprah instead of one of a young Whitney. Tobi flagged the error with an editor and suggested printing an apology, but there was backlash.

'Everyone was like, "She's got such an attitude! Who does she think she is?"' Tobi told me. 'I wanted the floor to swallow me up. I felt so silenced, like I should never have said anything. It was such a traumatic experience to me that the whole office was talking about how I had a nasty attitude, that I should know my place.'

Tobi was the only Black person working in that office. She still can't understand why her colleagues responded the way they did. They were all journalists, after all – surely presenting the facts and apologizing when you get it wrong is part of the job.

Tobi moved on to another magazine, and when her contract ended she found herself out of work and unable, despite applying for everything, to find another position. She did some research on the women who were being successful in securing these jobs in lifestyle journalism and discovered that, essentially, they were all very thin and very white. She decided to do something herself.

Tobi had noticed a lack of lifestyle magazines aimed at Black

British women: 'I'm super passionate about Black women, and always talking about how there's nothing for Black women, not in Britain. *Ebony* and *Essence* are amazing – but there's nothing here for me as a Black millennial that encompasses everything from careers to beauty, the whole spectrum of what it is to be a Black woman.'

Tobi gathered her 'super-talented' friends and put together a social media team, a writing team, a sub-ed team, and a designer. She got the website made on the cheap, and eight months later, she launched *Black Ballad* online.

Tobi couldn't find herself on the women's lifestyle shelf in the supermarket magazine aisle, and so had to create what was lacking. However, after she'd started *Black Ballad*, she found something else was missing: data. Not only were people like Tobi not represented on the magazine shelves, they weren't in the statistics and data that journalists use for research either.

Tobi was pushing for quality journalism, to match that in established publications such as the *Guardian*. She wanted to do investigative pieces, not just opinion pieces, but that required research, and therefore stats. One of *Black Ballad*'s first investigative pieces was about the Black experience in higher education, from the perspective of a student and lecturers. However, the person she commissioned struggled to find any real statistics about the challenges that Black students face in the UK, or even the number of Black lecturers working in UK universities. The researcher had to rely either on US stats or British stats that encompassed everybody.

To make a great platform and run quality journalism, Tobi needed good data to reflect what was going on in the Black community in Britain and beyond. 'Because numbers don't lie,' she told me. 'People can say, "You're a little bit emotional about that issue. Is it really like that?" You need the numbers to back you up.'

In 2020, *Black Ballad* won a grant from the Membership Puzzle Project in the US to look at a particular issue within the Black community in Britain. Tobi chose Black motherhood and surveyed over 2,500 women, uncovering the experiences of Black women's journeys through pregnancy and motherhood in the process.

Black Ballad was a small team, and the amount of new knowledge that came out of the survey had a big impact on them. They realized just how much they didn't know about the lives of Black women in Britain and Europe. They started to think about how they could distribute the data they'd collected, so that it could be used by the community, by academics, and by society in general.

Using social media to go beyond traditional publishing, Tobi has also been able to build a community of Black women, including a wide range of experiences, in a safe and non-judgemental space. On top of that, a £70,000 grant from Nesta, the innovation foundation, allowed *Black Ballad* to commission writers from around the UK, writing stories from their own areas.

'I'm for ever indebted to technology,' Tobi told me. 'It lowered the barriers for me to be able to start a publication. I would never have been able to afford the materials to create a print publication. Technology made a more even playing field for people like me.'

She also explained to me just how important it is to give power to other Black women in journalism, not just in a writing capacity, but in positions where they will actively be making decisions on the content. I asked her what success would look like for her. How will she know when she's done a good job? Her vision for the future is ambitious.

I believe that *Black Ballad* can be the leading publication for Black women in Britain and across Europe, and the diaspora. Where is the publication for Black women in Australia and New Zealand? The African American voice is very pronounced, very loud and clear. I think our Black British voice is clear and pronounced, but it's just not loud. I want to magnify those voices. I want us to be the number-one media company in those countries and across continents.

She'll know she's done when people start writing academic texts and books on the Black experience that aren't centred on the US and African Americans, and when there's enough rich data, qualitative as well as quantitative, from the stories *Black Ballad* has put together: 'Our experience in Britain is so rich, I think it deserves a platform. I just think it deserves to be docu-mented better.'

Tobi now has her lifestyle platform and a great following. She has the capacity to collect datasets, and she's creating and using them to make Black women's lives more visible. *Black Ballad* has just completed a successful equity crowdfund, raising around £300,000 from 1,400 investors, many of them Black women, which will enable the team to invest more heavily in the tech that will allow them to reach an even wider audience of Black women.

As Tobi's experience demonstrates, there's a lot of data that we just don't have, a lot of information that we haven't col-lected, and a lot of issues that have not been prioritized, seen as important or seen as worthy. If we don't think that a group of people is important or care that they exist, then it's pretty hard to build technology that doesn't end up doing some of the damaging and discriminatory things that we've seen and continue to see.

One recent example is the app unveiled by Google to help identify skin conditions. Although they claim their technology works for skin types 'from pale skin that does not tan to brown skin that rarely burns', they didn't use a truly diverse range to build their technology. Only 6.8 per cent of the people in Google's training dataset said they were Black, and none of them had skin that matched the darkest category, Type VI, in the standard Fitzpatrick classification system.

It's quite a telling story about what it is to be Black.

We've also seen problems with people trying to renew their UK passports online. The Home Office software repeatedly told Black people that their photos weren't acceptable because their mouths were open. Their mouths were not open, but the software (provided to the UK Government by a private company) hadn't been trained on enough faces that look like mine. BBC research, based on the Gender Shades study by Joy Buolamwini and Timnit Gebru, found that dark-skinned people were 50–60 per cent more likely to be told their uploaded photos don't meet the required standards.

Globally (because technology is global), you can't be successful in your product creation when you're failing to include a huge chunk of the world's population. Focusing on one ethnicity means that you're not building something that will fully work anywhere. The stats are hard to find because of differences in definition and ability to count but, proportionally speaking, if the world were 100 people, roughly eleven would be European, sixty would be Asian, fifteen would be African and fourteen would be from the Americas. By religion, thirty-one would be Christian, twenty-three Muslim, fifteen Hindu, seven Buddhist, eight other religions and belief systems, and the final sixteen unaffiliated. This should be part of our thinking when creating.

This is the hard edge of needing to hold tech accountable. A lot of it, and the decisions that are made around it, involve particular people in power – individuals who commission a particular system or decide what or how something should be built. That's an issue. The problem isn't just that their software doesn't know about my lip colour when I need a new passport. The issue is more that their system is going to assume I'm more likely to commit a crime. If datasets and software are being used to decide risks of reoffending, I might end up unnecessarily doing a prison sentence.

Facial-recognition software works quite well, but only if you're white and male. That's not good if you're Black or female and trying to unlock your phone or get into your house. And it's very bad if you're being tagged by a police facial-recognition system as matching somebody on their files.

Facial-recognition software recently misidentified a young Black teenage girl as having been involved in a brawl at an ice-rink in Michigan. She was rejected from the venue on arrival. That was her first visit to the ice-rink and her features didn't match those of the girl she was supposed to be. Because the software wasn't sensitive enough to make a strong identification, the girl's safety was also jeopardized when she was escorted out of the building onto the streets, alone.[9]

These are two real-world examples resulting from algorithms used by the police and court systems in the US and UK. The people programming the algorithms didn't set out to be racist, but they used historic data that was neither fair nor equal, without thinking about the fact that interactions between the police and the courts and the public have not been equal or fair in the past either.

You'll have noticed that the people who aren't being well served by these AI systems are also the people who are already disadvantaged and excluded in society. Black people in the US are arrested and imprisoned at far higher rates than Hispanic or white people. Though imprisonment rates are falling, in 2019 1.5 per cent of Black American adults were in prison, compared to 0.8 per cent of Hispanic adults and 0.25 per cent of white adults. Meanwhile, in the UK, Black people are over three times as likely as white people to be arrested.[10]

If the same AI system is used for hiring selections, then that's going to end up having an impact on Black people too. Someone like me won't be selected for a particular job because of the system's assumptions, because I wasn't built in as part of that policy.

If we're going to hold tech accountable, we need to recognize that systemic racism is already codified into the technology. The issues are the same for anyone who hasn't been considered, hasn't been prioritized or hasn't been seen as being as worthy as other humans. When we're building a system that makes decisions on human beings, it's important for *all* human beings to be acknowledged in its creation. We all need to be a part of making the right kinds of technical decisions, and in understanding the decisions that are being made about us.

Getting Started

See the fullness of humanity. Use technology to hear and see the differences in people around you. Deloitte's Diversify Your Feed tool is a good start for social media. Follow a few folks who have different views to yours. Subscribe to a Black-focused news outlet such as *Black Ballad* or *gal-dem*. Actively look for different angles on the same news story. Whether you fully understand the new perspective or not to start with, reading a story on, say, violence, written by an outlet that is focused on a particular community, can be eye-opening and help colour in your understanding of the fullness of humanity.

- Lend your support to accountability groups. Be on the lookout to support folks who are holding tech accountable, from the Institute for the Future of Work in the UK to the Algorithmic Justice League in the US. Sign petitions, write letters and subscribe to newsletters. Join the affinity groups in your workplace. Not all support needs to be financial, but a little bit can go a long way. So many of these organizations are run on a voluntary basis and don't have the support of big tech firms.

- Make sure you credit women and underrepresented folks whose ideas you like, when they inform your actions or work. Passive support and proactive support are possible with little effort, but at scale will ensure that we change the course of history. As you learn more, you'll be empowered to join the frontline – don't spend too much time comfortably supporting from the back!

9

WHO
GETS TO
CHOOSE?

Nothing is inevitable in the creation of a tool or a product.
There's nothing that *has* to happen. It's the choice of a person,
an organization or a group of people as to what gets created. At
Stemettes, when we're teaching young people to code, before
we give them a computer we get them to write a set of instructions for somebody who has never made a jam sandwich before,
or even seen one. We put a knife and a plate, two slices of bread
and a jar of jam in front of them as a visual aid. Sounds simple
enough, but there's a twist – they're not allowed to use the
words 'put', 'get', 'spread' or 'open'.

When they're finished, we get the girls to read out the
instructions, and a member of the team acts as a sandwich-
maker and follows them as literally as they can. If a step is
ambiguous or incomplete, the sandwich-maker either makes a
lot of mess or doesn't do anything. If the first step doesn't
explicitly say, 'pick up the knife in one hand', they might use
their elbows. If the spreading step reads, 'distribute the jam
evenly', without specifying 'on the bread', we end up with a lot
of jam everywhere.

These instructions are essentially an algorithm – a series of
choices. If you make the wrong choices, you end up with a huge

amount of mess and no end result. It's up to the person writing the algorithm to get it right.

It doesn't have to be a jam sandwich. It's up to you if you'd rather have a honey one, if you want to use brown bread or white, if you want to cut it on the diagonal or straight down the middle. Ultimately, it's your choice whether you even want to make a sandwich or something else entirely.

When we talk about creating technology, we're talking about the same considerations – it's all about looking at the options you have and the choices you make. And there are always options. Even if you're using massive sets of data, which is the nature of a lot of today's technology, it's up to you which ones you use, which ones you ascribe a greater value to, and which ones you combine. What technology does is determined and defined by its creator, and one of the most important considerations is who is in the room when those choices are being made.

Making the Right Choices

One thing you could do in your next ten minutes of learning is watch a TED talk by computer scientist Timnit Gebru called 'How Can We Stop Artificial Intelligence from Marginalizing Communities?'.[1] In it, Timnit Gebru compares the tech industry today to what happened during the early days of the automobile industry. Just like early motor cars, tech is being developed faster than its effects are being researched and regulated.

When first launched in 1931, there were just 2.3 million motor vehicles in Great Britain, yet over 7,000 people were being killed in road accidents each year. The technology came in before anyone had worked out the necessary rules and habits to make it safe. People weren't used to motorized vehicles travelling on their roads, and speed limits had never been enforced before. Even though the 1865 Red Flag Act had long ago reduced UK speed limits to 2 mph in towns and 4 mph in rural areas, roads remained dangerous.

Gradually, the technology itself became safer, with the introduction of seat belts, better brakes, lights, and so on. However, the social rules and conventions were just as important: driving on the same side of the road when more than one car is travelling in the same direction, road signs, rules for who gives way at a junction, and so on. Even though there are more and more vehicles on the road today, fewer people every year die in road accidents.

Those social rules and conventions were all reached by making choices. As were the new road systems that would protect pedestrians as well as drivers, and the new motor vehicle technology. Every time we make a choice, we should ask what are the implications of that choice, and there's one particular question we need to be asking a lot more: How are we including differences in the choices that we make? Or, to turn the question around, what kind of privileges are at work when it comes to the kind of people who get to make the choices, and what those choices are?

Privilege can mean advantage, being lucky, being born rich or healthy, or just getting the right opportunity at the right time. One of my privileges is that both of my parents went to university. This meant that tertiary education was always on my radar and appeared very achievable for me. In the society I live in, having a university degree affords me a higher earning potential and a particular status, as well as an affinity and understanding with certain people in the top strata of society. I'm still Black, a woman and clinically obese, but my parents' higher-education experiences have definitely given me advantages in life.

Privilege is also about society conferring a different status and special protection upon some individuals and groups of individuals. In medieval times a privilege was literally a legal right to do things that others weren't permitted to do, such as letting your pigs eat the acorns in the woods, or getting away with things that others couldn't, such as not paying tithes or taxes. Today, privilege is mostly informal and often unconscious. It's about getting away with a minor motoring offence because you're white, or being asked your opinion in a meeting because you're male.

When tech is built by people who have that kind of privilege, those people might never have considered the fact that other people don't have it. As we discussed in Chapter 8, not having to think about whether AI will recognize your face as a human face shouldn't be a privilege, it should just be the way things are for all of us. That's not where we're starting from, though. To get to where we want to be, we need to get those different faces and voices and experiences into the technical room and decision-making spaces.

Whenever technical choices are being made, whenever new tech is being created, there is the opportunity to think about difference. Some of the difference that you could bring to those decisions derives from the fact that you're a woman, and we've seen all the ways that women's perspectives are missing in tech, but there will also be other forms of difference that might not be directly related to who you are.

When you start getting into tech, and creating new tech, it's important to always bear that difference in mind. One example would be if you're building something for water. At higher temperatures water turns to steam, and at really low temperatures it turns to ice, so the product should consider water in *all* its states. If you're building something relating to women's health, bear in mind that pregnancy and menopause are also phases of female reproductive health, so it might perhaps be an idea to take into account women who aren't having periods.

It might also be worth considering women living with disabilities, or women experiencing menstrual disorders such as endometriosis. All kinds of individuals might want to use your technology, or might also be facing the problem that you're trying to solve, but are coming at it from different perspectives. Your creation process is going to be really important in terms of holding tech accountable, and ensuring that what you build is helpful and stands the test of time.

As well as all the other skills you're building, you need to develop your ability to spot the difference, to hear the difference. That way, you can exercise your capacity for choice-making in how you explore things, and in the technical decisions you're going to make. You can embrace difference, and build for it.

I think of this capacity to be intentional as a new frontier. It's the new space race, something that's in its infancy, and is still open to being influenced. Your privilege can be taking control on behalf of others, on behalf of the diversity and full range of people who might use the technology you create.

As well as the different types of folks in the present for whom you're creating tech, you might also be finding a new voice for those who were there in the past, but who still aren't represented in the tech you're now learning more about. The choices you make now will have an impact on the lives of a diverse range of people in the future. We can't ignore the social, moral and political stakes. Technology is often presented with certainty and scientific neutrality, but we need to acknowledge uncertainty and practise humility when it comes to the tech we create.[2]

Remember that technology is deterministic. It will perpetuate and disseminate any poor decisions that you make now, and it will magnify them. So make sure you're making the right decisions when it comes to the small stuff, because that will determine the next choices you get to make, and the ones after that, until they end up shaping things on a massive scale.

Power in (Small) Numbers

The number of people who get to make the important choices is ... small. They also tend to come from a very narrow slice of the world's population. The way that power is concentrated like this affects how accountable we can hold these individuals, and the technology they create.

The same holds true for the limited range of people who tend to be in government, and this problem is the impetus behind the 50:50 Parliament initiative here in the UK. The idea is that, since the population is a 50:50 ratio of men to women, the make-up of Parliament, which makes decisions on behalf of the population, should also be 50:50. That way, the needs and wants of the whole population, their concerns and their troubles, can be reflected in the decisions that are being made. Instead of making pandemic policies that result in more women losing their work – such as the closing-down of the beauty sector, for example, or assuming that women could take time off work for homeschooling – the needs of women would be considered right from the start. The more agency and power women have, the easier it will be to hold power to account for actions that do us harm.

I'd like to see the same thing happen in technology. A version of history has continually and very intentionally been sold to us, but it doesn't have to look that way going forward. We have choices. When you think about the impact that tech can have, it's obvious that that power shouldn't be concentrated in one type of person. The many experiences you have as a woman aren't unique to you, but they're very much hidden from those who are more likely to be in that 'ruling' class.

A friend of mine worked at a clothing retail site where she was the developer. On several occasions she had to explain how bra sizes work, because the team kept building filters and ways to store information about particular products that didn't take into account the fact that a bra size is made up of numbers as well as letters, in that particular order. She had to keep reminding the team about the importance of these sizes, because if a consumer is looking for a bra, size is the most crucial factor, because they need to know it's going to fit.

That team of developers didn't understand bra sizes because they had limited life experience, not because bra-wearing is something unique to you. In the same way, when politicians talk about personal safety, they too often lack knowledge that you have as a woman. There are things you instinctively know about what's safe and what isn't, whether you're travelling home on your own or are alone in a room with a certain person.

Let's look at a common scenario, where we might use Google Maps to plot our route home. A friend of mine, Jillian Kowal-chuk, founded the app Safe & the City, which provides users with safer, better-lit routes to walk in an unfamiliar area. She created this out of her own desire to feel more secure. It's not a feature that Google Maps deems important to include in their own app. When we consider the deaths of Sarah Everard, Bibaa Henry, Nicole Smallman and Sabina Nessa, there is also something to be said about how technology can be used to hold those who are meant to keep us safe accountable. It has since been revealed that the many discussions amongst police officers on technology platforms could have been used to flag and pre-empt the terrible tragedies that have since taken place.

The responsibility to keep people safe in public spaces goes beyond the culpability of those in positions of power, of course. Many other attackers post enough content online to set the red flags waving. Technology can be reactive, producing apps such as Safe & the City, or preventative, by analysing dangerous content when it appears. Good and inclusive technology could have played a part in ensuring these women were still with us.

The power to make choices needs to be distributed across many different axes in society. A huge hurdle is that new tech is often funded by venture capitalists (VCs) who take a chance on products or tech innovations that may never succeed. The majority of British VCs are white – in fact, three-quarters of London VCs (where most British ones are located) are white.

They're mostly men – less than one in seven individuals on investment committees are women, and over a third of UK VC companies in 2019 were exclusively male. US investment firms are no better. Women make up less than 10 per cent of VC partners, and four out of five VC companies have not a single Black investor on the team. They're also drawn from elite backgrounds and institutions. One in five UK VCs went to Oxford, Cambridge or Harvard.[3] These are the people making funding decisions about startups. Whether it's building more technology or reaching more users, whatever that company needs, money plays a vital role.

It's important to make sure that tech is not built by the few and feared by the many. We need to know how to disrupt this and we need to be deliberately using technology as a tool. It's not enough to accept that tech is universally positive because it's about modernity and progress. We need to be intentional about the potential, to use it as a force for change, and for social justice. If technology has been designed by men in the global North, we can't assume that it's going to be equally useful to all humanity. Technologies designed for the few by the few are constructed with many visible and invisible power dynamics. As we make our choices, as we build this technology, it's so important that we are vigilant about who is gaining power, who is maintaining power and who is losing power as a result of this technology.

When the Apple Card launched in 2019, it hit the news for the wrong reasons. Like most financial products, customers were offered different credit limits on their card, based on what an algorithm thought they could reliably afford to repay, but some high-profile customers reported that the algorithm was discriminating against female customers. The tech entrepreneur Steve Wozniak went public about the fact that he was offered a credit limit ten times bigger than his wife's, even though they have no separate finances. Steve Wozniak is, of course, the co-founder of ... Apple.

Historically, women haven't necessarily had as much money as men, and that shows up in credit-card data from the past. Whatever algorithm was setting the Apple Card credit limits was doubling down on that. By discriminating against the female half of heterosexual married couples, it was also perpetuating the stereotypical power dynamic in these relationships. The problem wasn't the technology, but the fact that the algorithm was perpetuating an underlying historical bias against women in the credit system. It's a good example of how historical patterns continue to disadvantage women, and highlights that even though spouses may have joint financial records, it's a common misconception that they will share the same credit limits. Instead of being transparent about how these credit decisions are made, Apple refused to engage.[4]

By taking CTRL, listening, understanding and being technically literate, we can get ourselves into the rooms where those decisions are made. The more we're able to bring the breadth of our experiences as women to shine a light on these power imbalances that are being perpetuated through technology by a small number of individuals, the more likely we are to secure the right kind of future for all.

It's not enough to sit by and just observe. Hard work is required and things won't change overnight, but investing in change by using our unique experiences will incrementally move the pendulum. What follows is an example of how by using our voices, we can effect change.

Choose to Challenge

Deborah Okenla, founder and CEO of Your Startup, Your Story (YSYS), a startup community for founders, developers, creatives and investors, used her voice and gathered the voices of others to call for change and make space for difference. Working in the tech and startup scene in London, she was very aware that most people who are offered the opportunity to have their startups funded are white men. So, when she saw the publicity for an event being run by City Hall, aimed at women entrepreneurs, her excitement quickly turned to frustration. All of the faces in the ad, apart from one, were those of white women. She recalled seeing the hashtag accompanying the photo – #behind everygreatcity – and thinking to herself, 'Well, that's not really reflective of the London that we advocate for.'

Deborah was already using WhatsApp groups to network and build a community of support, and as she shared the content of the ad with them, the disappointment and anger spread fast. There was outrage amongst the community members at the suggestion that behind every great city is only one type of woman: a white one.

When Deborah and I spoke, she told me, 'That doesn't inspire me, that doesn't inspire my sister, that doesn't inspire future generations to think that they could be behind a great city . . . I think that's what hurt me the most, because oftentimes the effects might not come on us, but it's on the generations to come.'

Not everyone in the WhatsApp networks got why Deborah felt this was so important. Some of the male members didn't see it as something they should care about. It was clear to Deborah that they simply weren't *able* to care because they benefited from the patriarchy that made initiatives like the one being held at City Hall necessary in the first place. She met up with Abadesi Osunsade, Vanessa Sanyauke and other Black women entrepreneurs to work out what action they could take: 'We're not just Black, we are also women, we are intersectional in our identities, dual and multi-layered. I thought, "We've got to do more."'

They decided to write an open letter.

At that point Meghan Markle was in the news for having written one to an advertising agency, so Deborah and her contemporaries decided to write straight to the Mayor of London, Sadiq Khan. Instead of simply pointing out the lack of diversity in the City Hall initiative, they wanted to offer constructive ideas about what he should be doing. Some of these suggestions were working with diverse communities, talking to grassroots organizations and showing that the application form is accessible.

Over twenty people from different campaigns and organizations put their name to the open letter. Deborah not only wanted to make sure that Sadiq Khan noticed it, but that other people would know he had seen it, and would expect him to respond, so they posted their letter to Twitter and @ mentioned him.

Their move caught the attention of social entrepreneur Natalie Campbell, who was doing other work with the Mayor. All of a sudden they were invited to City Hall to put forward their suggestions to Deputy Mayor Rajesh Agrawal about how to make London women entrepreneurship programmes more intersectional and accommodate women who looked like them. It was phenomenal, and so powerful to see a Black woman at the centre of that table bringing underrepresented voices together to talk about the issue. Deputy Mayor Agrawal listened carefully to all the points Deborah and her allies made.

Sadiq Khan didn't attend the meeting, but he tweeted, 'One letter can literally change the world.' Deborah tells me she always tells people: 'That opinion you want to share? Post it, share it. You can change the world. You can change the government. You can change so many different things.'

Getting into the room at City Hall wasn't enough for Deborah, Abadesi and the others. They wanted to keep the whole process open and inclusive, and remain accountable to the wider community. Every time there was an update or any changes, they would post about it, so that they brought the community alongside them. The impact of that open letter was the first Diverse Entrepreneurship Summit in City Hall. It's now called the Entrepreneurship Summit, and it's become an annual event. It brings together different accelerator programmes and startup support programmes for entrepreneurs who are trying to engage diverse audiences.

Accountability can be uncomfortable. You might feel anxious about confronting the individuals or institutions with whom you have an issue. Going out on a limb is tough, and doing what's right rather than what's cool, easiest or makes you the most money is hard when you're trying to hold others to account. You might be made to feel that your knowledge is lacking, that you don't understand the algorithm. It can sometimes be nerve-racking to ask the easy questions, never mind the difficult ones. But the more you do it, the better you'll become at it.

What Happens When We Don't Speak Up?

People love space science, and technology plays a huge part in it. We've been able to learn so much from our space missions and use that knowledge on Earth to solve problems. A few years ago, the European Space Agency landed a spaceship on a comet. It was an extraordinary feat of engineering, a big thing for the agency and a big news story.

The engineer who appeared on national television to discuss the landing wore a shirt printed with drawings of scantily clad women. In the wake of the interview, screengrabs of the footage were splashed all over social media with great frustration. The engineer's response was that he'd wanted to dress in something different to what the stereotypical scientist might wear. What he'd really done was reinforce the idea that tech is a man's world where women are viewed as no more than decoration. Rose Eveleth, a tech writer at *The Atlantic*, tweeted the picture with a caption that said it all: 'No no women are tooootally welcome in our community, just ask the dude in this shirt.'

The image sparked a plethora of questions in my head. First, what was going through the mind of the designer or retailer who sold the shirt (or the gift-giver)? Was any thought given to the kind of places this person might be seen wearing the shirt? My next thought was about the engineer's journey to work that morning. A big day for him. Folk at home might have noticed his shirt choice and said nothing. Or they might have asked him why he'd chosen that particular shirt for this big occasion. Had there been any double takes as he sat in the car at the traffic lights, or travelled on the bus or the train? Any passing comments?

The next stage in my thinking was this engineer linking up with colleagues who were excited for his TV appearance. Was there any discussion surrounding his shirt choice? How many of them might have been wearing similar items? How regularly do people wear clothes featuring sexually suggestive images in the workplace?

The final stage in my thought process followed him to the studio. One of the most important messages production crews like to send to a guest before a TV appearance relates to their attire. You must bring at least one spare outfit, in case something you've chosen to wear doesn't play nicely with the cameras – anything overly shiny, green, or with black and white stripes is always out. At the studio, did no one ask for his second outfit?

What was such a monumental day for the European Space Agency became even bigger, but for all the wrong reasons, in no small part because the television producers and other figures in this engineer's life failed to speak up. There were uncomfortable conversations that could have happened before his appearance, and that were clearly missed.

When it comes to taking action in the process of creating our tech, we must ask ourselves: What can we practise to hold tech spaces accountable? How do we question and challenge? How do we have those tough conversations? You'll find lots of practical advice and guidance on where to start in the Getting Started section over the page. Couple this with the section at the end of Chapter 8.

We can make sure that we think about the choices that are

being made, *before* the seat belts and the traffic lights and the rules of the road are built. We share the responsibility to make sure that difference is included, not just in what we create, but in what other people create. It's a big responsibility, but finding your voice will help to ensure you're up to the task.

Getting Started

Just as you wouldn't send out a document without running a spellcheck first, build a belonging check into your thinking process. It's an idea I picked up from Abadesi Osunsade, CEO of Hustle Crew and VP for Global Community and Belonging for Brandwatch. I asked her to explain how it works, and she broke it down into three steps:

1. Who's Not in the Room?

'One of the things that can be really helpful is just to think about who you might see on a bus, or on a train, who you might see in the supermarket, that you don't see in the room that you're in, doing this product meeting or having this marketing session or reviewing feedback. Who's out there that isn't in the room? And how can you ensure that type of person is represented when they're not in the room? We know that there are people with neurodiversity. We know that there are people in wheelchairs. We know that there are queer people, deaf people, blind people – we know all of these people are out there and need to interact with our products and services. But when we come into a meeting, and people like them are not there, how can we feel confident that we are anticipating the needs of that diverse group of people?'

2. What Are Your Biases?

'Take stock of the parts of you that represent dominant groups. That's where you're most likely to have bias that you cannot see or tell – bias that you are unaware of. To use my own example, I am university educated, so I don't have that experience that some self-taught folks have. People who didn't go to university, people who went straight into vocational work or maybe went to a bootcamp, have had to justify their intellect and their intelligence in a way that no one has ever asked me to do, because I have that credential.

'In a similar way, because I am cisgender, I identify with the body I was born into, people correctly guess my pronouns as she/her. I've never had to insist that we introduce ourselves, in a meeting, with our pronouns as well. That's something I should be more mindful of, because I want to normalize the idea that you don't need to assume that people know your pronouns.

'Ask yourself, "Where do I represent the dominant groups in society and the dominant groups in the workplace?" Because that's where you need to be most careful about the judgements that you make, and the things that you're thinking about.

'In a similar way, if you're a dominant gender, or a dominant race, there are going to be obstacles that others who are not in those groups have faced, which you have no experience of. And you need to empathize with that, so that you can create a recruitment strategy that will appeal to those individuals, or a performance-review strategy that takes into account those unique experiences.'

3. Own Your Identity

'We need to get more comfortable owning our identity. That's just a part of taking belonging seriously. Many people are still not comfortable talking about their race, their gender, their class. If you're not comfortable talking about it, how can you start to acknowledge the privilege and probable bias and prejudice that come with that? How can you be a champion of belonging if you're not understanding the very causes of a lack of greater belonging?

'This idea of owning our identity and our lived experience is such an important part of this journey. I'm not shying away from the fact that I'm a middle-class person, and my parents could afford to invest in things for me that other Black and Asian women like me did not have access to. I need to tell that part of the story so that other women out there don't compare their trajectory to mine, and feel like failures. I've had doors open for me that would never be opened for them. I can't shy away from that. I can't hide that, that doesn't help others, and it doesn't help me.'

How do you make sure that you've considered difference and you're ready for it, that you can embrace it? And how do you ensure that you're doing it in every decision that you make as a technologist? You make decisions, you make choices. Build that in as a habit from early in your technical journey – to always check for difference. That's the belonging check.

•

Facing the privilege you have can be hard to do as, by its nature, privilege is invisible. I regularly use an adapted version of an activity from thesafezoneproject.com with folks to help them break down how things that are 'normal' for them are not normal for others. It's easy to consider how the lives of people far away from you differ. Considering the privileges and disadvantages that play out on the streets near you is much harder.

Let's say you have £500 to spend and just ten minutes to decide which items from the following list you want or need in your life. Use a timer. Start the activity with the assumption that you have nothing on the list.

- Being open and having your partner(s) accepted by your family: £105
- Celebrating your marriage(s) with your family, friends and co-workers: £80
- Paid leave from your job when grieving the death of your partner(s): £100
- Having multiple positive TV role models: £110
- Adopting a child: £105
- Being able to feel safe in your interactions with police officers: £200
- Being able to travel, or show ID in restaurants or bars, without fear you'll be rejected: £100
- Being able to discuss and have access to multiple family-planning options: £120
- Receiving discounted homeowner insurance rates with your recognized partner(s): £100
- Raising children without worrying about state intervention: £180
- Using public toilets without fear of threat or punishment: £150
- Being able to access social services without fear of discrimination or being turned away: £100

Which items did you immediately jump to? Who might not have these privileges in your society? In your social circles?

At your workplace? Which ones do you not have (and how easy was it to imagine not having any of them)? Which of these privileges have already contributed to your own sense of identity and self? How do these privileges overlap with what you see in the news? Or what you see at work?

Calling out the small things can be much more comfortable than calling out big injustices and mistakes. Look for an opportunity to practise. Is there an assumption in a meeting you regularly attend that you can challenge without causing too much of a kerfuffle? Give it a go. See what happens. Then do the same thing the following week. After three weeks, go for a bigger, more uncomfortable conversation. As you continue to challenge assumptions, in different ways, note which ones gain ground and which ones don't. Highlight people's blind spots. Explain why a particular book or clothing choice might not be helpful for your niece or nephew.

These conversations will lead to discomfort and push-back from others. Sometimes you'll make a mistake, but doing so once and learning from it will allow you to make better mistakes next time.

Taking this kind of action armed with knowledge about your own privileges and with the support of your learning tribe (as we'll see in the next chapter) will set you up to be a force for good in the tech space. Perhaps take the time to reflect on some of the tech trends you've been discovering and the creative examples others have produced – are there any big opportunities to upgrade what they've brought into the tech sphere to better serve a particular forgotten demographic?

10

FINDING
YOUR
VOICE

I'm a member of the *Pop Idol* generation, so the analogy that follows appeals to me and I'm going to run with it . . . When you were young, did you fantasize about becoming a pop star (or, ahem, a rapper)? Those artists who did achieve their dream – millions of people listening to their music, kids with their picture on their wall, wearing their face on a T-shirt, or coming to their concerts – dreamed big and didn't give up.

My advice to anyone who wants to make their mark and make a change is to do exactly the same thing. Let your imagination run wild – not necessarily being a pop star, but being the person that you want to be.

What is it that you want to do? What is it that you want to try? Take a little bit of time to decide: What do you want to explore? What's got you excited so far? As you indulge your curiosity, the more you go through life, the more you see, the more you observe, the more you practise, the richer your dreams will become, the more detailed they'll get, the wider their scope will be.

In this chapter I want to focus on your personal CTRL journey. Where are you going, tech-wise? Would you like to take on a role in the tech world? Would you like to be able to apply technical knowledge to your life and hobbies in a more power-ful and informed way? Is there a part of your life that you've always wanted to have more control over, and do you want to explore how technical literacy might help you with that goal? Do you want to effect change in a real-world problem, and are you open to using technology as a tool to do so? I want to use the *Pop Idol* analogy to help you get started – to move from being comfortable with some aspects of technology to becoming competent in your own use of it.

The good news is there's much more room in tech than there is in the music business. The odds are on your side. We don't need that many pop stars, but we do need people who understand tech, who can use it and who can play a role in forming the next generation. There's no reason why one of those people can't be you. Did you know that in the UK's major cities, one job advert in five is for a tech role? The number of positions advertised is growing all the time, and changing all the time. There are new jobs today that didn't exist even five years ago.

In that sense, we're still following a trend that dates back as far as 1871. Census results since that point show that the rise of machines has resulted in the creation of jobs rather than making working humans obsolete. Twenty years ago, there weren't any social media managers, computer scientists, podcast producers, mobile app developers, Bolt or Uber drivers, developer evangelists, content moderators, virtual assistants, or any positions related to automated driving.[1]

How about a job programming drones to survey power lines? Maybe you fancy a job as a cloud architect? Why not? A cloud architect is the person responsible for configuring, managing and securing a group of servers on behalf of the millions of users who need access to the cloud.

In the past we stored all our files on our desktop PCs, and then, when we progressed to network servers, all the computers connected to that network could access the files. When there was only one server and it was in your house, if something happened, like a power cut or an accident with a cup of coffee, it was up to you to deal with it, but not any more.

We finally arrived at the cloud, a big group of servers that you don't own and you don't maintain. The cloud and its group of servers is owned by someone whose job it is to ensure there will always be enough space and that it's live and accessible twenty-four hours a day, seven days a week, twelve months a year. Still fancy the job?

Even if none of those ideas floats your boat, think about this: some fields are moving forward so quickly that new job roles are being advertised that didn't exist when you first started reading this book. So when you dream, go big. In your ideal world, where would you end up? What would be the change that you'd want to see? What part of the past would you preserve? What part of the present would you improve? What part of the future are you going to make?

As with *Pop Idol* prep, once you've found your dream, you need to be ready to use your tech voice, and you need to manoeuvre yourself into the right position to be able to use it.

Practice Makes Progress

Look at your tech journey as a development of your voice. You're learning to cultivate it and, as time goes on, you'll become more and more assured. Professional singers learn to eat and avoid particular foods, not to sing at full volume every day, to do the right vocal exercises so that they can sing their best at the right times.

Document what you've learned. Write it down so that you can say, 'I learned this, this is part of my voice, this is part of my technical capabilities, and here's how I can prove it', or, 'Here are my projects, here's my GitHub, here's the blog that I've written.'

Also think about the influence your new technical voice will have. Reflect on your history and who has inspired and influenced you. When you dream about being that great tech person of the future, who do you imagine standing alongside you? You're not trying to be somebody else, but other people's experiences can help you create your own story and be part of it too.

Consider all the things you've been through that have made you who you are and brought you to this point, and how you're going to continue to build on all that. Taking all these considerations into account, begin to pull together a group of mentors who reflect where you want to be and where you're coming from. You don't need to talk to all of them or hold regular sessions with them, although there's a plethora of dedicated mentoring programmes for folk in tech. Mentorship isn't purely about the relationships; read and watch their output and take nuggets of advice and guidance from it.

Finally, it's about learning the tech. Make sure to spend the time developing your tech voice – it's not going to just come and hit you. There are lots of things it will be helpful to be in the habit of doing as you make the transition to being a technical person. Whether it's participating in hackathons, learning from podcasts or getting more hands-on with tutorials, you'll be storing up more tech skills, more knowledge and, ultimately, more CTRL.

As a next step, share your ideas with others. Look at it as putting together your band, the people around you who you're going to play music with. Just as it's sometimes better to start your own group than look for one you fit in to, you might need to seek out the right people for your tech crew. Playing with others is an important part of experimenting with your voice. You'll grow in confidence and discover why you're entitled to build your voice, why you might not have done so before and what you're going to use it for.

Keeping those motivations in the front of your mind will spur you on. You'll have the confidence to practise challenging poor technical decisions when you see them. You'll be able to practise holding tech accountable. You'll be able to practise the decisions you make around which bits of tech you use.

Find Your Microphone(s)

You'll be entering the tech space like a singer comes into a rehearsal space. Maybe you're feeling like a newbie. You've done your practice projects, you've started to learn a language, new software or a technical framework. A degree of fluency in your chosen technologies is in sight. Now you need to find your microphone.

Having some technical knowledge and perspective is not enough. It's all about sharing and projecting what you know. That's when you might discover that you know more than you realize. Until you get hold of the microphone and broadcast your knowledge or perspective, you won't hear how it's being received or understand the scale of what you've learned. Your project might be small, but reactions are essential if you're to appreciate the value of your ideas to others.

There will be snippets you've learned from working on previous projects, things you've heard at a hackathon, on a podcast or have read somewhere. It's only when you're at the mic, sharing your technical voice with others, that everything you've absorbed will become apparent and your own voice will ring clearer. Sharing is part of the process of building literacy.

Let's use the example of *Legally Blonde*, the 2001 Hollywood film in which Reese Witherspoon's character, Elle, gets into Harvard Law School to try to win back her ex-boyfriend. Everybody thinks she's just a dumb blonde but, in the end, not only does she prove herself to be very smart but she also uses her knowledge of hairdressing to win a major court case while still a student. Her interest in beauty and fashion, which stopped people from taking her seriously, turned out to be a key attribute that she brought into the courtroom. Something no one else arguing the case had. (Oh, and her ex-boyfriend is revealed as shallow and not that smart, so when he asks her to take him back, she turns him down.)

The elements of your character and experience that make you feel as though you don't belong, or that you're not up to the competition, might turn out to be the things that give you the edge. You just need to find your microphones, your podium and your space to get your voice heard.

A great place to begin sharing your voice is tech rooms. When we talk about tech rooms, we must first acknowledge that technology creation happens in a lot of different places. There are the obvious technology companies, or technology departments of different companies, but there are many other venues.

Stemettes, for example, work with the STEM industry and companies therein, but also STEM academia and STEM entrepreneurship – these are tech rooms within Stemettes. If we look at the wider world of work, we have to take into account the public sector, which includes governance and legislation, and also the private sector, which includes industry and start-ups. The third sector is charity. So, if you're on the search for a space where you can apply your knowledge and make a difference, there are myriad places where technical decisions are being made on behalf of technology, for technology or with technology. Check out the Getting Started section on page 211 for inspiration.

I studied maths and computer science for my master's degree then worked in a technology department in a bank. I now run a tech third-sector organization that uses technology to give other people technical skills. As a trustee at the Institute for the Future of Work I feed into tech policy and tech regulation, not only for our country but under the G7 international banner.

These are my tech rooms – you'll have your own, different set, and anyone else you meet on your tech journey will have theirs. In your current workplace there might be opportunities for you to understand more about technology decisions that are being made, and the implications of technology for your security at work. In all of these places and for all of the technology being enacted, someone has made a decision in a room, physical or otherwise.

It's easy to visit physical tech rooms; you can sign up for all kinds of events and hear about new technology being made. You could also apply to visit a demo day at a hackathon and hear the ideas that people are pitching. Virtual tech rooms exist too, such as #ukedchat, for people who want to talk about education in the UK on social media.

The point of this book is not to encourage everyone into the tech industry and into a tech role, but to consider how tech might relate to what interests you, what you work on and how you live. If you add the word 'tech' to your area of work and do an online search, you'll probably find a group of rooms that have already been set up to discuss the implications of technology on that particular field, industry or role. If you're a lawyer, for example, take a look at RegTech and LegalTech. If you're a doctor, there's MedTech; for transport, try TransportTech and MobilityTech. There's EdTech for teachers, and so on. These rooms will give you information on events, podcasts, hashtags, hackathon events and policies around technology. Dive in. You'll be able to exercise more curiosity, learn even more and practise your new technical skills. It's always easier to start on any learning journey with things you know and are familiar with.

Technology is the whole field, but within that field there are many 'use cases' – simply put, an instance of a use of that tech. For example, Google has many use cases. Say there's an emergency – you might google someone who can help you. If you want to go shopping you might google the opening times of the nearest shop. It's one tool, but it can be used in several different ways. The same goes for technology – tech is the field but there are many different use cases to consider within it. What are the problems you want to solve? And where are the rooms in which people are talking about solving these issues?

DoNotPay, which is advertised as the world's first robot lawyer, is an AI program that helps you appeal parking tickets, and it can now solve a lot of other problems, such as getting refunds or not getting stuck in free trials that turn into regular payments for a service you no longer want.[2]

Also of interest is law firm BLP, Berwin Leighton Paisner, who are using AI to trawl through historical property records and land registry records to apply them to current property cases. Both of these platforms save a huge amount of human effort. No human being has to sift through every case in the land registry trying to filter, read and note all the different details. Instead, you can create an algorithm to search for particular words, context or types of cases. The AI can do it faster, and at all hours of the day, so the human being can spend time on higher-cognitive work instead.

The value that you will bring on your technical journey won't purely be based on your technical capability; it will be about all the other things you're able to add to it. Identify the cross-disciplinary approach to a problem, and use that as a starting place for your thinking. It will be at the core of your voice.

It's OK to feel that technical ability isn't perhaps something you were born with, or maybe you're still getting over generations of patriarchal damage or the way the system and power have played with tech and who gets to do tech. Start by thinking, 'What I do know is art', or 'What I do know is food'. The next step is to consider, with newfound curiosity around tech, 'Here's what I can add, here's how I can build, here's why I can create.' Explore what art plus tech means or what food plus tech means.

Ghislaine Boddington is one woman who came from a non-tech background. Like so many of the individuals featured in this book, she never studied computer science, mathematics or engineering at university, but she's been a pioneer of tech since the 1990s, and is still pioneering virtual reality, augmented reality, and what we're getting used to calling hybrid ways of communicating and sharing.

She remembers watching the Apollo moon landing as a child, but it wasn't the rocket or the technology that transported the astronauts there that caught her imagination. What struck her was how mission control was able to contact the team all the way from Earth. She credits this as the moment her interest in communicating across time and space was sparked.

Ghislaine trained as a dancer, and it was dance that she brought to her exploration of technology. In the 1990s she returned to that childhood fascination with communicating across great distances. Working with experimental and community dance companies, she became involved in some workshops that were using digital video.

She recounted to me how, while the dancers were watching back recordings of their performances, she came up with a revolutionary idea. The dancers could project moving images of themselves into a different room, which would allow other dancers to perform with them whilst being in that different space.

The fact that Ghislaine and I were chatting over Zoom for this interview helped her to talk me through how that first experimental setup worked. 'The camera that's filming you now,' she explained, 'will project you behind me so that I can dance with you in my room and vice versa. We did it with what's called BNC cabling between two studios. I think the first time was probably 1991. With no internet involved at all.'

Ghislaine was a member of Chisenhale Dance Space in East London at the time, and was already working with interdisciplinary groups. The dance space was home to a range of classes from Indian dance to African drumming. It was the innovative collective running the space that brought the group who were starting to work with technology over from New York. The power of networking to open up avenues for communication should never be underestimated.

It was the beginning of Ghislaine's journey in experimenting, exploring and building projects that combined dance and technology. To start with, she brought the dance and relied on other people, mostly men, to do the tech side: 'In the nineties, fifty per cent of us were the dance lot, and we were ninety per cent women, and fifty per cent were the technology lot and they were ninety per cent men. And that's how it was for fifteen years of my career. I was in gender-mixed groups, and there was equality. But the equality wasn't in the expertise. There weren't as many men doing dance. And there weren't as many women doing the tech side.'

Through a community web space in South London called Backspace, Ghislaine's collective made an early webpage, and became part of a young tech community. She discovered a mailing list for dance and tech, which opened the door to expanding the work she calls telepresence – where real and virtual dancers can move and create together across space. She explained to me how very quickly, rather than being on her own, she had connections across the globe who were keen to share their expertise and experiment with her.

Overcoming the challenges of great distances between performers was one thing but, as we found out with some of the technologies we used for communication during the pandemic, it's not so easy to conquer time.

'We were dealing with [. . .] massive lag,' explained Ghislaine. 'When you're working with these early technologies, as we are now with machine learning, there are lots of glitches.'

Machine learning is at the heart of the learning capabilities of some forms of AI. Let's say I was teaching you to play the violin. I might show you physically how to hold the instrument and where to place your fingers, but machine learning is akin to being shown a film of what violin playing looks like and then allowing AI to figure out how to hold the instrument and play it all by itself. It uses algorithms and statistics, and tries to look for patterns in data, then uses those patterns and maps them forward; this is how it learns. The algorithm fills in the gaps along the journey, but there is very little direct coaching.

Back to Ghislaine and her infuriating lag!

Her team was communicating via old ISDN cables between London and Helsinki, Lisbon and Kyoto, and the longer the distance, the greater the lag. If someone is dancing, the delay in what they're hearing and seeing puts them off their moves. To overcome this, the glitches due to the lag were written into the dance, and became part of the dance's aesthetics.

(Lag aesthetics is also related to latency in gaming. If you're using an older machine or a poorer internet line, you have something called latency – the gap between when you click to move, jump or shoot, and these actions happening in the game. In most games, latency will impact the way you play the game. To counter this, you might have to shoot or jump earlier than you need to, in order to take the lag into account. Being able to reduce the latency in gaming is a big issue because everyone wants a realistic experience. Conversely, increasing the lag might add to the difficulty level in the game you're trying to play.)

The next great boost to Ghislaine's experimental work was the nineties club scene and rave culture. A group that had just opened a club in New Oxford Street invited her team to experiment with tech at club nights every couple of months. Amongst their many experiments, Ghislaine told me, were robot scent machines that wandered around giving off different perfumes, and the Robo lights that lit the club in the right places, according to where people were in the space.

Ten years later, Ghislaine and her team were putting the Robo lights on the web so that people could control the lights in her spaces over the internet: '[It] was ridiculous, because people were just crazy and moved lights all over the place.' That may be, but it was also exciting, new and innovative, and allowed people who weren't in the space to feel as if they were.

Ghislaine is still using her artistic performance skills to drive her tech experimentation today. She's now an expert in virtual worlds and mixed realities, telepresence, robotics and wearables because she started using them years ago, when they were new. Guess what – she has still never written a line of computer code.

I hope her story demonstrates why it's important for you to embrace the knowledge that you already have, to express your perspective as it stands, and to use it as a way to enter these rooms. If you come into the room as a lawyer, or as a journalist, or a dancer, you'll likely apply technology to problems that you've identified and which others may not have ever considered. Be confident and draw on your own authentic experience.

There are countless other examples of people who have worked in myriad fields then gone on to use that knowledge in tech. An interest in dogs led Rikke Rosenlund to create the app Borrow My Doggy, which matches people who want to walk dogs with the owners of dogs who want them to be walked. Spanish teacher Ángela Ruiz Robles registered the patent for the first ever ebook in the 1950s. She felt bad for her students dragging their textbooks around with them, so she created a device to solve that problem. Her little machine was able to hold more than one book and, using a system of mechanical coil scrolls, books could be easily replaced, translated into several languages or even read aloud. Text size could be increased and the device also featured a small light that allowed you to read in the dark.

Be assured that there is something that you already know enough about. Maybe you're not an expert (yet), but there's definitely something in your knowledge and lived experience that relates in some way to technology. Take it and map it onto the tech that you're continually learning about. That will be what gives you the permission to speak up in tech spaces. But which tech spaces?

Well, if we carry on running with our *Pop Idol* analogy, if you're a musician, then those tech spaces might be music venues. Picking the right venue will give you a higher chance of building your confidence and your skills as you progress in your music career.

Choose a Venue

Since 2012 I've been a trustee of the UD Music Foundation, a charity working across East London to inform and support young people on their potential journeys into the music industry. Fun fact: the boys' school where I sat my GCSE computer science exam as a ten-year-old was attended by some of the biggest names in grime music – a genre that was born out of East London. The charity itself works with young people in the area to show them the wide variety of employment options they have beyond 'artist', even if they're inspired by the success of local people like Tinchy Stryder and Kano.

The reason I got involved with the charity was its emphasis on exploring options in music beyond the obvious. When you become an artist, you have to be open to possibilities – starting off playing in bars and doing the live circuit, and trying different approaches to see what works. Entering tech is the same. Once you're ready to put yourself out there, it's up to you to discover and choose the venue that works for you.

According to my mum, I wanted to be a weather presenter when I was a child. I loved watching them reading out the forecast, waving their hands around, pointing to different visuals. When I was thirteen, as part of the national career service called Connexions, we completed a questionnaire at school to discover what our future career could be. It asked questions such as 'Would you like to work outside?' (I said no) and 'Do you like numbers?' (I said yes).

The top two results for me were systems analyst and management consultant. I'd never heard of either. Helpfully, the program allowed me to click into each role and view a file of information. The average salary for a management consultant looked good, and after reading what the job entailed, I also figured out that I could choose to be a management consultant for Sainsbury's and get free groceries – I was sold.

Three years later, I did a paid tech internship at an investment bank and revised my ambition. I decided I wanted to be a technology management consultant for banks. Another three years later, as I was graduating from university, I changed my mind again – I wanted to do a straight technology role at the same bank. As I grew older and wiser, and as the industry expanded, so too did my options for finding my place in it.

Of course, there is no one right avenue to pursue. Your pathway, your journey, and the routes you explore out of those that are available to you might differ wildly from the options I have – even within the same industry. Some of the best options are tech spaces where everyone feels equally included and valued, but the reality is that not all of your options will provide this level of inclusion and value. The tech world still has a lot to do before everyone experiences the same level of equality across all the tech venues.

Nancy Ramsey and Pamela McCorduck, researchers at Anita B.org, formerly known as the Anita Borg Institute for Women and Technology, talk about 'micro-climates' to describe how different the atmosphere in a startup can be compared with that in an IT department in a big, non-tech company, or in academic research versus industrial research and development.[3] Different companies have very different cultures, and departments can vary even within the same building. There's no way such a big industry or field of activity could ever be homogenous, and everyone has their own idea about the kind of tech environment in which they will thrive.

As you start out, be open to trying things. Whether it's hackathon events, or non-profit organizations and groups, or a larger gathering such as a technology conference. Maybe a stage is the right place for you, talking about something exciting that's happening in your current industry, or perhaps you'd like to take part in roundtables that are already happening where you are.

Roundtables are great. Much like a conference where several people talk as equals about something, they usually provide the opportunity to listen and learn from an expert on the research they've done, or to hear from a legislator on issues that they're encountering. You might hear from another citizen on the impact that technology is having on them, and then discuss that input. If you're the citizen you might talk about how your experiences mirror or run counter to what has been put forward by the expert. Maybe a report comes out of the roundtable, or a blog, and decisions might even be made based on what was covered at the event. In addition to taking to the stage, you might get involved in testing a new tech or sharing knowledge via social media, or you might become involved in facilitating. Every one of these occasions is an opportunity to learn and influence.

From your starting point, you want to grow – either in terms of the size and importance of the projects you're working on, or in terms of the kind of tech you're tapping into. If you're an artist, you might be looking at new tech tools to use as your medium.

A few years ago I was invited to join the council at the Royal College of Art. STEAM is a large part of their strategic plan, bringing together the technical spaces of science, engineering and maths, and arts and design. The areas of overlap are far-reaching, from how to use STEAM technology to design spaces for the elderly to the use of smart materials in aerospace and transport vehicles of the future. Good art paired with good design and good tech solves problems.

Don't be afraid to make your mistakes on a smaller stage. That way, you'll not only learn from that mistake but you'll also see that the fallout in one area doesn't mean you'll have the same fallout when you go and have a crack at the same thing elsewhere. Find the space where you can experiment, try things out and meet people. Find the right tribe and make those connections.

Sometimes you have to set up your own venue. Sometimes you have to do your own thing. I created Stemettes because I retrospectively realized that kind of community didn't exist for me when I was younger, or didn't embrace me. I made the decision that it *should* exist – and I had enough agency, enough power, and enough skill to be able to set that up.

Abadesi Osunsade, CEO and founder of Hustle Crew, did a similar thing. I asked her what prompted her to start up herself, and she explained that she'd just quit a job at a startup that had a really toxic culture: 'I was the only Black employee there, and things that my colleagues thought were completely inno-cent things – for example, playing with my hair, without my permission – were actually really damaging to my productivity and my self-confidence. I could never succeed in explaining to them why that was. And that was one of many reasons why I eventually left, because it took too much energy trying to just do my job whilst also trying to foster belonging.'

That experience made Abadesi fall out of love with the tech industry. She felt traumatized by the experience, and it made her fearful about joining a new team in case the same thing happened again. Was it something she was doing wrong, or a systemic problem? She began to do some research, and found a book that resonated with her own experience. That book was *Reset* by Ellen Pao, former CEO of Reddit, which charted her experiences of discrimination in her career. Abadesi's discovery that what she'd been through was not an isolated experience made her realize that something bigger was at play.

Hustle Crew started off as Abadesi meeting with other women of colour in tech to discuss job hunting and how they could ensure their next team wasn't a toxic one. They soon discovered that they'd all had similarly negative experiences, but they also shared a high degree of ambition and a high desire to stay, make money and start businesses in this amazing industry to which they'd devoted so much energy.

The space that had been created for conversations about shared challenges, shared goals and shared ambitions started to gather momentum. The women met every month – a free event in a central London venue. It was a chance for them to check in, talk about their experiences and share opportunities: 'Finally, there were those who were just looking for similar faces. They had never seen other brown people, Black people, gay people in tech. And here we are, still going.'

Tech was also Abadesi's key to finding the people who form her community. She began blogging about her experiences at the startup and her frustrations around the lack of information about getting into tech. She told me she felt that one of the reasons there are so few Black people and Black women in tech is because it's not easy and obvious to find a path into the industry, especially if you're not someone with a technical degree.

As Abadesi discussed these issues in her blog posts and on social media, she found that others would comment and share them again. Soon she was collecting email addresses and within months, Hustle Crew had evolved into a mailing list of hundreds of people from around the world. It swiftly grew too big for the physical meetup once a month so they shifted their focus to allow the conversations to unfold on LinkedIn and Instagram.

The obvious demand for Hustle Crew made Abadesi think she could make it work as a self-supporting business, but when she tried to pitch it to investors, it seemed that no one was interested. No one thought that it could make money. VCs couldn't see why anyone would invest in something only for women or people of colour. How would the men feel? How would the white people feel?

The response made Abadesi rethink her plan. She decided to always have other projects and sources of income besides Hustle Crew: 'I never want to put myself in the position where my means of survival are dependent on a group of people who don't share my lived experience validating my truth. What happened in that first year of me trying and failing to pitch Hustle Crew, both to clients and to investors, was a real low point in terms of seeing how my identity is respected within society. It was really psychologically damaging.'

In spite of all the doubt, Hustle Crew does meet a need for a lot of people: 'I have a global community, thousands of people interacting with our content every day, showing up to events. It's validated enough for me to feel like we're on the right track.'

Deborah Okenla, founder and CEO of Your Startup, Your Story (YSYS), had a similar experience of needing to create her own space. She studied law at university then joined a big accountancy firm where she discovered the world of entrepreneurs. Deborah wasn't especially technical, but she tried to improve the company's system for handling immigration documents using Excel spreadsheets. Although her immediate manager was impressed, a senior manager actively discouraged Deborah's innovation. In a one-on-one meeting, during which she was told that the project was a waste of time, she realized there would never be room for innovation at the firm. Soon after the meeting, Deborah's manager was made redundant after twelve years at the company and Deborah decided that she didn't ever want to be dependent on just one company or one person for her livelihood.

'You've got to have something that no one can ever take away from you,' she told me. 'And then I came across the word hackathon on Eventbrite. It said, "Free pizza, beer, £70, three days, you're going to build a business." It had a really amazing, international, exciting, resilient vibe. "OK, I'm not necessarily a coder," I thought. "I don't have these technical skills. But I love this environment. And I want to stay here."'

In spite of all her skills and experience, Deborah had a hard time breaking into the tech entrepreneur scene. She did internships, worked on accelerator programmes with startups, and finally got headhunted by the company that had turned her down for an internship a couple of years previously. However, three things happened in one week that sparked a new project.

The first was that Deborah got made redundant from a company where her role was connecting investors to founders (a term commonly used for entrepreneurs in the technology world). Then, when she was in church, a week before her job came to an end, the sermon spoke to her: 'I remember them saying, whatever your title is today, it doesn't matter if someone takes it away. If you know that's your destiny, keep walking on that path.'

A few nights later, at a Valentine's Day event, she decided to slip away early to attend the last twenty minutes of a launch event for UK Black Tech. 'There was just a sea of Black people,' she told me. 'I'd never seen so many Black people in the room before. It was amazing. The energy in that room gave me enough strength to continue my last week.'

That experience also made her see the job she was leaving in a new light. One of her final tasks was to organize the last investor lounge connecting investors to founders. As she looked around, she realized she'd literally been connecting white guys to white guys. Occupying nearly every seat was one white male investor and one white male founder. Apart from the last table, where a woman called Check Warner, a VC from Ada Ventures, was seated.

Deborah's realization sparked an urge to connect and learn from other Black people in the industry. She reached out to contacts and women like Check Warner, and invited them to join a WhatsApp group where they could talk about startups and building technology businesses. She was amazed by the results: 'When you bring all these amazing people into one place, even more amazing things happen. I think because we have that commonality and a shared resilience, whether it's because of skills that we were lacking, or based on our race and our gender. That commonality brought us together.'

It's how Deborah came to found YSYS, which is, in her words, a startup community dedicated to connecting diverse people with opportunities in tech. YSYS has an ambitious target to help 100,000 people by 2023, and they are well on the way to achieving that goal.

Not everyone you meet will be welcoming and supportive. Some might even be openly hostile. Generally speaking, the closer people are to power, the more hostile they are towards newcomers, but that's not a hard and fast rule. You can also find really hostile places that are nowhere near power, and places that aren't that hostile where there is a lot of power, and where a lot of decisions are made. Don't be deterred, just keep moving until you find somewhere that suits you. It's exciting to try the different spaces out and see what they're like, and what connections you can make. Learning with others is so important.

The best places to be – the ones where you can supercharge your growth the most, and will also set you up for better success down the line – are the ones where you find your learning tribe. They'll be the places where you not only feel supported, but are also able to learn from the other perspectives that those people bring to the table, because that's what will enrich your understanding of technology much more.

As an example, perhaps you're someone who likes fishing,

and invented a glove with a built-in LED to help you tie knots in the dark. Your friend who likes cycling might see your invention and ask if you could make a version with yellow lights that come on when you squeeze your fist – essentially, wearable indicators for when you're riding on a bicycle. That connection helps you develop a new version of your product for fishing that you can turn on and off with one hand. Being able to help someone else use the same piece of tech for cycling is going to enrich how you see it for fishing. That cross-pollination of ideas can happen in an environment where there's no need to have a hierarchy.

The best atmosphere is one where everyone learns from each other. Those are the venues where you want to spend most of your time, where you're able to make really interesting connections and where it isn't about gatekeeping. Choose the right venues that don't end up crushing your soul.

●

If you end up creating a new initiative, you'll want to assemble a like-minded team. You may need to take on a co-founder to work intensively alongside you. Alice Bentinck set up Entrepreneur First to encourage more people to found their own tech businesses. However, when it became apparent that only one in five of the applicants were women, she set up another enterprise, Code First Girls, to give young women a quick introduction to writing computer code.

'The original idea was that we'll run this marketing campaign called Code First Girls, where we'll get women skilled up technically, and then they'll want to become founders,' she told me. That didn't quite happen. There was such high demand from young women who wanted to learn to code that they had to turn the campaign into its own social enterprise.

In Alice's words: 'The idea is that [coding is] a very low barrier to entry, so it's on campus, you're with a group of women who are your own age, it's an amazing community, and you very quickly learn how to build a website.' The Code First Girls initiative has now extended beyond campuses and every year it teaches several thousand women across the UK how to code.

Alice isn't somebody who has always been playing with tech. She didn't come from a technical background, and had to upskill. She took it on as a project one summer, helped by somebody who was studying computer science. He took her through the Stanford Computer Science 101 course, which is widely available online. In eight weeks Alice learned to build a website and all the basics.

'He taught me for four hours every day,' she explained. 'I dreaded it, but I'm so, so glad I did it. It helped me understand the process, and the language and the thinking behind how technology works. I'm not going to become a developer, and that's OK.'

Most of the women who do Code First Girls find it useful for general tech literacy, but for some it changes their life. Alice told me about a woman who came in as a declared technophobe. She'd always wanted to work in heritage buildings and had no interest in technology at all, but after doing Code First Girls, she fell in love with it. Eventually, she became a professional developer.

I wanted to know how Alice went about finding people to work with, and how the people who do the Entrepreneur First programme find, in a group of a hundred people, the collaborators who will become their co-founders. She explained that when you join, you don't have an idea, you don't have a team, you don't have anything. Selection is based on your founder potential. The first eight weeks are all about finding a co-founder in a process she describes as being like speed dating on steroids. During those eight weeks, most people go through about two and a half other potential co-founders, and about 80 per cent of people get into a team, even though they're strangers at the beginning.

'It's an intense, emotional process,' she admitted, 'because you're trying to do something quite complicated. You're trying to build a relationship with a person you don't know, alongside deciding an idea to work on. What we found is that you can do that with two people, but in a team of three it becomes incredibly complex. I'm so glad I have a co-founder, because being a founder is relentlessly hard. I don't know how people do it by themselves.'

Finding your learning tribe and founders is one of the last pieces of the puzzle. As it all comes together, there are considerations to be had relating to *how* you now work with this new group of people.

Share Your Working

Start by letting yourself dream about the technology rooms that you can end up in. Then develop your vision and set out what you're thinking, so that you know what you want to say and how you want to say it. Finally, get it out of your head and into the world. Get into those rooms and say what needs to be said. Whether it's the knowledge you already have, whether it's holding folks accountable, whether it's sharing the heritage that we have, or whether it's just empowering other people to be curious.

Make sure to share your learning – don't be a gatekeeper. My friend John Stepper's book, *Working Out Loud*, is all about working better by sharing not just the end product with others, but your thought process too. As well as being a generous process to help others learn from what you're doing, it also means you'll learn more along the way and that learning experience will be a richer one.

You don't have to share all your secret sources. Rest assured that there's more than one way to solve any problem, and if someone does copy your idea, they probably won't do it in the same way. They will most likely prioritize different areas, so sharing your thought process doesn't necessarily mean you'll lose your IP. You must protect your IP, however, as far as is possible, hopefully with advice from your mentors.

Find a comfortable way to be visible, so that you can be documented in a way that other women from history weren't. Hedge against the way that other people might want to erase your story or hide bits of what you are. Take control of it. Document it. Do it on social media, a blog, a website, or whatever new tech platforms have appeared by the time you're reading this book. You could have ten followers or you could have 10,000 followers, but it's not just about the potential engagement. You're sharing not because those numbers matter, but so that there's a record of what you're doing, and because your thinking can add to that body of knowledge. So much of the female experience hasn't been documented, written down or seen as important.

In spite of all the gatekeepers, document what's important to you. It will help you cement your thoughts and refine your voice. When you go into other rooms, it will help you document your mistakes (and associated learnings) for the rooms after that, and finally, it will help you build your tribe. It will attract other people who are having similar thoughts and who are also being curious. Being curious together is powerful.

Getting Started

A big step for any problem you know about, that you're trying to solve with tech, using what you've learned, is to test and try. Going to the right kind of venues means that if you've built something, you're able to test it with others.

Alpha testing is when you test as you go. It's a way of developing. Get into a habit of testing what you're doing. If you're thinking about difference, you can test against it, and that way you can see the limits of what you're doing. You can see the extra features that you might want to try or amend next time around.

And then you try it with others. This is beta testing. You can't be precious and scared about going out with your idea, you can't be scared about your voice being heard. Some of the tools you already use or come across on your technical journey are 'in beta'. This means you're helping their creators test the tech! Over the years at Stemettes we've met all manner of testers working in gaming companies, banks, aircraft companies, chocolate factories . . . So don't be scared to test. Testing and trying is all part of the process. The more you test and try, the less scary it gets. Just like taking auditions for *Pop Idol* and similar shows, the more you do, the less daunting it is. It's just a test.

The final point is measuring the feedback. It really helps to have a 'growth mindset'. Psychologist Carol Dweck asserted that if you take yourself out of your comfort zone, that is where the magic happens. A growth mindset means that you want to continue getting better. And you can only get better if you keep sharing, keep making, keep testing, keep trying.

When you give your thing to someone to test, you're not doing it so they can evaluate you, you're doing it so you can take that feedback, and you can come back better. You want to end up in a feedback loop, you want to have that continuous improvement. You're learning to detach your sense of value from your failures. And you're learning that it's a way we work with technology.

There's a new version of Facebook out every two weeks because they're continuously testing and measuring. They try and they fail. And then they come back and issue you a whole new version. Part of maintaining your voice is that there are always mistakes, nothing is ever perfect. If Meta isn't afraid to try and test and fail (on such a major scale), neither should you be.

- Work on your 'growth mindset'. When it comes to taking CTRL, this equates to approaching your technical journey as one where you are trying to know more and get better. That's it. The destination isn't important – ending up an expert isn't really the goal. You just want to know more today than you did yesterday, and know more this month than you did last month. You can appreciate and recognize that progress is about the stages of the journey itself. Keeping your notes and taking stock of everything you've done to date will help you to develop this mindset. Writing down your achievements and periodically reflecting on them will strengthen it. Finding your tech voice means acknowledging that that voice will develop and become refined over time as you grow, and therefore doesn't need to be perfect from day one.

o Discover your communities. Finding a tribe or crew is important, and there are many ways to meet folks to learn with – offline or online. Listen to podcasts, sign up for courses or browse event-listing sites such as Meetup and Eventbrite. Groups might coordinate themselves via Slack, WhatsApp, Facebook, or a more custom online forum platform like Mighty Networks.

o Go along to some events. You can find out about what's going on on social media, hear recommendations from your favourite podcasts, read about events in magazines. Perhaps start with small venues, small groups, small zooms. Keep searching, try and try again. Things happen in small towns as well as in big cities, so there will be something within reach of wherever you live. If there isn't an event you can physically attend, join online. If the right community doesn't exist, consider setting it up yourself, in your area.

o Take three topics from your musings as you've been reading this book and search for them on a podcast platform, a video platform, an events platform and a social media platform. Now search the topics and add the name of the area where you live. Once you've done that, search the same topics, adding 'women' before them. You should now have a longlist of communities to plug in to. Not all of

them will be active. Not all of them will be the perfect fit
for you. Which ones show up regularly? Which ones have
enough content or explanation for you to know they're
worth a try?

- Once you've whittled things down to a shortlist, do a
  standard search-engine search (DuckDuckGo, Ecosia,
  Bing or Google). What upcoming events are there? What
  can you attend? What can you join?

- On your favourite social media platform, follow the
  leaders and people you see talking about these topics.
  Then, if your social media platform allows, follow the
  topic-related hashtags. Follow to learn.

- With all the ups and downs of life, my gratitude journal is
  something I fill in regularly to keep me buoyant. It's a list of
  things (small and big) that I'm thankful for. Being grateful is
  one of the principles from the Working Out Loud framework
  (available at workingoutloud.com). It's a fantastic way to
  connect with people you're learning from, too. Take the
  opportunity to find your voice by experimenting with your
  online profiles and personas. If you've kept your learnings
  analogue/on paper until now, see what you can try to share
  online. Gratitude is a great exercise to practise – thank
  someone whose resources you've found helpful, then share
  what you actually learned.

- Find a forum you are either a member of or eligible to be
  a member of because of the work you do or who you are.

You might belong to LinkedIn, BYP (Black Young Professionals) Network or The Dots, a professional network for people in the creative industries. Find someone you would like to thank professionally for helping you in some way – maybe for something they posted, a podcast, a video or an article. The point is to be specific and show gratitude to someone you don't know on an online platform. Did you use their advice? Did they make you feel better? This activity is about building a network by showing generosity. There is no agenda and it breaks down the barrier of posting on a social platform. You might hear back but you might not. A key part of this exercise is to build resilience and confidence as you go.

- Join a hackathon or a code-athon – they're the same thing. Join a creative workshop. You don't have to do everything on your own, you can learn by workshopping with others, discussing with friends and colleagues. Meetup and Eventbrite are incredible places to find events like this and, more often than not, you won't even need to leave your house.

- Find a hack in your niche, or one specifically for women: from Wikipedia editathons, to coding workshops to coding day courses, you'll find something that floats your boat.

GOOD
TECH AND
GOOD
HABITS

You might have read about the ten-thousand-hour rule, which Malcolm Gladwell popularized in his book *Outliers*, to emphasize that being an expert is less about natural talent and more about putting in work over time. He was struck by a study of musicians by psychologist Anders Ericsson, who concluded that intense practice, over at least ten years, could explain a lot of what we usually think of as raw talent.

If you do want to be a tech expert, you can get there by practising and building your skills. Remember that even experts started somewhere. They got the basics right, they deliberately built good habits, they let their curiosity keep their interest alive, and they didn't give up after the first week.

Martha Lane Fox set up Lastminute.com in the same year that Google launched, when only one person in eleven had an internet connection at home.[1] She and her business partner weren't technology experts. They both had to learn the basics, back when those basics were much simpler than they are today. Now Martha Lane Fox is a strong voice in the tech space, pushing to get the world online. Let her story show that there's nothing to stop you from setting out on a similar journey.

However, Professor Ericsson also pointed out that repeating the same thing for ten thousand hours won't get you very far . . . It's no good just sitting at your computer for ten hours a week without being intentional about what you're doing, which is why having a framework for your learning is important. If you're learning to code, avoid repeating the same tutorial over and over again; look instead for more complex ones to keep building your skills. It's essential to keep moving forward.

Embracing Tech for Good

Tech for Good is a developing movement that aims to 'consciously build tech that solves problems, that doesn't create problems'. The movement itself has two sides to it. There are generations of bad tech – awful things have happened because of technology being weaponized, for example – but it doesn't have to be like that. Tech for Good is all about asking, 'Who wants this change? Who wants to change what they're doing, how they're doing things, where they're at?' A core part of the movement's thinking began with the notion that technology can be built for public good, rather than purely for money-making and power-wielding purposes.

There's a lot to be said for using technology as a tool to fight for the right side, something that lies at the heart of the international project Code for All, whose mission is 'to drive change through digital technology, citizen participation, collaborative decision-making and good governance to deliver solutions for social challenges while improving the relationship between governments and citizens'. Democracy, collaboration, support and openness are its core values, and it has a network of organizations in over thirty countries around the world, each with its own clear mission statement.

Code for Nigeria uses data to give citizens local and personal information to help them make better-informed decisions about their bread-and-butter issues. It's about amplifying the voices of local citizens. Code for Romania has thousands of volunteers creating open-source digital tools to solve social problems. They believe that technology is one way of enabling citizens to engage more meaningfully in the public sphere and make a positive impact on their communities. Code for America's motto reads, 'Build the right thing and build the thing right.' In the Caribbean, SlashRoots uses the principles and practices of the digital age to create a more equitable, inclusive and sustainable Caribbean society.

This global mission is partly about goals – what problems are trying to be solved, and who is being helped with the tech – but it's also about building the tech in the right way, so the whole process – of finding out what people want and need, of working in a team and handing over the tech to be used – is also done the right way. These organizations work with volunteers in the communities the tech is designed to serve. They're always trying to have an inclusive workforce and to keep learning.

This is the way things are going more widely – tech is becoming more and more important to democracy. Barack Obama's presidential campaigns pioneered data use to target and engage voters. More recently, Dutch politician Jesse Klaver copied Obama's campaign tactics and even used the tech company – Blue State Digital – that worked on Obama's successful 2012 campaign. He's now in parliament as leader of the GroenLinks (GreenLeft) party.

A particularly great example of good tech is the Do Not Do That! bot, built by a couple of kids for a coding competition a few years ago. We know how much some people suffer at the hands of trolls on social media. This bot looked for trolls making threats or saying nasty things, and very simply but effectively tweeted back, 'Do Not Do That!'

Then there's Tracy Chou, an engineer who worked for Facebook and Pinterest, who wanted to do something about online trolls too. She built an app called Block Party, which you can add on to Twitter to filter out harassment or bullying. She used her tech skills and personal experience of trolls to design a tool that doesn't place the burden to resolve the issue on the person being abused. Abusive messages are saved in a folder so that they can be deleted en masse when you want to.

For now, Block Party is an add-on app, but Tracy hopes that future platforms will incorporate her tech features into the way they are built, and make the experience better for users who find themselves the victims of online abuse.

Similarly, activist Seyi Akiwowo set up Glitch, an award-winning UK charity championing digital citizenship as a way to counter online abuse, especially that experienced by Black women. As well as reports and campaigns, Glitch offers free toolkits that anyone can use to build strategies against online abuse.

For all the harm that technology can do, we can also spend time playing on those platforms to counter that harm. Think of it as an investment of your time, fighting for change. Sometimes developing our own knowledge of technology to counter the bad side feels like hand-to-hand combat, but it's work that needs to be done.

It's not necessarily a service we should be providing for free, but there is scope for doing that work on a voluntary basis, as a community service. If you would happily volunteer your time and your skills to help a charity or a community project, what's so different about using your tech skills to help?

The other side of Tech for Good that has been a powerful thing to see over the last couple of years is individuals entering tech companies that have questionable practices and then forcing their hand from inside. Tech employees at Google, Amazon and Netflix have staged walkouts in protest at some of the companies' decisions. This is a longer play. It means getting into the company in question, rising through the ranks, and acquiring more agency and more influence. At that point, they're able to say, for example, that the company shouldn't be working with certain parties. Or they're able to say, 'We'll build it a different way', rather than throwing the baby out with the bathwater.

Lots of people and organizations are working on this ethical side of how to do good with the tech rather than making things worse. There's a big opportunity to look at that work and learn from some of the new thinking.

It's worth remembering that you're not learning from something that's completed; this is all still live and evolving. You still have an opportunity to shape a lot of what's happening in this space, especially if you're someone who doesn't necessarily consider themselves technical. You might not be coming into the sphere with the inherited knowledge of what other technologies might have done. You're not thinking it's just about computer science and missing the wider implications of what's being built.

As you learn, it's important to be conscious of the more

ethical Tech for Good stance. In the years to come, I think we'll see people taking a better approach, engaging in tech citizenship and taking a greater responsibility for the ways in which they apply technology.

What Does 'Good' Look Like?

Good tech isn't something we've explored or prioritized as much as we should. However, as women, we're able to bring a fresh perspective that's been missing in this space for so long on what *is* good, and is there only one definition of good? If there isn't, then what does 'good' look like? How are you able to identify it? How are you able to work towards it?

Here are my suggestions:

- Good tech makes a difference in the quality of people's lives – for the better.
- Good tech incorporates the difference in those different types of lives.
- Good tech leaves things better than they were, and doesn't maintain the status quo. Not only is it not harmful, it's an improvement.

As we know, good tech isn't necessarily what gets adopted. It's not necessarily what gets to scale, or necessarily what becomes a household name. It's not about being bigger, making more money, or being harder, faster or stronger. It is, however, tech that genuinely makes a difference.

Be conscious of this distinction. Use it as a lens, as you observe and research, and as you look into use cases. Being able to spot what good is is like developing an ear for music. There's certainly a subjective element, but you learn to distinguish between good singers and bad singers. You may not like someone's voice but you can recognize its quality.

As an example, as much as the way that the Facebook platform operates, scares and frustrates me, I can appreciate the glimmers of good that happen on there. It's a good distinction to be able to make, and one that reflects our level of agency when it comes to our interaction with the platform. We don't have to feel at its mercy.

Being aware of the distinction also means that when I'm involved in making or influencing technical decisions, I can take my learning from the bad and make sure I don't replicate it. I often ponder what I would have said if I was in the room when certain tech companies were founded.

'We're going to create a platform that allows ANYONE to say ANYTHING to ANYBODY at ANY time.'

It doesn't sound good. I know what It's like to have things shouted at me in the street. The thought of creating a technical space where the same thing happens sets all of my alarm bells ringing. I imagine it sets off some of yours too. Yet here we are with a plethora of ways to say anything to anyone at any time.

•

It will come as no surprise to you that often good tech can be made by bringing a fresh women's perspective to an issue. I talked to Professor Noémie Elhadad, a computer scientist working with the medical school at Columbia University. Working together across disciplines is one of the things that keeps her there.

On my podcast, Noémie told me the story of how she came to

the work she's doing now. All through her years as an under-graduate to being a professor, she has lived with endometriosis – a painful women's health condition where tissue similar to that which lines the uterus grows outside it. It can disrupt all sorts of bodily functions and generally interferes with living a normal life. You probably know somebody who suffers from it.

'It's not a rare disease in any way,' Noémie told me. 'Right now, it's estimated to be an issue for six to ten per cent of women in reproductive age, which is pretty high. And there's hardly any research in endometriosis – not for lack of interest, but for lack of funding. As a patient, I was frustrated, I was angry, I felt like I was alone.'

Noémie decided to do something about it, using her tech skills and knowledge to tackle the problem. She found that in the medical literature there was a lack of representation of the lived experience of patients and identified a real need to document those experiences to better understand what it is to have endometriosis. It led her to create Phendo, an app that patients can use to record their own experience of endometriosis, and contribute that data to research that could help them and others.

Noémie's department, Biomedical Informatics, also has access to the medical records of patients who have been to the associated hospital. The patients' notes are written by doctors, typed into the computer or dictated, so Noémie is using her specialism, Natural Language Processing (NLP), to design a program that allows computers to extract information from records written by humans, for humans. They can then compare the symptoms documented by clinicians with what the patients are telling them through Phendo.

Noémie wanted to keep the Phendo app simple: 'We decided

not to use too many cutting-edge AI or machine-learning approaches to it. It was this very simple idea of "You're a patient, you have an experience of disease, just tell me about it." And that's it.'

She is using her tech knowledge on a problem of which she has first-hand experience, but she can also see that it's an approach that could work on other problems. 'I think what's so exciting with this approach is that you can apply it to many questions,' she told me. 'It's a methodology, it's a way of thinking about advancing medicine. For me, that's the biggest deal. As much as clinical trials are the gold standard for understanding how disease works and how interventions and treatments work, we don't have enough funds, or time, to do a clinical trial for every type of patient out there.'

As a computer scientist working in medicine, Noémie can also see another limitation that her approach could help to overcome. She discussed with me the restrictions that come with clinical trials and their eligibility criteria, and how this often results in a lack of diversity in patients. What Noémie is doing is the opposite, thriving on a much larger and more diverse sample of data.

Involving patients in a project such as Phendo creates a different relationship, a different power dynamic, to traditional clinical trials. Noémie explained, 'The big difference with this population of patients who have a disease and are frustrated, is that they're in it for something, they're waiting for something back. We want to be partners together in understanding what this disease is. And as a patient myself, I had a lot of trust from fellow patients.'

At first Noémie was hesitant to disclose that she also had a diagnosis of endometriosis, but soon found that this link meant she was very much in touch with her subjects. She could show empathy and approach them as a partner: 'In retrospect, it was the right choice to really open myself up. I don't really enjoy talking about my uterus, but I'm going to do it, and I'm going to talk about my period and my pain, and all the ways in which endometriosis has affected me, because I want others to understand.'

This approach also means Noémie sees the importance of sharing what she and her team learn with as wide an audience as possible: 'We do a lot of small meetups and talk to different patient communities. We also write a blog. We're about to put out a summary of two research papers that got published recently and make a lay version of it that explains what it means for patients.[2] And surprisingly we're pretty good at disseminating through Instagram – it's like science by Twitter but it works. We can have very interesting discussions with patients through Instagram.'

If you build anything that doesn't overtly show that it's ready for difference, or built around difference, it's not going to sound good. 'Good' means that you've considered that difference. 'Good' means that you're ready for a wide variety of use cases, and that you've considered the majority of examples that your tech might be used for. If you haven't done that and not been able to go beyond the default, then, given the plurality we have as human beings and the heterogeneous nature of whatever your tech is being applied to, it won't be good.

This matters the most when we're talking about living beings. If you're applying the technology to something that doesn't touch humans, or doesn't impact humans at all, then the bar is set lower. If, however, any kind of human life is involved, or there are any consequences for human beings, then you have a responsibility to make sure that it is good.

Late to the Game? No Problem

There's a difference between knowing that something sounds good when you're creating the tech, and evaluating tech that has already been made, is being sold to you, or is being introduced for you to use. You won't have the same level of choice as if you were building it yourself, but there is still a choice in how you use it, or even *whether* you use it. That's the difference between being able to identify the good in tech versus being able to make sure that a piece of tech *is* good.

When we talk about identifying good tech, especially in the context of women, examples of women not being part of the building process always show up in the way that the tech is put together. Whether it's the registration system at your gym that assumes that you're male if you've selected Dr as your title, so you're then locked out of the female changing rooms.[3] Or the voice-recognition systems that struggle to understand female voices.[4] Or the virtual-reality headsets that cause cyber sickness for the 90 per cent of women whose pupils are set closer together than the headset's default settings.[5]

It happens because at no time during the development process do people *listen* in order to ensure they are building something that sounds good.

As we look across technologies and at using tech to solve our problems, we can see that tech is not inherently bad. It's all about the ways in which it can be used. A knife can be used to help feed someone, or it can be used to harm them. Folks who create tech talk about user error, but often we should be talking about creator error.

As we've said previously, a lot of the tech we use is missing many perspectives. When you're evaluating the building process, ask, 'Does this measure up to me? Does this measure up to that different perspective? How would this work out in that use case, on that device, on that platform, in that country?'

We've seen examples of not considering, not thinking and not asking the right questions. We understand that not considering tech from different perspectives limits the difference it can make to the quality of women's lives. When you check for those different perspectives, you're making a pre-emptive strike against poor tech choices. What you are picking, engaging with, choosing to use and choosing to build on makes a difference.

That doesn't always mean simply not using something. It might mean taking it up but hedging against what it doesn't provide. It might mean building something on top of it to improve it.

Good Tech Habits – It's About Quality Over Quantity

It's my belief that your personal qualities are linked to the quality of your digital habits. Philosophers since Aristotle have talked about a good person having good habits, and not just because you get into the habit of doing good things, such as cleaning your teeth or thanking the driver when you get off the bus. It's also about getting into the habit of paying attention to the right things, so you can deliberately do the good thing, because you were listening, paying attention and asking the right questions.

Instead of trying to develop lots of good little tech habits, what's important is the depth or the value of them, and having at least one good tech habit that you're able to develop over time. Developing this quality filter, this ear for good, will help you keep thinking about the point of trying to make good tech. Practice makes better, if not perfect. This is about continually improving and evolving with the field. You'll also become better at being able to sniff out good, or hear it.

Having a 'growth mindset', the term coined by psychologist Carol Dweck, means that you're able to look back at last week, or last month, and say, 'I've spotted this thing now that I wouldn't have spotted a month ago.' It's how you'll know you're making progress on your own 'good filter', for the tech you're evaluating and for the tech you're building, for the tech you're exploring and the way you're using tech as a tool. Even for the tech you're still just dreaming of. The habit of listening, looking and sniffing for what's good will get stronger the more you use it.

Using the same growth mindset, you need to become comfortable with being outside your comfort zone (something of a contradiction in terms, I know). If you don't know whether something is going to be good, or what the implications could be if it's not, that's fine. Step outside your comfort zone, learn about it, do some background research. Have a think, talk to people, engage with others in the ethics communities and institutions. In the UK, we've got, amongst others, the Alan Turing Institute and the Ada Lovelace Institute, which you can turn to. Watch some online lectures, read through some papers, have a look at what's already been said on the issue and what others are thinking, then try to evaluate it for yourself.

The Getting Started section opposite will give you advice and tips for putting some of the above into action. What we've covered in this chapter will also provide you with a great foundation for becoming a pioneer of change, which we'll talk about next.

Getting Started

It's a powerful thing to develop good habits. Keep building those habits, because they will end up making tech work for you, and will ensure you're in CTRL. Here's a set of habits worth building in order to futureproof yourself and your tech journey.

- Build, measure, learn: this is an idea that ties into the continuous improvement that happens within the tech industry, and comes from *The Lean Startup* by Eric Ries. Lots of people like to say that they're using this process, but whether they're actually continuously improving is up for debate. The idea of build, measure, learn is that, whatever you do, it's always an experiment. You never know what's going to happen, and you don't always know how it's happened. Give yourself permission to build, to try something out, and then evaluate it. The point is that you tried and then learned from your evaluation. Then, you take that learning into building or trying something else. This cyclical way of looking at things is the way tech happens.

- Get used to challenging the 'why' on particular tech. If you're a manager, or in a position to ask questions, have a look at the technology that's being used in your workplace, or anywhere else you're involved with. Get your Good Tech filter working. Does it sound good? If you can find gaps, or potential harms, maybe challenge 'why' that particular tech is being used or what gaps might exist. Try out your Good Tech filter in the design process, maybe at a hackathon.

- Digital collaboration tools at work are one of my favourite ways to take CTRL. A lot of organizations are beginning to use them, and they can help you to connect with people across your organization (if it's a large one) and connect better with your colleagues generally (if your organization is small). If there's not one at work, then there are several contained communities or forums, on platforms such as LinkedIn, where you can practise extending your influence and connections. They're a nicer test ground compared with the really big social media platforms, which can sometimes be overwhelming. Spend time on one of these and learn quirks as you go – it's very powerful. Be sure to carefully read through the features of the platform you're on, so you can send emojis and GIFs and enrich your learning journey.

- Fake news and misinformation have flourished on the internet. There's so much information online – how can you be sure it's reliable? The answer is you never can be. Even reputable sites make mistakes. So all information needs to be taken with a pinch of salt. The more information you handle, the easier you'll find doing this. Getting used to comparing information from many different sources is the way to go. Lifelong learning is necessary, and a big part of being in CTRL, because things are constantly changing. Check the current syllabus for a subject you studied at school. How much of it is familiar to you? How much of this knowledge have you used in the intervening years? How recently has the Wikipedia page been updated for a topic within that subject?

- Many of the important habits worth developing revolve around online safety and security. Cybersecurity is a massive field that, even if it hasn't been on your curiosity radar so far, will definitely be a part of your processes and considerations at work. A resource I've found fascinating when it comes to considering safe devices for the home, and for discovering who is using what data, is Privacy Not Included from the Mozilla Foundation. It'll inform the way you bring new devices into your home – and will help you form good habits around asking the right questions of technology.

- There are also goals around habits, whether it's switching news subscriptions or choosing to spend your money with a different outlet or vendor. When I read Dale Carnegie's *How to Win Friends and Influence People*, shortly after I graduated, my favourite thing was to read a chapter or principle then spend the next two weeks trying it out on folks around me. I changed how I wrote emails, how I 'argued', and even how I thought through work relationships to great effect. Experimenting in that way gave me something more to think about, to be excited about. The experiments were harmless but insightful.

12

BE A
CHANGE
PIONEER

I've always been obsessed with making change happen. And I've always loved technology as a tool for precisely that purpose. It's something I recognize as a privilege. Making the decision to be a change pioneer is the easy part. The harder bit is deciding what change you want to effect, but it's good to be as specific as possible.

Take, as an example, the US Suffragettes. There were many things that they wanted to change, and they didn't all agree on everything. It might not have been their intention, but initially, only women who owned land were allowed the vote. However, it was intentional that Black women were not part of their remit. They didn't all agree on the fact that Black women should be entitled to the vote – so it wasn't *all* women they were campaigning for, just white women. The women who succeeded defined their objective clearly and could narrow it down to a simple slogan (despite the caveats listed above): votes for women.

Defining your scope is something to consider right from the start. Refine and focus your objectives. What is the change you want to make happen? Often it relates to your lived experience. Sometimes it relates to experiences you've learned about – and you want to help others. It's up to you to exercise your choice on what problem you are trying to solve.

I spoke to Emma Lawton, a designer, writer and speaker. I see her as a change pioneer because she is refining other people's tools to improve the lives of people with Parkinson's. Emma has a watch named after her, although, as she points out, it doesn't tell the time. She described it to me as having quite a space-age look to it, with a white circle on top and six haptics, so you can have vibration points that sit on the wrist.

Haiyan Zhang, a designer and engineer at Microsoft, worked with Emma on creating the watch to help Emma manage her Parkinson's. The secret of the watch's success lies in the tiny vibrations emitted from the watch to reduce tremors caused by the disease. The vibrations almost distract the brain from creating the tremor – in a similar way to how King George VI's stammer was halted by listening to music while he spoke.

As a graphic designer, a diagnosis of Parkinson's at the age of twenty-nine was a blow to Emma's career plans. By the time she met Haiyan she was struggling to write or draw by hand. Technology helped her regain some of her capabilities, but her experience also gave her completely new insights into people who benefit from technology. She told me that it changed how she felt about users and grew her interest in user-first technology, which led her to a new job, working for the charity focused on her medical condition.

'They made a role for me at Parkinson's UK,' she told me. 'I was working there as a freelance designer and we were getting loads of phone calls from people asking, "What else is there tech-wise that we can use? What would you recommend?"'

People were hesitant to recommend anything. If you were to suggest an app that reminds a patient to take their medication and the app stopped getting updated and stopped working properly, you would run the risk of dangerous consequences. The issue led to Emma's new role in verifying whether certain technology is genuinely useful for individuals with Parkinson's. She would work with people living with the disease to test whether the tech was safe and whether the business was sustainable enough that they'd keep updating it.

Like Noémie Elhadad, Emma realized that bringing together people who might want to use the technology with experts (who could assess things like safety, privacy and reliability) would combine different voices and experiences, and produce the best possible result. So Emma became Devices and Apps lead at Parkinson's UK and has had her eyes opened to the range of things that tech can do. 'I suddenly realized the real power of technology. You can help people live fairly normal lives. I feel like I'm still living a fairly Independent life, that I maybe would need more help with if there wasn't such a thing as technology.'

With her insight, I asked Emma what tips she would give somebody wanting to develop tech for people with Parkinson's. She told me simplicity is key: 'Everyone tries to create that all-singing, all-dancing app, and actually the most successful ones are a single-purpose app or solution.' She also issued a plea for tech with stylish design: 'Don't forget that you're designing for people who have taste as well as an illness.'

These are all tips that anybody wanting to develop tech, for any user or purpose, could take on board. Keep it as simple as you can and remember you're designing for humans, not one-dimensional (and one-coloured) robots.

•

Where you want to take CTRL might come as a result of something you've personally experienced. Some people see a problem in the world and want to create something that sparks change. I spoke with another inspirational woman taking CTRL, Anisah Osman Britton, a true change pioneer in the field of breaking down the borders between women in different countries.

Anisah founded 23 Code Street because she wanted to create a safe space for women to be a part of tech and creating tech. She also wanted to make a difference to the lives of women in India, where she has family connections. Of all the startups and clients she'd worked with, one particular project set her on her journey to becoming a change pioneer. She'd found herself seated at a table with eight men, talking about periods for an NHS project. She told me how she remembered going home that day and thinking, 'I can't be the only person to talk for women at these tables.'

She started to imagine what it would be like to create her own project to address the diversity issue in tech and the ways in which gender disparity affects the products and services. In the end, she quit her job. She didn't know what the precise nature of her project would be, but she knew that it would be about giving women more of a voice and more control in tech.

In 2016 Anisah launched 23 Code Street, a coding school for all women, which starts them off on the path to becoming a software engineer, with the additional promise that for every paying student the enterprise will also teach digital skills to a woman in the slums of India. 'I initially thought we were just going to work with women in India,' she told me, 'but I have a bit of a problem with charitable giving and not being able to be self-reliant.'

She felt there was an uncomfortable juxtaposition between women having more control through tech and women being reliant on handouts. While Indian women were her focus, she didn't want to run the school purely as a charity, so she turned it into a social enterprise where the money she charges women in the UK pays for the women in India to become skilled. She saw that there were plenty of women in the UK who also needed these technology skills to be able to move up in their careers: '23 Code Street came out of a need for a safe space for women to learn, specifically. They didn't have to want to be developers – that was always key. I wanted to teach people to have a seat at the table and have the skills to talk about technology, and understand it and not be hoodwinked.'

Anisah started her enterprise with a lot of enthusiasm, a lot of help from people who supported the idea, and not much else. Her former boss gave her £5,000. 'So we started with that,' she told me, 'and I lived on a boat, and I had a laptop. We started to build the landing page, the logo and the identity. We didn't pay for space for our courses for a very long time, because people believed in what we were doing. A lot of people helped and a lot of connections got it off the ground.'

Because Anisah had identified her goals and her values right from the start, she knew what her non-negotiables were. She knew she wanted to do something in India that was sustainable rather than relying on charity. She also wanted it to involve women closest to the problem, and to give them the tools to support themselves.

Working in both the UK and India helped resource the work with Indian women. 'It was always a one-for-one model,' Anisah told me. 'But we started in India with a bunch of partners on the ground. I never wanted us to own the teaching there. We had to work with locals – it couldn't seem like white charity. Everyone had to look like the people that they were teaching. Just so it felt inclusive.'

Anisah went out to India and met with local experts and smaller NGOs to find partners on the ground. She had a clear sense of who she would and wouldn't work with. I asked what happened when she was approached by organizations that didn't match their criteria. 'The answer was always, "We're not the right partner for you,"' she replied. '"But do put your money into people and charities that are looking for it."'

The beauty of understanding tech, and having this tool, is that you can solve so many problems with it. You can be as altruistic as you like, because tech, in its very nature, is incredibly altruistic. It's important to exercise the right choice.

Fully research and truly understand the problem you're trying to solve, and the different ways that might happen, before you start laying technology on top of it. Ultimately, it's not the tech itself that's going to solve your issue. Tech is one of the tools you can use – and it's a pretty powerful one at that – but the real revolution is going to be in humans and human behaviour, human change and human systems.

Why wouldn't you want to pioneer change, whether it's to preserve the past, to enjoy more of the present, or to have an impact on the future? Taking CTRL will involve doing your research and talking to folks, to explore their perspective on problems. As you start to make change happen, you will start to change too.

From Ideas Person to Ideas Controller

You've decided your scope, you've worked out the change you want to make happen. What next?

Some people think that to be a change pioneer you have to be an ideas person. You might be, but I don't think it's always necessary. Some people will naturally start thinking of inventing something or putting something new together, but that's not the only way to solve problems. Other people are ideas controllers, where you have a blueprint for others to work from.

This is something we see across technology, and across STEM. You're never truly starting from scratch. You might be building on top of structures that other people have created, or on top of theories that other people have proved. You might even be building on lessons learned from what other people have done.

So don't be disheartened and feel like being a change pioneer means that you need to start with a blank piece of paper. Innovation isn't just about creating new things. It's about making changes to existing things, and edits to what's already there.

Borrowing from *The Lean Startup* approach to developing tech – build, test, learn – think of your idea as prototyping until you get to something called the minimum viable product. You don't jump from zero to 100 – you first get to ten. The question you should be asking yourself is, 'What's the minimum number of features needed for this idea, this concept, this change, to prove the point of what I'm trying to do?'

This approach formed the core of three ideas I brought to Stemettes. I'd been inspired by what I'd seen in the US at the

Grace Hopper Celebration of Women in Computing, and I wanted to translate some parts of the event for a slightly younger audience (the conferences at GHC are mostly for students and tech executives) and make them happen here in the UK. I asked myself, 'How do we repackage this? How do we change this? How do we edit this? I then looked for three elements of the event that I could try to translate to a younger audience.' Originally, those elements were a panel event, a hackathon and a show. Nine years on, we still do the panels, the hackathon, and much more besides. We decided to drop the show because it didn't fit in with the other things we do – it didn't directly translate to the UK. I documented our early work and learnings, and they're still visible on the Stemettes blog.

You've got to be ready to throw away ideas, even as you're trying them out, and especially as you're starting out. Other elements will remain at the core, and you will simply evolve around them. Allow yourself to take an iterative approach. Folks who have started companies will tell you how they didn't immediately build a full app on, say, everything to do with motherhood. They perhaps started with pregnancy, and focused on a smaller element. That's how you need to think. What's a smaller aspect of the thing that you want to change? Start there – and build from it.

If you have the big vision, the big idea from the start, that's great, but don't forget that there are steps you will need to take towards realizing it, and that will take time. Take advantage of the lessons you can learn in the early stages, when the stakes are lower. They'll give you more confidence for when you move on to bigger steps, later on.

Remember never to lose sight of the set of values that are

the basis for what you're doing. Some companies display their set of values on a wall, or you might see them on the back of your ID card: they'll be reduced to five different words, or a catchy phrase. Apple wants you to 'think different'. The International Olympic Committee's motto is 'faster, higher, stronger'. Organizations usually host their values on their website. Code for Pakistan lists six: integrity, equality, community-building, collaboration, openness, optimism. Code for Sierra Leone has just three: agency, action, ecosystems.

You don't need to reduce your values to a few memorable words or phrases, but you do need to know what's at the heart of what you're trying to do. What's the core of your idea? What's unique about what you're doing? And what are the things that matter most to you in the implementation of what you're doing?

Values can change over time, but if you're clear on what they are it makes it easier for other folks to know if those values align with their own. If they do, then it'll be easier for them to join you, give you the right kind of feedback, feed in to what you're doing and understand what might happen next.

At this point in your journey to become a change pioneer, you're in a position to put together your proof of concept, or a minimum viable product for change. As we touched upon earlier, a minimal viable product is the simplest, smallest product or service you can create that doesn't embody the full set of your ambitions but acts as *enough* of a representation of them for people to understand or use the product.

If you have all of these elements, reaching this point will mean you're almost ready to release your idea and allow others to work on it alongside you. Once you've put together your minimum viable product you've done all the hard work. You can still be in control of the action and the change that is happening under the banner of what you are trying to build, but the rest of the work can be implemented by other people without you as the engine driving production forwards. Your load will be lighter, and you can be the ideas controller rather than the enactor.

In the early days of Stemettes we were really clear about what we were trying to solve, our remit and our goals. We were also really clear about our motto: 'free, fun, food'.

'Free' came from the idea that if I'm trying to convince someone to do something, or if I'm trying to inform them, they shouldn't have to pay for the privilege of me evangelizing to them. It makes no sense to me to charge people to come to our events, and during the sessions it costs nothing to participate and the laptops are free to use. 'Fun' came from the fact that other people working in the tech space were hosting very curriculum-focused events, which felt very serious, like an academic course or a lesson. Kids already go to lessons, so why would they willingly choose to attend more, even if they were free? Fun and enjoyment had to be at the heart of the learning experience. In a different, fun environment you are likely to learn much more, so having a positive STEM experience over a serious one was essential. Finally, I believe that food, or breaking bread with others, helps to forge connections between people. I like eating free food because it tastes better than food you've paid for. Also, if you know you're going to get a hot meal when you're at an event, it's one less thing to worry about. You can abandon yourself to the sessions without stressing about when and where you're going to grab a sandwich.

Our first event was on Pancake Day and we served unlimited pancakes! We had temporarily covered major parts of Maslow's Hierarchy of Needs[1] and the delegates were able to concentrate on enjoying themselves and picking up whatever skills we were encouraging in our environment. We knew our approach was very, very different to that of other courses, so it became our USP. We attracted people by promising free fun and free food. If we'd put STEM front and centre, we might not have been so successful.

We actually started off with something about lipstick, handbags and shoes, and it didn't take us long to realize why we might not want to lean hard into a stereotype like that. That being said, where we ended up was still quite different to how other STEM outreach organizations were approaching the same problem of trying to engage with girls. Our rationale was that these groups were focusing on knowledge and subject content so much that they were forgetting the other things that might motivate human beings and draw people in. That point of difference is something we've stuck to.

We also saw the value of me having a Twitter account and the value of pushing our ideas and our work on social media – me having a blog, using my own LinkedIn, using some of my existing platforms, was all part of the documenting process. It allowed me to communicate Stemettes' ideas and share our values, which made it easier for other people to be drawn into what we're doing and be a part of it.

I went from being the single, central ideas person to being more of an ideas controller and an implementation person.

Say 'No!' to Brilliant Jerks

There's an old proverb from Burkina Faso that roughly translates to: 'If you want to go faster, go on your own, but if you want to go further, go with others.' You can't effect change alone.

In technical fields, nothing is accomplished by one person operating on their own, however much we might hold in our minds the stereotype of the lone genius inventor. We like to have heroes, and figureheads are important, as they allow people to be drawn in by an individual, and drawn to a movement in a more personal way. However, getting stuff done is really about collaboration, bringing people together and working together.

The story we hear about Facebook is that Mark Zuckerberg came up with the idea on his own, but the Hollywood movie *The Social Network* tells a different story – that in fact, he was working with other people, and the seed of the idea was someone else's. In my experience, that idea of lone geniuses is nonsense, and it leads to really bad technical decisions being made.

When you have someone who's really great at one aspect of their job, you end up valuing their skill sets above the combined knowledge and experience of the group. I've heard these people referred to as 'brilliant jerks'. Idolizing them is one thing that we've got quite wrong in the tech industry. Technology is a collaborative enterprise and no one builds something good entirely on their own. It takes teamwork. The perspectives and voices of others are essential if you're to produce a good piece of tech that works for the full range of people who might end up using or being affected by it. This isn't 'design by committee' but rather the collaborative effort of a team of specialists. We can use the catering industry as an analogy here – each kitchen features a chef de cuisine, sous chefs, chefs de partie, tasters and sommeliers, each with their own area of expertise.

As your sphere of influence grows, as you explore the technology industry and find yourself in tech environments, be aware of those brilliant jerks, and of cultures and environments that idolize them. Make sure that you design with multiple perspectives in mind, and remember that tech alone won't solve the problem. Foster a culture of collaboration in everything you do.

Collaboration means that when you are thinking of ideas or in a development process, no one person's views and skills are valued more than others'. You might be the ideas controller, and the buck stops with you, but you need to have as much input as possible into what you're doing. Having the right number of collaborators will mean you can balance more things at once, but you need to be able to manage that collaboration. You might choose to use a framework – one of the agile frameworks, for example, which is an iterative and incremental software-development approach – to manage your work over a longer period of time. The core principles of agile are:

- A focus on user needs
- To deliver iteratively
- To keep improving how your team works
- To fail fast and learn quickly
- To keep planning

If you spend enough time in technology rooms, you'll eventually hear the word 'agile' being bandied about. In the olden days, we ran IT projects in a very linear fashion. You did the analysis –

which involved learning about why an IT project had been requested and why it was needed. Then you'd do a design stage – where you'd decide on how the technology was going to be built, and would draw up plans for it. After that was an implementation phase, which involved building the technology. Then it would be tested against what you said in the analysis. After passing tests it would be evaluated, and that was the end of the IT project.

Given that IT projects differ very much from building projects, this method caused issues – what if the world had changed slightly by the time you got to the implementation stage? You'd have to go back to analysis and start again, wasting a big part of the design stage. In IT we were working on products, not projects in the traditional sense. These products would change over time, during the course of the project, in a way that buildings don't. When a construction project is over, the building is open for use and there are no new amendments other than maintenance. Technology projects build products that evolve over time – with new features and significant enhancements.

In the nineties, a group of folks brought together some ideas to change this process fundamentally – focusing on product management rather than project management. The agile framework was born and the whole industry slowly rotated to face it. As a newbie entering this world, agile is a brilliant thing for you to explore. A series of ideas and new words, such as 'scrum', 'kanban' and 'backlog', became commonplace.

(A scrum is a methodology for helping teams work and iterate together in two-week sprints. A kanban is a way of visualizing all the pieces of work being done by a team that provides transparency and subsequently allows the team to see their capacity and prioritize accordingly. A backlog is a list of priorities of upcoming work and features to be carried out by a team.)

As a change pioneer, if you embrace the agile framework and build your technology during your two-week sprint, you will be developing and working on the specific features outlined in your backlog. However, because you can balance only so much on your plate at any given time, rather than trying to boil the whole ocean at once, you will work iteratively to build your technology in chunks. This means that you can start from the core of your idea, from your minimum viable product, and go from there. Once you have that core product or small nugget of an idea, as soon as you have extra time and resources, you can add a new feature. All the new features you want to build can become a product roadmap, and that's how you'll know what's next for your plate.

When you take a collaborative approach to design, and instil a culture of collaboration in your working life, good change happens. If we were to look at technologies that have done well, we'd see that the ideas could have come from anywhere. It's never purely about technical prowess. Deciding who to work with is something that we are still learning at Stemettes. There are so many factors to consider.

Considerations for Collaboration

Whenever we enter into a new partnership at Stemettes, we begin by sitting down with the prospective partner and evaluating how much **time**, **space** and **money** they – and we – are able to give to the particular initiative or intervention.

Time relates to how many people our prospective partner can offer as, for example, volunteers on programmes as mentors and role models in the partnership. How many folks will be able to help liaise with us and ensure we properly represent the opportunities available with that partner to our young people?

Space is about what they can offer in terms of physically hosting events in the programme. We don't host our own events as all of our interventions are created with collaboration in mind, so we wouldn't want to work in a nondescript 'Stemettes' space away from where the 'STEM' happens. Where is the space the partner has? Is it safe for young people? Is it accessible? Is there an internet connection?

Money is the final piece of the puzzle. We have to be sustainable and I pay all of my staff at least a living wage. Will this partner be able to help cover our costs to bring our STEM outreach expertise, safeguarding protocols, aftercare, community and event skills to the programmes in the partnership?

These elements are never considered in isolation. We struggle to work with partners who have, say, a lot of time but no space and no funds, unless we can bring in another partner who has space and funds but no time.

There will always be constraints on how much you can collaborate with different folks – based on whatever your model of managing collaboration looks like. You need to work out what your constraints might be and then set your non-negotiable boundaries. Your ideas, values and priorities, the type of change you want to make and where you've set your scope – all of these considerations will help you to determine who your first line of collaborators might be. Then your second line, third or fourth line.

Do this early on, and be clear on those non-negotiables. It will make it so much easier for you to say, for example, 'We won't collaborate with organizations that work just with boys.' In turn, that will make it easier for you to use your resources efficiently, and easier for other folks to accept that they might not be the right organization for you to partner with. On the flip side, non-negotiables also make it easy to confidently say yes. They allow potential collaborators to understand how they can work with you and the value they're bringing.

Own those non-negotiables – the minimum that you are prepared to accept, and the values that you're able to bring to others. Ask yourself: What have we proved that we're good at? What have we learned from our experiments? What do we know we can offer to others? Beyond those time, space and money questions, what other things are we missing out on and need to have in order to be a change pioneer?

As you use technology to do your research and understand the problem you want to tackle, you might find gaps in what you're working on. You might decide to collaborate with somebody if they can fill some of your gaps – or maybe you can fill gaps that they have. However, there's also a wild card: serendipity. Sometimes an opportunity for collaboration might present itself, where it's not immediately obvious what the benefit might be. I call it magnanimous collaboration. About twice a month, I'll accept a request and do it as a freebie. I'll do it to put some good back into the universe, to help somebody else out, and I won't expect anything in return.

I don't consider it charity – it's more like leaving a bit of your garden to grow wild, which results in more flowers, and more bees, which then pollinate the rest of your garden. There will be occasions when one of those freebies will lead to something I wouldn't ever have predicted. If I never did those things, there would be fewer chances for something completely unexpected but incredibly positive to happen.

Intentionally Including

We served unlimited pancakes at the Stemettes launch partly because it was Pancake Day, but also because food is one of our core tenets. One of the partners we worked with gave us £100, and that allowed us to pay someone to make pancakes for us for two or three hours, with all the toppings we wanted. Which is very Stemettes.

When I first started the organization, a 'hack culture' existed where there would be beer and pizza on tap at events, and you'd stay for hours, even working through the night. There was a running joke that coders were machines that turned coffee into code. I realized that if we were going to run similar events with young people, they couldn't have beer and they couldn't have coffee. So we asked ourselves, what can their fuel be? We wanted something that would both give them energy and keep them happy and enthusiastic.

In the end, we settled on sweets – Haribo, in particular. Our vision was that while the kids were listening to Justin Bieber, or whoever, they'd have their sweets, and would be living their best life getting technical at a Stemettes event.

Very early on I realized that some kids can't have Haribo because they eat halal or kosher. Our next thought was to offer some kind of chocolate, but then we discovered vegetarian Haribo, so we were able to offer those as well. Everyone got their sugar if they wanted sugar. If they didn't want it, we sometimes had fruit too. But kids are kids – they mostly wanted sugar.

Down the line, I spoke at an event that also included the founders of a new confectionary company, Candy Kittens. Not long afterwards, a delivery arrived for me. It was a metre-long cardboard box from the company, packed full of sweets, all of which were vegan. The accompanying note read, 'We love what you said, we love what you do, and we love that you love food. Why don't we do something together?'

Send me free food and I'll be yours for ever. It was also a solution to a problem we didn't know we had until that point. It helped us to understand a little bit more about what equitable practice could look like.

Intentionally including folks is something I talk about to companies and organizations. The first stage of being inclusive means considering difference – recognizing that some people can't eat Haribo, and making sure to offer an alternative, and that is fine. However, the next level, the deeper level, is offering something that works universally and promotes a proper sense of belonging within our community.

That doesn't mean compromise. In fact, making something that genuinely works for everyone is better than compromise. To use a maths analogy, rather than the lowest common denominator, it's the highest common factor. It's trying something different that will allow everyone to partake in the same way – one that makes sense for all. During the pandemic, in order to continue working in an equitable way, we posted laptops out to Stemettes participants and worked with partners to buy laptops so that girls could continue to be involved by working remotely.

We've always maintained that if you're going to visit a Stem-ettes space you can come empty-handed. We will feed you, we will give you a laptop, we will give you a good time, and you won't even have to pay to be there. As supportive as they were, my parents wouldn't have paid for me to attend coding classes regularly, or lessons like the ones we host at Stemettes. With five children in the family, that wasn't something they were able to spend money on. Keeping Stemettes free isn't going to solve all problems of accessibility, but it definitely removes one major barrier for the folks we're trying to support.

Intentional inclusion isn't just about thinking how people are accessing your service or using your product, it's also about how you're including the different types of people you might need as part of your desire to effect change. Including everyone isn't a favour you're doing for them, it's a practice that's equally valuable to you – in that it helps you to make the changes you want without missing out perspectives that you need.

Keep looking for difference across and beyond the benefi-ciaries of the change you're working on. Who isn't coming? Why might they not be coming? What barriers could be keeping them away? Given that you need that difference to build the best possible product, it's worth investing in accessibility and allowing different folks to come in. Bend over backwards to include them. It's also the right thing to do.

Equitable practice starts with not assuming things are equal. People haven't come from the same baseline. The assumptions you might have about access, whether that's about going on a ski trip every year, having a laptop, or being able to travel to London, won't hold true for everybody.

Not everybody will need the extra provision, but there are

people who will. Bake that extra provision into everything you do, then everyone can partake on the same level.

The value of intentional inclusion is that there will be a richness in what you're doing, and a resilience in the change that you're making. Both your feedback loop and your continuous improvement will be richer, because there will be more checks and balances, and more people to help you evaluate your product, improve and refine it.

The Need for Equity

Since 2017, Stemettes has been part of a project, run by the University College London Institute of Education and the University of Michigan, that looks at Youth Equity in STEM Outreach. Equity is defined as 'the quality of being equal or fair or right with impartiality and even-handed dealing', and exploring equity is vital for success.[2]

The project has looked at how STEM outreach in informal settings – rather than in school – is a powerful thing when it focuses on the experiences and perspectives of young people. In other words, the focus is not on the people who 'normally' do STEM and what they see as important. Instead, the focus is on *you* and what *you* see as important. The researchers spoke to my team, and teams at other informal STEM organizations, to understand how to centre STEM outreach on young people and achieve different outcomes from traditional outreach. Other UK partners on the research have been Hanwell Zoo, We The Curious, and Knowle West Media Centre.

Following the in-depth research into what we all do and how we do it, the university researchers came up with a STEM Equity

Compass. If you're looking to centre your STEM outreach work on young people, rather than using traditional methods you can use it as a tool to ensure that you're heading in the right direction. It points the way to better working practices in STEM participation – practices that are equitable. And while it's designed for STEM outreach – and for children in particular – the tool can be applied in lots of different situations. You might consider solving problems around the access disabled women have to their money, for example. This compass will help you to ensure you're engaging properly and equitably across that group of women. It has eight points:

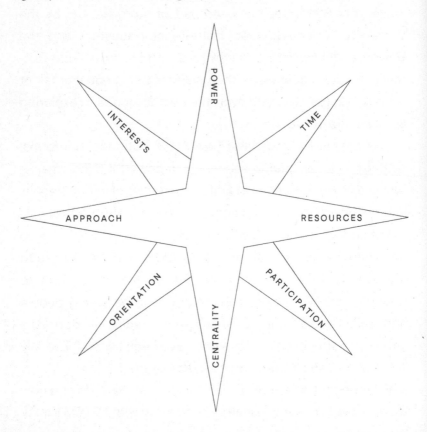

Power and *Interests* are quite self-explanatory. Will your work serve the interests of those who are already dominant? Or will it give people real power over their own lives – the power to effect change?

The answers to those questions should inform your *approach* – how you see your work contributing to the situation.

Orientation is about looking beyond how things work for an individual, and asking how things work for the people around them. In Stemettes we call them influencers; think not just about the individual, but about their context, their setting. Influencers are the parents, guardians, teachers and peers of the young people for whom Stemettes runs programmes.

Centrality is asking yourself whether you're just co-opting people as token representatives. Are you giving them a walk-on part, or making space for them to play a major role, take centre stage, write their own script?

With *Participation*, ask yourself: Is a change being made *to* the particular people or the young people or the underserved community? Is it being made *for* them? Or is it being made *with* them? How much are they involved in decision-making? How much are they producers, as well as consumers, of what you're doing? Is your practice tokenistic or exploitative? How much is the identity and the agency of your beneficiaries and value partners being supported by what you're doing?

Resources being directed at more privileged groups of individuals is one of the trends you need to be trying to change – not just in compensation for inequality, but in a way that puts those resources in the hands of less privileged groups to use in their own ways.

And *Time* reminds us that this is a long game. Short-term

results can be important to boost confidence and show what's possible, but long-term change won't happen in weeks or months.

Setting equitable practice at the centre of what you're trying to do *will* pay off. If you're going to make long-lasting change, or are striving for change that makes things better rather than maintaining the status quo, or if you want to effect change for a group of people, equitable practice means that you include them and their interests. A big part of taking CTRL and using your technical literacy to take CTRL is not purely about the technical skills themselves or about your perspectives, it's about the others you're able to work with, and technology *does* allow you to collaborate in very good ways. These principles, however, sit outside the technology. The technology is a tool, not an answer in and of itself. A tool that can be used across all parts of life – one of which is the workplace, as we'll see in the next chapter.

Getting Started

Making a difference in the lives of others has been a really good source of motivation for me. No matter what I might come up against – patriarchy, racism, exhaustion – it has become my driving force. It's made it easy for me to keep going and keep pushing, keep changing and keep pioneering. There are so many problems to solve – we're not about to run out of things that need changing. Don't ever feel like you're too small to make a difference. There's so much room, so many gaps, so many holes, that whatever you end up doing, you'll be able to make a change, with technology as one of your tools. This isn't purely about you starting something alone. You can engage with change that other people are effecting, learn from others and be part of what is already being done.

○ Match your curiosity and tech understanding with some of the other environments for change that are happening. Find some of the other individuals who are trying to make things happen, trying to explore their own equitable practice and trying to investigate what collaboration might look like. Improve, iterate or evolve what's already happening. How will you support or engage with others?

○ Seek difference and make change in your everyday. It's in the decisions that you make, it's in who you choose to support, it's in how you spend and where you spend, because how you make your purchasing decisions is another way to be a change pioneer.

○ Explore other people's values. Look at some of the people you admire the most, and find out who is working with them and collaborating with them.

○ As you try things out, measure the results, adjust your approach then try again. You're measuring up against what other people are doing. Where does what you want to do, what you care about and your research fit into this bigger picture? How does being collaborative, iterative and inclusive fit into the way that you're living?

○ Agile is open source, which means that it's available for free in its entirety. We run Agile courses for Stemettes with qualifications provider QA. You can find lots online – or check if your company has Agile courses you can join. Find podcasts, YouTube channels and Twitter accounts, and when you've had enough, stop. If you can't get enough, then why not look for Agile roles you can get stuck into – like a scrum master.

○ Have a closer look at the **STEM** Equity Compass on page 260. Although it's intended for **STEM** outreach, quite a lot of it could apply to the change you're trying to effect – especially if you've chosen a problem that affects a group with less privilege. How can you head in a more equitable direction using the eight points? Use the tool to review others working in the space or to review an organization you're already involved with.

Assuming you have your idea, and have decided on your scope and a name by this point, make it real. I normally do a few digital checks before I lock in a name for something.

First is the domain. Namecheap, GoDaddy and 1&1 are sites where you can buy a .com. Is the .com for your name already taken? How about the .org or .co.uk? Add it to your basket but don't purchase it just yet.

Check all the social media platforms – is your idea's username held by someone else? You don't want confusion from your collaborators, so be sure you have a clear space to set up shop. Once you've done that, register a free email address for the name you like, which also won't confuse people on the socials. This will be where enquiries can be received while you set up. We still have the original Stemettes Gmail account that people send emails to, even though we now have team@stemettes.org.

Use that free email address to register your domain and your social accounts. It's now real. The change is beginning – and from this point it will be much easier for collaboration to happen. Follow tutorials for setting up your website or blog – remember you have no-code and low-code options before you find a technical collaborator to take over from you.

13

THE
FUTURE
OF WORK

You can read so much about the future of love, family, food, sports, and many other subjects, all based on the tech that we're building now and the decisions we're currently making. It's the future of work that interests me the most, though – I've become obsessed with it.

The World Economic Forum predicts that by 2025, 85 million human jobs will have been taken over by machines,[1] and you might have read some reports or seen news headlines that effectively amount to 'The robots are coming and will marry our grandchildren'. It would seem that we're losing CTRL.

Between 2007 and 2018, around 60 per cent of secretarial and administrative jobs in the US disappeared, for example. Over half of all switchboard operator jobs were lost. MIT professor Daron Acemoglu thinks the kind of work that is taken up by robots tends to be lower paid and lower status, so this trend effectively widens inequality and hits the disadvantaged harder. However, that's not the entire picture. The next jobs to be taken over by machines will be the better-paid positions, such as those held by lawyers and journalists.[2]

We've had industrial revolutions before. The first replaced muscle power, primitive wind and water mills with steam to power factories and new forms of transport. The second electrified machinery, as well as bringing bright, reliable light whenever we wanted it. The third brought in electronics and automation.

Industries that used to depend on human muscle power have become increasingly reliant on these different technologies. Examples abound. Human computers – mostly women using slide rules and pencils – used to calculate advanced mathematical problems such as the trajectory of spacecraft. These women did the 'computers" job before being replaced by the electronic computers that we recognize today. In shops, self-checkouts have taken the jobs of many cashiers, and ATMs and online banking have almost completely replaced the need for bricks-and-mortar bank branches. In car manufacturing, whole factories are now staffed by robots, with just a few humans on site to program and repair the machines.

It's not the first time that we've encountered this narrative of 'the robots are coming' and been scared that they're going to take our jobs. The sci-fi genre is full of fiction-that-could-become-reality narratives that further feed the fear.

In theory, there's no reason why the whole of the London Underground couldn't run using driverless trains, in the way the Docklands Light Railway does, but the idea of such a vast and complex transport network operating without a single driver is a fearsome one for many.

I remember when I found out that it used to be someone's job in bowling alleys to stand the pins back up once they'd been knocked down. It had never occurred to me that that job had never *not* been done by a machine. It's just one of many roles that have completely disappeared – lamplighters, telegraph operators and lift attendants, for instance.

Lift attendants are a particularly interesting example, because we have to remember the days before all that was needed to speed you to your floor was a button. These attendants had to learn how to operate the lifts by manipulating a series of levers, as well as how to safely line up the lift compartment with the floor. Ice-cutters also became redundant; we now have fridges. It makes me wonder what jobs all those people went on to do.

The more we look at the headlines with their scary reports and figures for how many jobs will be lost, and the more videos we see of, say, robot dogs figuring out how to open doors for other robot dogs, the more you might end up believing that we're actually losing control at work to the robots.

Do have a look at the robot dogs if you're not already aware of them. Robot makers Boston Dynamics regularly post videos featuring their robot 'dogs' exploring uncharted terrain using robotics and AI to move and observe as they carry out their task of identifying bombs. They manage to negotiate rubble and climb across uneven surfaces, and can even correct themselves if they trip.

One particular video, which was apparently very disturbing to some viewers, shows a couple of the dogs working their way through a building. The dogs weren't being remotely operated, but one with an 'arm' used its AI and robotic dexterity to turn the handle of a door, displaying exceptional fine motor skills and strength. This same robotic dog opened the door, but before it went through, it allowed its 'mate' to pass through first. It was this very human impulse to be of service to others that was so troubling. We're not used to these images of powerful machines, much stronger than human beings, making complex decisions, navigating spaces, and behaving in human ways, *autonomously.*

Another great but troubling example is Facebook's chat-bots. Facebook created them to negotiate with humans on advertising prices but then set them on each other as part of the research project. They very quickly developed their own shorthand that their creators couldn't understand – almost like toddlers creating their own secret language.[3] If bots can talk to each other in a way we can't understand, and if robot dogs are efficient in solving physical problems fairly quickly, what's to say they wouldn't be able to take over the world, let alone your job?

The Covid-19 pandemic accelerated the growing trend of turning to robots for assistance. If human beings aren't able to come in to work, but *someone* needs to come in (because money still has to be made), that's an obvious job for robots to take over. However, the majority of folks go to work to earn money to live. Can you see the problem?

You might have seen statistics like 90 per cent of jobs will require digital skills ten years from now, but the World Economic Forum also tells us '50 per cent of jobs will be changed by automation – but only 5 per cent eliminated.'[4] The reassuring outlook is that while jobs are being taken over and performed by technology, more and more roles need humans to work with that technology.

Pretty much all jobs these days require some sort of tech knowledge, whether it's marketing agencies using technology to bid for advertising space, or legal firms using technology to scan through documents and papers to extract evidence. Job titles such as advertising executive or solicitor might not have changed, but the nature of the work – and the skills required to do it – has.

Similarly, if you're a doctor, you can now use AI to help you diagnose conditions from images and scans, as well as keeping digital patient records. If you're a plumber, and you don't use a navigation app to help you travel to your next job, you'll likely be spending more time in traffic than you need to. In any field, you may also be operating illegally or below the latest professional standards if you don't have a way of accessing and keeping up to date with changing regulations, perhaps by receiving an email newsletter.

Those jobs that aren't already largely automated soon will be. Other roles won't disappear entirely, but they'll hire fewer people to do them. Even the jobs that will still be here will demand a whole new range of skills to work with the technology as it comes in.

Klaus Schwab, founder of the World Economic Forum, has called this the Fourth Industrial Revolution – the digital revolution. 'It is characterized by a fusion of technologies that is blurring the lines between the physical, digital, and biological spheres,' he says.[5] Whatever kind of work you do, or want to do in the future, now you know that this Fourth Industrial Revolution is upon us, it's imperative that your understanding allows you to remain in CTRL. Research how it's going to affect you. Read into it, listen to what other people have to say, and try to engage.

As Klaus Schwab tells us:

We stand on the brink of a technological revolution that will fundamentally alter the way we live, work, and relate to one another. In its scale, scope and complexity, the transformation will be unlike anything humankind has experienced before. We do not yet know just how it will unfold, but one thing is clear: the response to it must be integrated and comprehensive, involving all stakeholders of the global polity, from the public and private sectors to academia and civil society.

The Fourth Industrial Revolution builds on the Third, a digital revolution that has been in motion since the middle of the twentieth century. What makes this a revolution in its own right is the speed of the current breakthroughs. There is no historical precedent for the pace at which we're moving. Schwab continues:

> When compared with previous industrial revolutions, the Fourth is evolving at an *exponential* rather than a *linear* pace. Moreover, it is disrupting almost every industry in every country. And the breadth and depth of these changes herald the transformation of entire systems of production, management, and governance.

It's well within the realms of possibility that billions of people are connected by all manner of mobile devices that have a lot of power to process information, store that information and allow unlimited access to knowledge. If you couple this with the different types of technology out there – some of which we've covered in this book, such as AI, robotics and the Internet of Things, and many others you will discover on your journey – this is the scale of the revolution we're facing. It's a revolution you are living through, and you're also able to shape it and be a part of it. It will impact your work and your life certainly. Maybe it already has.

Thanks to my work with a range of young people at Stemettes, the future-of-work concept fell onto my curiosity plate. Success for us looks like a greater number of those young people deciding to choose a STEM-related career in academia, entrepreneurship or industry. It's easier to see what we're preparing the twenty-five-year-olds for in their working life, but the world we're preparing the five-year-olds for is less of a known quantity.

In the thirteen years it'll take them to reach 'working age', a key question is: What will their aspirations be? How will those aspirations translate into gainful employment? What am I selling to them? What am I preparing them for? But also, what should their future employers be preparing to expect?

Whenever I talked about these considerations at various events and roundtables, discussions began to centre on the Fourth Industrial Revolution. I knew that technologies that had previously been purely theoretical (and which I had only played with in practicals on my computer science course at university) were now becoming reality – exactly as Schwab predicted.

Technical capability has advanced not only to make these things real, but also to a level that means it's possible for them to work at scale, and in a way that can have a huge impact on the world, including the world of work. Far from dealing with theories, we're now looking at practical considerations for the careers of my current cohort of five-year-old Stemettes.

●

Work is important. It can be one of the things that define us, but that is changing too. Having a particular job is becoming less important to our sense of identity, and these days, the average graduate can expect to change their job six times over the course of their working life. As our relationship with our work changes, what happens to our sense of identity? In a hundred years, will it still be linked to the job we do, or will it be about something completely different?

Also, if the robots take all the positions, what will we do with our time? How will we make money to live? The idea of the four-day workweek is already being posited as one solution to this problem. Think about what it would be like to have robots that can do enough of your job that you don't need to turn up for work every day of the week! It sounds great, if you're still getting paid the same amount, but if not, could you live on 80 per cent of your earnings? Along with the opportunity come, well, problems.

Most industries have a hierarchy that you move up as you learn more about the job and gain more experience. Generally, you start by doing the grunt work and, once you've paid your dues, learning by doing the unskilled work, you progress to do the more skilled part of the job. If there's a robot doing the grunt work and paying your dues for you, how do you decide who gets promoted, and who doesn't? How do you learn what's in all those legal papers that need sorting, if a robot is reading them for you?

Routine tasks will be done by robots not only because their labour is cheaper and they don't complain about not getting a lunch break, but also because they perform certain work better than we do. They don't get distracted or bored. They can handle huge quantitles of data. Will that mean that we get to focus on higher-level things instead? One optimistic vision is that instead of picking up bowling pins, those individuals who lost their jobs as a result of automation are now doing cognitively higher-level or creative work. Perhaps the Fifth Industrial Revolution will be upon us when robots get creative and take over those jobs as well.

That day might come sooner than we think. For the 2017 National Day celebrations in Luxembourg, a full orchestra and choir performed a piece of music. It was impressive stuff, all the more so because the entire piece was composed by an algorithm set to analyse music from the past and create something new that humans would enjoy.[6] For this special occasion, AIVA – the Artificial Intelligence Virtual Assistant – was given the brief of 'celebratory and rousing', and it totally filled it.

Of all the jobs we might expect AI to take from a human, composer wouldn't be my first thought. However, AIVA was able to put together a piece of music in a way that doesn't sound like a computer composed it. So maybe we are losing control. Maybe the robots are taking over.

Robots Aren't in Control of Themselves

If we are losing CTRL, the truth is that it isn't because of the robots or the tech, it's because of choices. Who gains or loses control is determined by the choices that are being made about how technology is being used, how it's going to be applied, and the problems it's going to be solving. The changes we're seeing in the world of work aren't inevitable, and they don't have to happen in the ways that they're happening right now. Just as you make a series of choices as a change pioneer, defining your scope and your focus, there are choices to be made about the scope of technology at work.

The transformation of work through technology isn't something that you have to fear, but it is something to examine carefully. Look at what choices have been made. How are you able to influence them? How are you able to make sure they're good ones, and that the right technology is chosen to do the right things?

In September 2016, Tom Watson, the former deputy leader of the Labour Party, convened the Future of Work Commission, which looked to ensure that the march of technological change did not adversely affect workers. He noted that we could proactively consider how tech might change the world of work for the better, and a Good Work Charter evolved.[7] I, along with the other Future of Work commissioners chosen by Tom, identified an opportunity to interrogate the checks and balances, and the issues we need to consider to ensure that people continue to have good work. Having a slightly better understanding of the expectations of five-, six-, seven- and eight-year-old girls than many of the folks involved in discussions about the future of work gave me an edge and a perspective that was desperately needed.

In my position as a trustee of what is now the Institute for the Future of Work (IFOW), I really enjoy taking a dive deep into these issues and having linkups and robust conversations with legal professionals, educators and economists. Our exchanges translate into policy and legal suggestions, which get fed into national and governmental policy. They also feed into wider public knowledge of the implications of technology on the future workplace.

Consider tech's current role – we've already seen how email has changed the way that work is done. We no longer have to type up memos and wait for them to be delivered around the building, or try to catch someone on the phone. We can now send text to lots of people in an instant. We use email to communicate decisions, share minutes and have all manner of discussions, but when we leave our companies, the whole thread of the decision-making process becomes lost in our abandoned inboxes. Unless another colleague at the company was present at those meetings and a part of those threads, your successor won't be privy to that decision-making information.

Being able to apply social networks within the workplace has also changed the way we might communicate and share ideas. Let's say you micro-blog the ideas from a meeting you've just been in, where decisions were made, or tag the people you made the decision with – a record of process will last beyond your presence in the company.

I once had a job that involved working with individuals across various different departments within the company, and we were encouraged to use not only email but also an internal 'social web'. On one occasion, someone at work blogged on it about the eighty-page slide presentations that were being printed out for every person attending a meeting. Why, she asked, did we need these unwieldly printouts, which were also being displayed on people's devices as well as on the screen at the front of the room, when most of the meeting attendees would only throw them away afterwards? As a result of her interrogation of this practice, this mass printing effort was halted immediately. Workers were quite happy to print off a sheet or two if they needed a physical copy, and make notes on their devices. Going forward, I wonder what other small suggestions might shape our future workplaces.

People are using technology in the workplace to carry out many tasks that were denied to them in the past, and now, as well as helping with the actual work we do, technology is also being used to manage the workforce, as in the case of employee polling events or company-wide surveys. When we talk about bringing technology into the workplace, these examples help to show where efficiency has been improved, and a layer of transparency has been added for managers to judge the thinking of the workforce and improve accountability when it comes to decision-making. The nature of work itself has changed, but it's not just technology that has had a hand in that – the way it's applied has also had an effect. Something that is set to continue.

It's worth reflecting upon some of the other technology trends you've seen and which we've discussed in other chapters; if you had the ability to use 3D printing in your workplace, how might it change the way that you work? If you have the kind of job where you regularly lose pieces of machinery in your office, might you be able to 3D print them, rather than wait for replacement parts to be delivered? If you're working for the National Grid, could virtual-reality training replace real-life power cuts so that you can practise your diagnostic skills?

It's also worth examining what the implications of these technologies might be for the workplace of the future if we project forward ten or fifteen years. If we can wear our tech, then maybe we won't need ID cards? We'll be able to access our offices without the need to swipe, and our whereabouts inside the building will also be tracked, in case we're needed.

Maybe your workspace will be better designed, based on the clusters of people working around you, and the way you use your space will be modified.

One way to try to imagine how this evolving tech might affect your workplace is to consider that most algorithms used to help make decisions at work tend to do one of six things to resources:

- Restrict
- Recommend
- Record
- Rate
- Replace
- Reward

According to the IFOW equality task force paper 'Mind the Gap', these principles represent the kinds of decisions we use technology to help us make. We might restrict worker access to certain areas of decision-making, we might recommend who to hire, or rate those who already work for us. We might use technology to replace workers where we believe the technology might do a better job, and finally, we use technology to choose who to reward.[8]

A good example of the principle of 'recording' concerns lift maintenance. In the past, lift maintenance happened on a regular basis, whether that was every six months, or every three years. Nowadays, the 'usage' of the lift is tracked, so, based on the data collected and what the algorithm is able to process, the decision on when the lift needs servicing can be very specific.

For the principle of 'replacement' we might look to Singapore, where AI is used to track driverless trains. If anything on the train ever comes loose or breaks, the train knows to park itself back at the depot at the end of its journey, order a replacement part and wait for it to arrive. This technology has done away with the need for human participation in a decision-making process that would have been entirely manual in the past.

At the beginning of 2020, the Institute for the Future of Work published a paper containing three case studies that show us why it's really important to consider the impacts of technology at work.[9] They also demand that we consider the fact that robots aren't in control of themselves. Someone has to code them. The paper was designed to enhance public understanding of machine learning at work, and to specifically advance policy response by identifying key issues. The case studies included job advertising, hiring, and what we call talent management or workforce management.

The first case study about job advertising featured a company with a job vacancy it wanted to fill through advertising. The job might have been based in Birmingham, for example, so the company wanted people who were old enough to work to see the advert, and for the person they appointed to live within a commutable distance. The company defined their own criteria, none of which were illegal, such as showing the job only to a specific race, or only to women.

They used a social network to advertise the position and the network selected its own criteria for success, which is where the hiring company ran into trouble. At the end of the day, an advert is an advert, and the social media company wanted to show it to people who were more likely to make the hiring company pay out on that advert. The social network was concerned with who and how many viewers clicked on or liked the job, which was a big part of the measure of success for them, but not for the hiring company. So, the advert was shown only to the people the algorithm decided were most likely to click on it (based on the audience's personal interests, which they had already shared on social media).

The algorithm isn't interested in who an individual is, or their protected characteristics. It cares only about whether they are more or less likely to click on an ad. So, actually, when you put up an ad, even though you don't intend to discriminate, it sometimes happens without you even realizing it, because the network's idea of success and yours don't fully align.

Because women tend to click on ads for lower-paid positions, the result of this particular case study was that the advert got shown to women who were lower-paid. That wasn't the fault, or the intention, of the recruiting company, but it meant that the way the ads were sent out was gendered. The application success and job satisfaction were also gendered.

The second case study related to an algorithm called Thor, which was also used in the hiring process. Say a telecoms company wanted to use an algorithm to help them with their hiring decisions, so they started with their existing employees. They looked at the customer ratings of those employees, with their permission, and they looked at their social media profiles. They then used that data to train the algorithm on what success looked like at that company.

This was a challenge because not all employees' social media profiles contain the same amount of information. Consequently, the information used to train algorithms is patchy, and more so for certain demographics because in the early days of

Facebook, those individuals who had had social media profiles the longest were those who had been to the universities that were introduced to the Facebook network early on. If you were to use those profiles as your dataset, it would mean that the amount of information you had on the people who attended those universities would be greater than what you had on those who didn't.

The algorithm determined that a very specific demographic ended up as the definition of success. When that algorithm was applied to the hiring process, people who hadn't attended those particular institutions were deemed not to fit the profile of someone who would be successful at the company.

Essentially, the company didn't hire anyone who wasn't a white man. There were no Black women for the algorithm to pattern match against. The algorithm therefore was deciding that a Black woman who didn't have the 'right' education or who had a less populated social media profile didn't meet the criteria for success according to the data it was given.

The third case study looked at talent management – in particular, a retail company that was combining lots of different datasets on people in their workplace, and who they were chatting to on and off the shop floor. Using facial-recognition software, they also had data on where employees were in the store at any given time, and used it to analyse their moods and predict their behaviour.

The company fed all this different data into an algorithm that helped them manage their workforce. In practice this equated to setting shifts, employees' pay and, ultimately, determining their prospects of promotion.

When so many different datasets are being pumped in, it's

almost impossible to tell what data is being regarded as important by the algorithm. It's hard to know what ends up being useful in making predictions about employees and what is being drawn on most heavily to make decisions. Neither employer nor employee knows what has had the greatest contribution to that decision, even though it affects both of them.

It's not that we don't have any control over algorithms, rather most algorithms work with a much greater amount of data than can be processed by a human being. There are too many different factors and too many different types of information for a human to hold in their head at one time! A complex mathematical calculation is at work, and simply removing datasets in order to try to understand what the algorithm has done will essentially reduce the algorithm's efficacy (even though it makes it easier for a human to wrap their head around what's going on). The way the field works at the moment means that if we want to take more control of how an algorithm comes to its decisions, we would have to completely reimagine how we build algorithms in the first place.

Over time, this particular algorithm also 'learned' how to predict which employees were likely to leave unless they were given a pay rise or promotion. Using information from these individuals' workplace accounts and job tenure, the algorithm would suggest the minimum pay rise to try to retain folks it had identified might want to leave. You can imagine why it's not fair to award pay and promotions in this way (especially against the background of persistent gender and ethnicity pay gaps). The importance of a job and the importance of an income varies between different people, so any negotiations around pay, for example, might be constrained by how much you rely on your job. You might not be able to afford to quit and bide your time until a better-paid alternative comes along.

Another unexplained effect of the algorithm was shift allocations. All in, folks from Black and Asian and ethnic minority backgrounds were given more frequent shift changes and were also less likely to be promoted. Nobody could point to why, because the program had just taken all the data and spat out its results. As we've already discussed, there is much to be said about how inaccurate facial recognition is for those with darker skin. So many considerations that had a material effect on the lives of workers weren't taken into account when rolling out the algorithm.

Going forward, something called 'exception handling' is going to be a much more common role in the workplace. When a computer is making decisions or processing data, most of the work falls within what it might deem a 'normal' range, whereas there are lots of examples in real life which operate outside of 'normal' – you can't cover every eventuality with a line of code. There are many instances when an 'exception' is raised, which is when the computer cannot handle a real-life situation – a problem that is too far removed from what it has been told to expect. A human being is then called upon to override, or decide what should happen. You can imagine how there are going to be plentiful roles in the field of exception handling.

Say you're at the supermarket self-checkouts and you're scanning some items. After each scan, you place the item in the bagging area. Tragedy strikes – the checkout isn't convinced you put the last item in the right place. A supermarket employee comes over, checks your screen, checks your scanned items and then handles the exception the self-checkout has taken to

the last scanned item. Swipe, tap, exception handled – you continue to pay for your shopping and leave the supermarket.

Those software crashes that we currently see in the small,
like at the supermarket, are going to be magnified when it
comes to the wider social issues – from credit decisions and
hiring decisions, to decisions on health or education provision. Things will fail in a quite spectacular fashion. However
well robots might do our jobs, it's not always good to hand
things over to them completely without being ready to override them.

A prime example, with mercifully rare but tragic consequences,
is autopilot technology. Commercial aircraft fly by autopilot most
of the time. Automated systems can even land a plane safely at
an airport. However, when autopilots fail, it's important that
human pilots are able to take the controls. One used his experience as a fighter pilot to save a plane full of passengers when the
autopilot malfunctioned over the Indian Ocean.[10]

In another example, in 2019, two Boeing 737 MAX aircraft
crashed, killing everyone on board, when the automatic systems wrongly interpreted sensor data showing the airspeed
was too low to keep the plane flying.[11] On both occasions, the
autopilot pointed the nose of the plane towards the ground,
which is what a pilot would normally do to gain airspeed. On
both occasions, the ground was too close.

In 2009, Air France flight AF447 from Rio de Janeiro to Paris
plunged into the sea, killing everyone on board, when the autopilot cut out and the human crew didn't know how to fly safely
without it. Air France and Airbus may stand trial for manslaugh-
ter of the 228 people on board. In the wake of the crash
investigation, experts warned that more and more pilots were

flying without the necessary experience to know what to do when they couldn't rely on automated systems.[12]

Going forward, we will need to ensure we set the right frameworks and standards concerning our use of algorithms, to uphold the very basic requirement of being able to keep people safe around the technology we are creating and implementing, expanding upon Asimov's Three Laws of Robotics.[13] Sometimes, it's a matter of life and death.

I, for one, would like women to take CTRL by being at the decision-making table and being a part of that important process. Given we have not had a seat in the past, I'm excited to see how you might help fill in the gaps and paint a proper picture of the considerations we need to make, the frameworks we have to instate, and everything else we need to bake into these algorithms.

Work Responsibly

Given that the robots aren't in control, that it isn't inevitable that they ever will be, and that there are so many consequences of automation for human life, we each need to take our share of responsibility for the future of work.

At the IFOW, we're looking at the impact on the individual of not applying this hiring technology properly. We're also looking at the impact on the company because, of course, what happens at company level has an impact on wider society. It's a cycle – individuals affected by poor technology decisions affect the success and outputs of a company; poor technology decisions by a company affect the wider society that company is serving; and poor technology decisions across society affect the individuals.

We all have a sphere of influence, and we shouldn't, especially as women, underestimate how much influence we have. So, what does it mean to be responsible at work? How are we able to take CTRL?

Sticking with my work at the IFOW, we also continue to discuss issues that are going to be relevant in the coming years. The first, of course, is the need for diversity amongst the people building and making decisions about technology. The second is the need to audit your use of technology, especially the algorithms and AI that are helping you make decisions.

Currently, impact assessments are one of the best tools to consider the limitations of the technology *being used* to make decisions. The best impact assessments identify ways to figure out how to tweak the method in which technology *is being used* to minimize negative impact. This should be done regularly, so that you can continue to be aware of the impact of the use of that technology. Ask the following questions of your tech: How does it work? Why does it work? How does it make decisions? What is being fed in and what's the quality of what's being fed in? What's the bias baked into what's being fed in? Who has created it? What are the assumptions it's been built on?

The questions about bias and assumptions in the data are especially important, because so much of what we do with tech ends up being global. Discrimination law looks very different in the US to the UK, and very different again in Nigeria. For example, the UK's Equalities Act features nine protected characteristics – age, disability, race, religion or belief, gender reassignment, sex, sexual orientation, marriage and civil partnership, pregnancy and maternity. Every country's laws will share some of these characteristics, and will exclude others. If different countries have different protected characteristics, then what is lawful in one country might not be in another. What is fair in one place may not be fair in another.

Ask yourself who has built the tech. What assumptions have they coded into what they're doing? Who is part of their team? And where else is the tech being used? How it is being used elsewhere might give you some clues about how it could end up working in your own organization. You can't just accept what the sales team tells you.

What follows is an example of where a failure to audit tech ended in catastrophe. Microsoft wanted to demonstrate the prowess of its AI research team, so it built a Twitter bot, Tay, to interact with people on Twitter, respond to users' queries, and learn from those interactions to become progressively smarter. It took just sixteen hours for Tay to become the most awful racist bot. Other Twitter users worked out that Tay would pick up on whatever they tweeted, because the bot was only repeating the incendiary remarks of users who interacted with it.[14]

Tay was, very simply, an algorithm, unaware of racism, sexism, politics or the difference between right and wrong. Clearly, Microsoft should have worked a lot harder before launching it, and asked themselves a few key questions, such as: Why are we making Tay? How will Tay distinguish between right and wrong? Microsoft knows how Twitter works, and about the bad behaviour and the trolling that occurs far and wide across the platform. Did they not think about how Tay would handle these behaviours? They should have considered exception handling.

Why weren't checks and balances established early on in Tay's creation? The way that things went very wrong is precisely why tech audits are vital when it comes to ensuring you don't build something that is so very offensive.

Once you've done your initial audit, and raised any issues about the tech that you think need to be resolved, or at least flagged, you can't relax and think the case is closed. Be aware that whatever use you might be bringing the tech in for won't necessarily be what you end up using it for in a year's time, or two years', or ten years'. Keep thinking critically: How is this going to be useful for us? What are the different use cases that might emerge at a later date? Also remember that as technology is constantly being updated, an audit on version 1 of what you're considering could produce different results to the audit of version 2. While you're doing your development, share your process. Work out loud. When you iterate on this auditing, you learn from each successive audit.

The next thing is to track things, not people. Resist allowing technology to make unchecked decisions on human beings, who are too complex and too complicated. Even though there are existing legal and ethical frameworks to protect human beings, none of them are foolproof enough for the ways in which technology is implemented.

Remember the case studies we looked at, relating to the algorithms used for hiring people, or for monitoring their work? If you're going to track people, or if you don't have the influence to stop your company from tracking people, you can still draw a line at technology making decisions about people. Yes, the whole point of artificial intelligence is for it to be able to make decisions like a human being, but we're not there yet. In a strange way, I think we might get there, but we are probably a millennium away. Let AI make decisions on food or energy or whatever. Let it take the data and interpret the results, but don't let it make decisions about people.

Allowing that to happen would be giving too much power to any algorithm, especially when we think about the power structures that are already in play, and the lack of accountability you would normally have. You can't possibly know every impact a decision might have, and the damage it might do, by which time, it's far too late.

It's not all about dangers and warnings, though. Every new use of tech is an opportunity. Bringing new tech into the workplace is your chance to decide what best practice could look like, and what the most exciting and effective options are for how you're going to use the tech. Is there an old problem that can now be solved? Is there an opportunity to build something new around the weaknesses of some other tech that you're considering?

One more challenge that we talk about at the IFOW is how we should try to be doing better with tech in the workplace, not just maintaining the status quo. Having a voice means you can make sure that technology brings an improvement, not just a replacement, and definitely not something that will make things worse. If it's not making things better, we shouldn't be using it. Asking 'Is there an improvement?' is a backstop. What does improvement look like? How are we defining 'better'? The more different people are involved in defining 'better', the more people will find that it does, in practice, make things better for them.

Here's a brief example. Textio is an AI tool that will read through the job description you're intending on posting, and see if it contains any gendered language that might be influencing people reading it. Typically, when you write a job description, you'll likely use particular adjectives and nouns, such as 'ambitious' or 'team'. You might not have intended them to be gendered, but statistically speaking, they could change the number of applications you get and the type of people you get them from. Words like 'team' tend to encourage more women to apply. 'Support' is female-coded, 'leader' is male-coded.[15]

Textio can make sure your job description appeals to a wider range of applicants, in a less biased way. It also looks out for age and ability bias, and improves your job advert in a way that is similar to how the spellcheck function makes your writing better. Also, the decision it makes is on the job description, not on the individual. It might have implications for the prospective applicants reading the ad, depending on how you decide to use the tool, but it's not making decisions about people directly. That's really important.

The Rest Is Still Unwritten

Maybe you're still thinking that new technology is an issue for people who write computer code and program algorithms, but this is an issue for you, too. Think of it like this: You don't have to be an immigration lawyer to have an opinion on immigration. In fact, very few people have access to the amount of detail that an immigration lawyer needs in order to make informed decisions on immigration, but we all get to vote on the matter, so it's something that we should all at least be thinking about. We should be trying to ask some questions about the impact different immigration policies might have on different groups of individuals, and we should want to make sure that new policies make things better, not worse. In much the same way, when new technology comes in, or when tech is used in new ways, it affects a lot of people, not just those who write the computer code.

As well as being a trustee for the IFOW, I'm also part of the Global Partnership on AI, a group of G7-and-beyond countries that are trying to make some global decisions and groundwork on what good AI looks like. We don't have all the answers. Rather, there is a raging ongoing debate being had. As we consider how technology will affect ourselves and others, things become heated and it gets tough. But we are doing it together.

One debate surrounds universal basic income and whether, if robots are taking jobs, we should tax the companies operating the robots. Should we just accept that not everyone will have a job all the time? If so, it would make sense to pay everyone a minimum income that they can live on, regardless of the work they're doing. Obviously that would cost a lot of money. Employers who replace humans with robots could be asked to pay a robot tax. However, that might encourage companies to keep people in unproductive jobs, instead of developing new technology and new jobs we've not considered before now. If millions of people are no longer able to work, is this liberating them or doing them a disservice?

Another Global Partnership on AI discussion we had was about whether an algorithm can actually pick out good hires or match jobs to people better than a human being. Yes, it might be able to process more data about a person or a job, but how does it know what 'good', 'great' or 'better' means? Is it whether someone has been to university? Is it their previous work experience?

Is it the language they use to answer questions at an interview? Is it the qualities or character traits they say they have? Or is it about the qualities they communicate on their CV?

If, as humans, we haven't got to the bottom of that 'something' that makes someone the right candidate for the job, then how can we train an algorithm to do it? Is the fairest way to randomize job allocations? Is a random selection the only way to know we haven't discriminated at all?

Delve into conversations such as these – whatever field you are in. A basic tech literacy will mean that you will become better at asking the right questions, and your knowledge of the detail will grow as a result.

It's key to remember how much of the future hasn't been decided yet, so now is a really great time to get involved. The workplace is a good place to begin to understand the implications of the Fourth Industrial Revolution and start to figure out how you will take control going forward. If you're an employer, you should already be skilling-up your workforce, but as an individual, see if there are opportunities for you across your workplace. You'll be able to study these issues up close and learn lessons that you can apply to what's going on outside work. Find the rooms where these discussions are happening in your workplace – perhaps that means joining roundtables with your union or sitting on employee representative boards.

Seeing Work from the Outside In

One of my fellow IFOW trustees is Graeme Nuttall OBE, who has done lots of work on employee ownership of companies, which the Institute believes is a big part of where things might be heading. The logic is that if employees own the company and have some CTRL over technology doing more of the work, then how might the use of technology differ? What would employees do with that sort of agency?

At the IFOW we often talk to unions, which were incredibly powerful back when mining was such a huge part of the UK's economy, and still have clout in certain industries. I do wonder how we might now apply some of the positive aspects of those times and those industries to our current industrial revolution. Mining supported entire communities, and a strong sense of identity and belonging came from the economic support and opportunities offered by being a miner or living near a mine. This collective power translated into political power, which, for a time, ran alongside the more traditional forms of power that we recognize today.

There was a time when rising through the ranks of a union was a very recognizable alternative route to becoming a politician. It's now very rare to see someone in the House of Commons who has ever had a manual job. Can technology allow us to gather, disseminate ideas and take back a form of CTRL for workers that has slipped from our grasp?

It's worth having your voice heard in spaces outside of your workplace, too. What cross-industry technology discussions are lacking your perspective?

Back in 2015, I spent a day with one of Stemettes' partners who had taken the time to do an in-depth review of why they didn't have many women in their technology department. One of the biggest complaints from hiring managers was the lack of women candidates put forward by the company's preferred recruitment suppliers on what were rather rigid and restricted lists. For any new role being advertised, the recruitment companies were allowed to propose only three candidates each – and those candidates were seldom women.

About a week later, a lady called Sinead Bunting, who worked at one of the biggest recruitment companies in the UK, reached out to Stemettes. She had recently learned about the lack of women in tech and was incensed. Straight away, I saw my opportunity to solve two problems at once. I laid out to her the frustrations of the hiring managers at the Stemettes partner company and suggested that recruitment companies like hers should do better in situations with limited candidate suggestions. A light bulb went on, and a month or two later, she had taken my suggestion and run with it. The Tech Talent Charter was born.

Sinead gathered more recruiters and got to work drawing up the charter of new habits for companies to develop. It included using structured interviews for recruitment and promotions, working for culture *add* and not culture *fit* (recruiting people who are going to add to the culture rather than just fit into it), and reviewing the inadvertently gendered language people were using in their job descriptions. Considering neurodiverse candidates and not marking people down for lack of eye contact in interviews was included, as was establishing diverse panels for recruitment, advertising job listings on non-traditional channels, and training and hiring managers and recruiters to play their part in solving at least some of the women-in-tech problems.

By 2020 the Tech Talent Charter had more than 300 signatories across the public, private and third (voluntary) sectors, who had pledged to follow a now-extensive playbook for better practice in diversity and inclusion across technology. These signatories have pledged to submit data on an annual basis and be held accountable for following good practice.

Debbie Forster MBE, the current CEO of the Tech Talent Charter, was part of the initial discussions on what form the charter should take. She grew up in the US and, in one meeting, she referenced something called the Rooney Rule, which was introduced in 2003 and named after Dan Rooney, who used to work at the NFL.

The NFL was benefiting from diverse teams of players across the league. Many of the NFL team coaches were ex-players themselves, and so the NFL coaches also made up a diverse group of people. This all changed, however, with head coaches. Many of them were ex-coaches, but most of them were white. Dan Rooney decided to enforce a rule – recruitment rounds for new head coaches weren't complete until at least one coach of colour had been interviewed. Fairly quickly, the diversity of head coaches improved.

We added the Rooney Rule to our charter, and the UK Football Association has now also taken it on. This cross-pollination of ideas between the NFL and the Tech Talent Charter, then on to technology companies and the Football Association, is exciting. Build those good habits of being a cross-pollinator and watch the magic happen.

When it comes to making the world of work better for everyone, including policies relating to child or parental care, leave and flexible working, there is still so much to be done. Talking about tech is an opportunity to be part of shaping those norms and policies. Consider statutory paternity leave in the UK. We've had it since 2003, but it's not necessarily taken up by those entitled to it. Why not? Could we use tech in a way that helps parents share childcare more equally? Could we use technology to influence the financial implications of taking on caring responsibilities?

The answers to these questions might be found by polling and surveying why people aren't taking up options you have in your policies. It might involve analysing data around folks who have come back after taking leave, to try to understand some of their needs, which might be missing in your implementation of the policy. It might be using technology to help support people with their leave and their care responsibilities. It might be using technology to help people find support for their leave responsibilities, or to train folks how to prepare for the financial implications of being away from work.

You don't have to be on the board of an organization to have your voice heard; everyone can be a change-maker, everyone can be a pioneer. Your workplace is one of the places you can learn your trade as a change pioneer. Some employers embrace the concept of the Intrapreneur – someone working inside a company to develop an innovative idea or project that will enhance the company.

The most important thing to remember about the future is that it should not be taken as given. Nothing is a foregone conclusion. Lots of people are still trying to work it out. And it could be that you and your perspectives, and what you've learned and what you know, end up being part of the solution.

Getting Started

Taking CTRL at your workplace and shaping the future of work is easier with a core set of principles to refer to. The Good Work Charter from the IFOW is a fantastic tool. Have a careful look at the ten principles that describe what 'good' looks like at work:

1.   Access – Everyone should have access to good work.
2.   Fair Pay – Everyone should be fairly paid.
3.   Fair Conditions – Everyone should work in fair conditions set out on fair terms.
4.   Equality – Everyone should be treated equally and without discrimination.
5.   Dignity – Work should promote dignity.
6.   Autonomy – Work should promote autonomy.
7.   Wellbeing – Work should promote physical and mental wellbeing.
8.   Support – Everyone should have access to institutions and people who can represent their interests.
9.   Participation – Everyone should be able to take part in determining and improving working conditions.
10. Learning – Everyone should have access to lifelong learning and career guidance.

When you're doing your tech audit, or considering how tech might change your working life (or the lives of people who work with you, or those who might come after you), think about these ten headings. It might be exciting to bring in some new tech that will transform how you do things, but remember, it's always about people and choices, and the impact those choices will have on human beings.

Can you evaluate some of the uses of technology in your workplace against each of the ten areas? How many of those uses directly contradict what defines good work? Having practised tough conversations in Chapter 9, can you add these principles to some of your discussions? How might the employee council or technology audit teams at your place of work use your tough questions to do better? What changes do you need to see? What data are they collecting about you and your colleagues? Do you know how the data is being used? How can the ideas and exercises at the end of Chapter 11 be used for this?

- Be a better ally. Beyond having tough conversations, you can also be an ally. It's more uplifting and just as important. Follow @betterallies on your preferred social media platform, or subscribe to their newsletter. Set yourself a challenge to build a new habit every thirty days. How can you show up for folks with less privilege than you at work?

- Experiment with your influence. What's your sphere of technical influence? When I first spoke to Sinead Bunting, I hadn't intended for the Tech Talent Charter to come into existence. However, I was in the right place at the right time to be able to join the dots. What places do you have access to? Which focus groups and roundtables are you being invited to? Which ones are happening at work and align with the external communities you've tapped into as part of Chapter 10? If these groups don't exist at work then maybe you should gather some friends and set one up? Or you could pose a question on your digital collaboration platform. Attend internal events at your company and ask questions. Start small – see what happens next.

Conclusion

Being in CTRL

Each of the stories I've shared about technical women throughout herstory excites me and shows the rich heritage you'll have as a woman in CTRL. They demonstrate what has already been possible and offer lessons to be learned. For me, they form a huge part of my resilience.

Being in CTRL will make a big difference to your life. As a student, Savinay, who we met in Chapter 4, shared her thoughts with me: 'Being in CTRL means having greater access to and understanding of the world. All of these computer programs are written by people. The biases we see in tech become problems that amplify themselves. If you care about improving that in your field, you have to have the technical agency to do it.'

My digital literacy and technical agency allow me to approach my work, and life in general, with confidence. It's almost like a 'superpower' that means I can add something to the conversation or compensate for any shortcomings.

I find myself in many rooms I had no intention of entering and talking to people I had no idea I would ever meet. At the end of my first year running Stemettes I was surprised to find myself at 10 Downing Street discussing tech, and I never imagined for one second that Lewis Hamilton would ask me to join The Hamilton Commission, whose remit is to aid Black people in getting into motorsport. I didn't know I would be invited to talk to tech companies about cultural change, equity, diversity and inclusion, but also the future of work.

Others in my situation might decline invitations such as these, asserting they know nothing or very little about the area into which they have been invited, but my love and use of tech, and my desire to engage others in technology puts me into these spaces time and again, with powerful results. I've been given opportunities to share that love, inspire others with it, and encourage others to join me on the journey and learn the skills. Rather than focusing on what I don't know, my learnings and knowledge from across the field allow me to apply what I do know to new situations. They allow me to have something technical to contribute and to approach problem-solving in a way that's useful in these new situations. From representing information in easy-to-interpret formats, to applying a way to support folks into STEM – or even motorsport. From understanding how to break down a large problem into smaller, easier-to-solve issues iteratively, to using the way technologists learn from experiments to encourage others to experiment with their careers, decisions and influence.

There are times when my technical knowledge means I can use a tool quickly to prove someone's point, or further interrogate or explain a complex idea. There are parallels with my technical knowledge to be drawn everywhere. My CTRL is evolving continuously as I learn more about technology and its uses. On occasion, my ability to troubleshoot has saved the day, too. Never underestimate the value of switching a device off and on again to solve a technical problem!

For Jenny Griffiths, CEO and founder of Snap Vision, being in CTRL is making sure she's always learning, staying curious and keeping pace with new things going on in technology. She doesn't want to be stuck in the past on her thinking about, for example, AI, and wants it to be changing at the same rate that the subject of AI is changing.

In her words: 'Staying in CTRL is making sure I'm learning, keeping my love of technology going, and trying to make sure I'm passing on that love and that enthusiasm to younger generations and people who aren't as engaged in technology.'

Having the agency that CTRL affords you means that there's a confidence and ease in situations which you really want others to experience.

Curator Ghislaine Boddington has a similar take. For her, being in CTRL makes her feel confident, and that she has a job to help other people feel confident about it too, by demystifying it. She doesn't want people to feel stupid if they don't have CTRL, nor does she think people should be left out. That being said, being in CTRL doesn't mean you'll *never* feel left out. It will, however, mean that you can shape who isn't left out in the future.

For Deborah Okenla, founder and CEO of YSYS, being in CTRL has meant that she can take control and use technology to advocate for herself and her community. There are platforms that already exist, and the power is in how you use those platforms. Her advice is to use them to make new friends, drive campaigns, grow community and spread impact, without having to reinvent the wheel. She reasons, 'In our small way, we've contributed to the success of these platforms, so why not use them to carry our voices?'

Being in CTRL means you can use your voice. Or, as Abadesi Osunsade, founder of Hustle Crew, told me, 'Being in CTRL is having my authority respected. I'm not always going to be the most important person in the room, but when I am the most important person on the subject being asked of me, I want to be listened to and heard. I want to be seen, I want to be believed. Being in CTRL allows that to be a reality for me.'

When you're taken seriously in a way you might not have been before, you'll also be able to ensure women – and other people – aren't taken advantage of. As Ghislaine explained to me, women not yet in CTRL 'shouldn't be left out of the next ten years of decisions about our identities and how we are represented in digital form – whether we own ourselves and whether we have any say over our virtual physical form'.

Ghislaine is an expert in virtual, hybrid and mixed realities, which is exactly where we are headed, post-pandemic. In the past, our physical selves went to work, and when we didn't go in, we weren't there. We still had access to email and messaging apps such as Slack, and these were a fair digital representation of workers. However, as we move towards a hybrid way of working, we will be increasingly represented not just physically but also digitally. Ghislaine has worked with avatars and digital-world representations of who we are, but avatars for work are different, and Ghislaine believes we should have some say over our digital representation – over the data that is collected around our virtual being, what it looks like and who owns it. It's going to be a new part of the way we turn up for work, so we must have agency over it. This agency mirrors the control that women *didn't* have in the erasure of our history – or our herstory – and the rich heritage of what we have done before.

We need to be careful not to become owned exclusively by big corporations.

Being in CTRL means you can be closer to ownership, and in the driving seat. Abadesi also told me: 'My digital literacy allows me to turn ideas into reality. Being able to access the internet on my laptop and build a no-code website in a weekend – five years on, we're a six-figure-revenue company, with a team of more than ten people. Being in CTRL is the ability to manifest in real time. I make it, it's real.'

Anisah Osman Britton, founder of 23 Code Street, concurred: 'I don't need to rely on anyone else to realize my visions. It's been a key part of changing career. It's also about being about to relinquish control to other women, to let them take charge of what they see as the future. My guiding force has been – can I give other women the power to take CTRL?'

Finally, being in CTRL has enriched my relationship with myself. Knowing that I can close down social media, or subscribe only to things that make me laugh or help me learn, has allowed me to protect my personal space and evolve my self-care.

Abadesi sums it up best: 'Me being willing to say no to the wrong opportunities, or say no to protect my time. Being in CTRL allows me to create boundaries that protect my productivity and my health, and actually maintain those boundaries, too. I do not feel guilty about them and I do not feel bad about them and I do not let people push back on them or convince me that [they] aren't important.'

These are the benefits of being in CTRL – crashing down as many barriers as have been put up as enemies of progress. Ultimately, our digital literacy is about changing the world with technology as a tool – one woman at a time.

What Dame Stephanie Shirley achieved in the sixties, founding her all-woman software company at a time when she couldn't open a bank account without the consent of her husband or father, provides a backdrop for women in the 2020s. The story of you taking CTRL will be wonderful for future generations to look back on. We're so fortunate to be able to now control our own narratives and have the privilege of leaving these stories behind. We don't need to rely on those in power to look favourably on our stories. We don't need to worry about erasure, as happened with Marie-Sophie Germain. It simply won't happen if we take CTRL and document the journey as we go.

Passing these stories forward will be part of how we secure our personal legacy. It'll be our gift to the generations to come and will help to ensure that a better future – one which the next set of women deserve and where problems have been ironed out – is built. We'll be able to solve better problems, and not just the ones we created. Better problems include the UN SDGs (United Nations Sustainable Development Goals), such as people having access to clean water, which is a far better problem to solve than who can get to space first.

As we look to the future, I'm also reminded of the scene in *Hidden Figures* when Dorothy shows a book on Fortran, one of the first coding languages, to the rest of the women in the African-American 'West Area Computers' group. They all skill-up so that when the IBM computers arrive to 'take their jobs', they're ready to step straight into new roles, controlling their machine replacements.

The women I speak to can all see the short-term, medium-term and long-term effects of women being in CTRL, en masse.

It's not just about stepping straight into new jobs as the old ones disappear.

Sharmadean Reid of Beautystack said we'd see 'products which are truly designed from a diverse mindset, like buttons for smaller fingers'. Devices that work in women's hands and designs for our bodies, rather than, for example, PPE that doesn't fit and fails to protect.

We'll also know that women are in CTRL when innovation comes out, serves all of us and we're no longer an afterthought when it comes to new products. This aligns with historian Mar Hicks's view: 'Seeing women in positions where they have a technical background but are now influencing policy and legislation across the next decade. This is where we're heading.'

Ghislaine is excited to see women take on the 'strength and ability to own a multi-identity and be themselves in different forms in different places, as needed'. Imagine, she asks of us, having the 'courage, inspirational thinking, curiosity and intelligence of women distributed through the physical and virtual worlds. And all of this whilst being owned by the women themselves.'

Deborah is looking forward to women in CTRL meaning women collectively feeling more rested, with sustainable lifestyles: 'I think of a working mother who has more control of day-to-day life using technology. She uses her fitness tracker on a run, then is able to check her good smartphone once in the office, getting the right emails and without unnecessary struggle, because she's used the tools to create balance in her life.'

Longer-term, women being in CTRL might mean that we look back at this period of history in disbelief. Jenny is looking forward to a time when we don't even talk about these issues any more, and girls are picking technical routes 'without much fanfare'.

Savinay sums it up succinctly. We'd see 'more balance across so many fields, in ways we probably can't even think of. Widening participation and differing perspectives will fundamentally change entire fields of discovery as we know them.'

•

When I left my tech job to go full-time at Stemettes, it was after a few months of soul searching. At work, my managers, mentors and a few peers had spent a huge amount of time begging me not to go. They almost managed to convince me that if I left to run a social enterprise, I'd be completely losing the technical nature of my career. Running tech events and being in the tech third sector wasn't authentically technical enough, they told me.

It didn't take me long to figure out that with technical roles, you can either stay in the technicality and 'deep tech' of what's going on, or you can take alternative routes. Many of the folk trying to convince me to 'stay technical' were in management and quite far from the frontlines of coding, doing technical research and experimentation, writing code, project management, solving errors and handling exceptions, technical troubleshooting and error messages – the technical coalface! Elitism isn't unique to the technology world, but is so deep-rooted that you will certainly encounter opposition regardless of the route you choose. See this as a journey, with different points and stops along the way. So much of it is new that whatever journey you go on, you'll end up somewhere you never would have imagined.

Looking back, I knew when I was at university that one day

I wanted to be an entrepreneur. I didn't know that social entrepreneurship would be for me, or that it would even allow me to pay more than one salary. I had no idea there was a tech third sector or that many of the projects I now work on were options for gainful employment. Those same people who wanted to make me feel as if I was losing my technical kudos are the same ones who are now telling me excitedly how inspired their children are about their tech futures, thanks to Stemettes.

It's your control, your agency, your choice, your curiosity and your journey. Don't let anyone make you feel like your choices led by curiosity are poor ones, or that they will ruin your career. You have to make mistakes to be able to learn from them. Every step is an opportunity to learn, and the freedom you have in making those calculated choices is a big form of CTRL.

When we run Stemette sessions and young people realize that dividers put up between themselves and tech – or between subjects such as art and tech – aren't real, it's really gratifying to see. They realize that a love for the environment can be reflected in working at the right kind of energy company on tech systems that minimize energy usage. They see the options available to them for what they can do next – in a way that parents, teachers and the media haven't been able (or sometimes willing) to convey. They see how biology and technology come together in biotech. They see how financial companies can be started to do good with money, rather than just focusing on making more of it.

The choices are endless. Having said that, it won't be an adventure without obstacles. It won't be without mistakes, and parts of it won't be without encountering resistance. Even nowadays, the horror stories from women doing technical things are many and far-reaching.[1] You'll hear these stories in the communities you join – about being chronically undermined; having your ideas ignored or stolen; being sexually harassed by people who are supposed to be in positions of power in your department; or being 'doxxed', so that you are attacked not only by one person, but your detractor will encourage others to come after you as well. There will also be the classic mansplaining about the things you do in your job every day, and let's not forget being overlooked for promotion, again and again and again. You'll have some frustrating, infuriating experiences along the way. They'll knock your confidence. They'll leave you with imposter syndrome. You'll have to do things that are tough and uncomfortable, and will make you fearful or unconfident.

But herstory tells us that it'll be worth it.

Peace, aimafidon

Glossary

It might seem as if the world of tech comes with its own language, and any newcomer to the field might be thrown by the sheer amount of jargon and strange terminology. The list that follows will hopefully serve as a useful guide as you navigate the landscape of unfamiliar terms and acronyms. Not all of them will be found in this book, but are included to give you a helping hand.

2FA Two-factor authentication. Using two different methods to be able to log in to a service. You might enter a password on the website then receive a text message to your mobile device with a one-time passcode that you also need to enter within a particular timeframe.

3D printing Creating a physical object from a digital model of it. You can print in all kinds of materials, from metals to silicon, to plastic to food. See page 76.

4G Fourth-generation cellular network – common across the UK in 2022. Higher speeds than 3G.

5G Fifth-generation cellular network. Higher speeds possible than the 4G network. Introduced in 2019 and still being rolled out in 2022.

A/B testing Being able to show to users different versions of the same product, in order to determine which version is most effective, or ascertain the ways that users react differently to the versions.

Agile A framework for building tech products that is very flexible and allows you to build iteratively, change direction and add features. See page 251.

Algorithm A series of instructions that can be followed to produce a particular output. Can be very simple – a few steps with one outcome – or incredibly complex – making several calculations and comparisons to create several outcomes.

Alpha testing   The first set of tests you do when creating a tech product, as the person who is creating the product. Followed by beta testing.

API   Application Programming Interface. A pre-agreed, well-defined way that two pieces of software can 'talk' to each other and share information, so they can work together or be connected. For example, the Google Maps API allows you to build software that uses the information in their maps.

App   Short for application. Commonly refers to software on a mobile device. Each app performs a particular set of functions, as defined and created by its developer. Could be any piece of software on any type of device.

AR   Augmented Reality. An extra layer – sounds, videos or images – on the real world, experienced through technology. Quite a lot of social-media filters operate this way. Your face is in the real world, and the bunny ears you can see on your head on the screen have 'augmented' reality.

AI   Artificial Intelligence is the field of computing that aims to emulate the level of intelligence humans display when making decisions. Specialized intelligence is what we have – where AI can make decisions in particular situations, such as during a game of chess or when driving a vehicle. General intelligence is where AI can make decisions across a number of realms, like humans do.

Autonomous vehicle   A vehicle that is able to control and direct itself without human intervention. Driverless cars are an example of an autonomous vehicle.

Avatar   A virtual representation of a person. Could be 2D – like a profile picture – or a 3D model, used for virtual worlds.

Backend   The part of a tech system that does the processing of information. Opposite of the frontend.

Backlog   A list of additional features or improvements that are due to be added to a tech product. Almost like the to-do list of things you still need to complete. Organized and visible to the entire tech team, so the work can be prioritized, shared . . . and carried out.

Beta testing   Testing a tech product with a sample of target users. Normally done after alpha testing, and before release (or further testing). When a product is in beta it means that you're using it to help test it.

Big data   Working with huge datasets that are collected quickly and on a large scale, and therefore difficult to process and understand using simple spreadsheet software or by hand.

Bitcoin   A (digital) cryptocurrency that has value due to a limited supply and a lot of interest. Recognized in El Salvador as legal tender. Not backed by a central bank like normal currencies are. See page 79.

Blockchain   A digital ledger that is tamper-proof and widely viewable. Typically stores transactions, but this technology can be used to track pretty much anything. See page 79.

Browser   Software used to view and navigate the World Wide Web. Examples include Microsoft Edge, Mozilla Firefox, Apple Safari, Brave and Google Chrome.

BYOD   Bring Your Own Device. Work technology used to be issued by employers and was meant to be used for work purposes only, to protect data and ensure employees had access to the same technology. However, BYOD policy allows you to bring your own devices and securely host work information on them.

Cache   Temporary memory used by your computer to hold things that might be reused again in the short term.

Certification   Courses and qualifications specific to a particular technology company's set of products and frameworks. Popular certifications are Cybersecurity, Databases, Agile, Coding and DevOps. Popular providers are Cisco, Salesforce and Microsoft.

Characters   A symbol, letter, number, punctuation, space, sign or mark that can be displayed. Character counts and character limits can be incredibly useful to help enforce security and provide structure.

Cloud (cloud-based)   Rather than storing information and data on your own devices and hardware that you own physically – and being restricted by their capacity and location – you can store them on someone else's cluster of devices. This means that you don't need to carry out maintenance and only pay for the storage you're using, while you use it.

CMS Content Management System. Software used to manage, store and modify digital content, such as text, images, videos and sound, usually for the purposes of websites. WordPress, Squarespace, Wix, Shopify and Drupal are popular CMSs.

Coding The act of writing programming languages that are understandable by computers.

Commit To add changes to a coding project (usually refers to GitHub).

Cookie A file stored on your computer by a website, in order for it to recognize you. Can last anywhere from a few hours to a few months. Cookies are what allow retail sites to remember what's in your shopping basket, and membership sites to keep you logged in.

CRM Customer Relationship Manager. Software that allows a company to keep track of communications with its customers (and future customers). Essentially used for orders, marketing and purchase aftercare.

Cryptocurrency Digital currencies that are backed by a complex algorithm and a decentralized system (not a central bank), and are intentionally difficult to fake or tamper with. Available from crypto exchanges and crypto brokers. They can be traded in the same way that stocks are, and their value fluctuates wildly.

CSS Cascading Style Sheets. Used on the web to 'style' pages – from the colours and fonts used, right through to the way elements are laid out across a webpage. The online web tutorial website W3Schools (www.w3schools.com) has the lowdown on all things CSS.

Cyber All things digital.

Cybersecurity Relating to securing digital assets and spaces. Covers a range of types of defences, and circumstances to be defended from. Wide field of work, study and innovation.

Dataset A collection of information in a form that is easy for a computer or algorithm to process.

DDoS Distributed Denial of Service. A type of cyber attack where several requests are made on one particular service, network or server (perhaps a website) at the same time, overloading it and stopping legitimate users from being able to access the service. A bit like making reservations for every table at a restaurant, then not showing up, so the restaurant isn't able to accommodate genuine, paying diners.

Decryption   The opposite of encryption – unscrambling a message that has been secured. Normally done by using a decryption algorithm, involving a key.

Deterministic   The logic that the same input will always result in the same output. It's the repeatability we see across so much of computer science, and which has cemented our reliance on technology. Two iPhone models work the same way, and typing a letter on the keyboard will always produce the same letter on the screen.

Encryption   To securely scramble a message so that even if it is seen by someone who is not the intended recipient, they cannot interpret what the message says. Normally achieved using an encryption algorithm and a key.

Field   The boxes in a form, often represented as a column in the table of information collected from a form.

GDPR   General Data Protection Regulation. A set of provisions, principles and rights to protect people's data from being used in ways they have not consented to. The aim is to preserve privacy in an increasingly digital world where data is constantly being collected, stored, transferred and used. Enforced by the ICO in the UK, with equivalent regulations across the world.

GIF   Graphic Interchange Format. A way of storing an image that also allows for animated images. Pronounced 'jif'. Has become a way of communicating far more than what words are able to convey. If a picture is worth a thousand words, then a GIF might be worth millions.

GitHub   An online repository for (mostly coding) projects that allows for open collaboration. Allows users to view a history of edits to the project and documentation relating to it.

Hack/Hackathon/Hack Day   An event where people come together to riff on tech product ideas and build prototypes in a very short space of time. A bit like time spent in garages playing musical instruments, it's non-committal – the worst-case scenario is that you enjoy some time with friends and learn a new chord or technique; best-case scenario is that you create, record and release what becomes an all-time hit. Prizes for hackathon winners vary from cash to technology to jobs. See page 86.

Hashtag   A way to describe a piece of content and group it with other pieces of content of the same type.

HTML   Hypertext Markup Language. The language of the web, understood and interpreted by browsers. Despite not being regarded as a programming language in the traditional sense (as there is no major processing going on), it allows you to 'mark up' content in the way you'd like the browser to display it, so is still a language understood by the computer! See page 17.

http(s)   HyperText Transfer Protocol (secure). The way that information is sent (transferred) across the internet. The secure part ensures the transfer is done in a protected way and is not intercepted by malicious users.

IDE   Integrated Development Environment. Useful software used to write code, which allows you to view mistakes, save your code in the correct format and also run the code to see it work. See page 29.

IoT   Internet of Things. The existence of devices and technology that can connect to the internet and communicate with other devices and technology without the need for constant human interaction. Also referred to as smart technologies. See page 83.

IP address   Internet Protocol address. Every device connected to the internet (or a computer network) is assigned a unique numerical identifier, a bit like a postcode, so that information being sent knows where to go.

Java   A programming language (not related to JavaScript), which is used to create software. Owned and maintained by Oracle.

JavaScript   A programming language, which is not Java, that is often used on the web for the processing and movement of elements.

Latency   The delay between a command being sent and it being executed. Usually a tiny amount of time, but the more data and more complex the command, the greater the latency. Very obvious in games and other high-data scenarios. See page 194.

Library   A set of files and standards that can be reused across different tech projects.

Machine learning   A way of creating algorithms where they 'learn' over time from datasets or outside inputs and refine their decision-making process.

Metadata   Data about a piece of data. For example, most photos have metadata attached to them that includes when and where the image was taken, as well as the camera used. The data itself is the image and the pixels; the metadata is the information *about* the image.

Metaverse   The entire 3D virtual world. Essentially cyberspace. Beyond this, definitions vary and the tech world is still figuring out what this might fully mean in practice.

MVP   Minimum Viable Product. The most basic version of a product that illustrates what it is eventually trying to achieve. Different from a proof of concept in that it is usable by end users.

Nanodegree   Short course that allows you to pick up the basics and foundations of a particular technical skill. Recognized by industry and employers. *See also* Certification.

Native   Used to describe software written in the language of the platform on which it is based, rather than translated for that platform, or even web-based. For example, you can have a Native iOS app that is written in Swift, the iOS language specifically developed by Apple for use on Apple products. You can also use a browser on your iOS device to get the same service, but via the web (written in the language of the web).

Network   A collection of computers connected together in order to share resources. The internet is one example.

NFC   Near Field Communication. Wireless communication between devices that are close to each other.

NFT   Non Fungible Token. Piece of data stored on a blockchain which can be traded.

NLP   Natural Language Processing. A field within computer science that aims to successfully process and understand human languages. This is a challenge, given how many different languages there are, which follow loose rules, contain slang and idioms, and are constantly evolving.

Open source   A style of technology where the source coding behind the technology can be viewed and accessed by anyone. It allows folks to remix the technology, and also ensures it is more secure and robust as it can be tested by anyone.

Optimization   Ensuring something runs very efficiently under a set of defined circumstances. For example, by making optimization tweaks you can adjust an image so that it can be sent quicker, will display better on certain types of screens or can be printed using less ink.

Phishing   Pronounced 'fishing'. A type of cyber attack in which someone pretends to be from a company or reputable organization and 'phishes' for data by asking you to reveal private or sensitive information. The bait is an official-looking communication and your personal data is the fish they're trying to catch.

Pixel   The smallest measurement unit of an image. An image 50 pixels by 50 pixels is square and made up of 2,500 pixels in total.

Podcast   An audio series that you can subscribe to and listen back to as you wish. Usually publicly accessible via podcast platforms, although some are behind paywalls.

Primary key   A unique piece of information for each record (row) in your dataset.

Python   A popular programming language.

QA   Quality Assurance. The process of testing your product to ensure it contains no major bugs or errors and works as intended.

Responsive   Interfaces that adapt to the screen on which they are being viewed. Visiting the same responsive website from a phone, tablet or computer will ensure you can see the information displayed in a way that fits your screen.

Retrospective   Agile term for reviewing work on a tech product at the end of an iteration.

Ruby on Rails   A coding language used mostly for creating complex websites that provide a service.

SaaS   Software as a Service. Instead of buying some software and installing it on your device for ever, you pay on a subscription basis to use it only when you need to, without needing to update it regularly or store it.

Scrum   Agile framework that covers creating a tech product in an interactive way.

SEO   Search Engine Optimization. Tuning your content and/or webpages to ensure they are well received and viewed by search engines, and can be found more easily by web users.

Sprint   Agile term for a smaller timeframe in which smaller tech product goals can be achieved. Also known as iterations.

Stack   The list of technologies that have been used to create a tech product. Usually a collection of programming languages and where the code is located.

Startup   A new company that has been formed to create and distribute a particular set of new tech products.

STEAM   Science, Technology, Engineering, Arts and Maths. A broad field bringing these skill sets together that requires collaboration, creativity and communication.

STEM   Science, Technology, Engineering and Maths. A broad field bringing these skill sets together that enables creativity and altruism.

Terminal   A computer terminal is a device into which you can enter data and commands.

UI   User Interface. The part of an application or computer system that a user sees and interacts with. Well-designed ones make life easy for a user, poorly designed ones harm the efficacy of the system.

UX   User Experience. How a user experiences a tech product and feels about its interface.

Virtual Reality   A combination of audio and visual outputs that allows a human to feel as if they are somewhere else. Commonly in the form of 3D video and audio that reacts to the motion of the user. VR headsets are also common. Has uses across the fields of gaming and work. See page 86.

VPN   Virtual Private Network. A simulated network that allows the device to access resources that its normal network can't get to. Commonly used for accessing (private) work systems from a personal device via the internet, or for accessing information reserved for users in one particular country.

Waterfall   An older style of technology project management that sequentially went through analysis, design, implementation, testing and evaluation stages. Notoriously inflexible.

Web 2.0   The current (2022) version of the World Wide Web. In Web 1.0 users could mostly read information across websites, but not contribute to them. In Web 2.0, users can communicate fairly easily with others across a number of platforms.

Web 3.0   In Web 3.0, the upcoming version of the web, users will be able to communicate freely without being restricted by platforms (so they can easily move their communications from one platform to another) and will be able to earn money for their contributions.

Wiki   A database and website written collaboratively.

Wikipedia   The web's open encyclopedia, which is editable and updated by volunteers.

Wireframe   A sketch of a technical interface that shows where elements such as buttons, headers, images and text will go. Aims to give people an idea of what the product will look like.

www   The World Wide Web – a part of the internet where information is stored in webpages and can be easily navigated by users. Accessed via a web browser.

Zip   A way to compress at least one large file or folder into one smaller file. Named because 'to zip' means to move at high speeds.

Recommended Reading, Watching and Listening

Introduction

Read
- Everyday Sexism Project: www.everydaysexism.com

Chapter 1: Be Curious

Watch
- *The Gadget Show*
- BBC *Click*

Listen
- *Women Tech Charge* podcast
- *Techish* podcast
- *Digital Planet* podcast

Also try out the following note-taking apps and search engines:
- Evernote
- Google Keep
- Microsoft OneNote
- Notion
- Trello
- Ecosia
- DuckDuckGo
- Bing

Chapter 2: Choose to Engage

Read

- Essential Digital Skills Framework; https://www.gov.uk/government/publications/essential-digital-skills-framework/essential-digital-skills-framework
- Institute of Coding; https://instituteofcoding.org
- Learn My Way; https://www.learnmyway.com
- Lloyds Bank Academy; https://www.lloydsbankacademy.co.uk
- The Skills Toolkit; https://nationalcareers.service.gov.uk/find-a-course/the-skills-toolkit

Chapter 3: Whose Gate Is It Anyway?

Read

- Chang, E., *Brotopia: Breaking Up the Boys' Club of Silicon Valley* (Portfolio, 2018)
- Cheng, E., *X+Y: A Mathematician's Manifesto for Rethinking Gender* (Profile Books, 2020)
- Saini, A., *Inferior: How Science Got Women Wrong* (Fourth Estate, 2017)
- Free Tech Books; https://www.freetechbooks.com

Watch

- *Bombshell: The Hedy Lamarr Story*, dir. Dean, A. (USA, 2017)
- Develop With Amina Aweis; https://www.youtube.com/c/DevelopwithAmina
- Jennifer Opal; https://www.youtube.com/c/JenniferOpal
- Lenora Porter; https://www.youtube.com/channel/UCfxFXSW7jbecnoE5zdRup5Q

Also search YouTube for [insert your own particular interest] tutorials. On Instagram follow the Intro to Tech, Women in Tech crew. Start with HerHelloWorld (@herhelloworld) and BecomingSamantha

(@samimafidon), and go from there, across the hashtags #breakintotech, #technewbie and #workingintech. Also explore the following online learning resources:

- Codecademy; https://www.codecademy.com
- Coursera; www.coursera.org
- Dash by General Assembly; https://dash.generalassemb.ly
- edX, including Harvard's Introduction to Computer Science course, for free; https://www.edx.org/course/introduction-computer-science-harvardx-cs50x
- FutureLearn; www.futurelearn.com
- LinkedIn Learning; https://www.linkedin.com/learning
- SoloLearn: Learn to Code; www.sololearn.com
- Udacity; www.udacity.com
- Udemy; www.udemy.com

Tech Will Save Us (www.techwillsaveus.com) is a company that manufactures DIY gadget kits. Experiment with STEM toys such as (but not limited to) Bare Conductive, Kano, Adafruit and Raspberry Pi.

Chapter 4: The Tech That's Shaping Our World

Read

- Fry, H., *Hello World: How to Be Human in the Age of the Machine* (Doubleday, 2018)
- Goldstaub, T., *How to Talk to Robots: A Girl's Guide to a Future Dominated by AI* (Fourth Estate, 2020)
- ProductHunt; www.producthunt.com

Chapter 5: A Woman's Work

Read

- Criado Perez, C., *Invisible Women: Exposing Data Bias in a World Designed for Men* (Chatto & Windus, 2019)

- Ashby, M., Charnock, A., et al., *Women Invent the Future: A Science Fiction Anthology* (Doteveryone, 2019)
- Shirley, S., *Let It Go* (Acorn Books, 2012)

Watch
- *Black Mirror* (2011– TV series)
- *Doctor Who* (1963– TV series)
- *Knight Rider* (1982 TV series)
- *Terminator 2: Judgment Day*, dir. Cameron, J. (USA, 1991)

Chapter 6: The Herstory of Tech

Read
- Hicks, M., *Programmed Inequality: How Britain Discarded Women Technologists and Lost Its Edge in Computing* (MIT Press, 2017)
- Lee Shetterly, M., *Hidden Figures: The American Dream and the Untold Story of the Black Women Mathematicians Who Helped Win the Space Race* (William Collins, 2017)
- 'The Women and Non-binary People That Inspire Us Here at Stemettes HQ', *Stemettes Zine*; https://stemettes.org/zine/articles-category/profile/

Watch
- *Hidden Figures*, dir. Melfi, T. (USA, 2016)

Chapter 7: The Value of Women

Read
- UN Sustainable Development Goals; https://sdgs.un.org/goals

Chapter 8: Holding Tech Accountable

Read

- O'Neil, C., *Weapons of Math Destruction: How Big Data Increases Inequality and Threatens Democracy* (Penguin, 2016)
- Peters, B., Philip, K., Hicks, M., and Mullaney, T. S. (eds), *Your Computer Is on Fire* (MIT Press, 2021)
- Prescod-Weinstein, C., *The Disordered Cosmos: A Journey into Dark Matter, Spacetime and Dreams Deferred* (Bold Type Books, 2021)
- Saini, A., *Superior: The Return of Race Science* (Fourth Estate, 2019)
- Wachter-Boettcher, S., *Technically Wrong: Sexist Apps, Biased Algorithms and Other Threats of Toxic Tech* (W. W. Norton & Co., 2017)
- *Black Ballad* (via subscription)
- *Gal-dem* (via subscription)

Watch

- *Coded Bias*, dir. Kantayya, S. (USA, 2020)
- Buolamwini, J., 'How I'm Fighting Bias in Algorithms', TEDx Talk, November 2016

Chapter 9: Who Gets to Choose?

Read

- Atcheson, S., *Demanding More: Why Diversity and Inclusion Don't Happen and What You Can Do About It* (Kogan Page, 2021)
- Catlin, K., *Better Allies: Everyday Actions to Create Engaging, Inclusive Workplaces* (Karen Catlin Consulting, 2019)

Watch

- Gebru, T., 'How Can We Stop Artificial Intelligence from Marginalizing Communities?', TEDx Talk, June 2018

Chapter 10: Finding Your Voice

Read
- Osunsade, A., *Dream Big, Hustle Hard: The Millennial Woman's Guide to Success in Tech* (CreateSpace, 2019)
- Stepper, J., *Working Out Loud: For a Better Career and Life* (Ikigal Press, 2015)

Watch
- Develop with Amina; https://www.youtube.com/c/developwith amina
- *Legally Blonde*, dir. Luketic, R. (USA, 2001)

Investigate professional certifications across top-level tech providers such as Salesforce, Microsoft and Cisco.

Chapter 11: Good Tech and Good Habits

Read
- Mozilla, 'Privacy Not Included'; https://foundation.mozilla.org/en/privacynotincluded/

Watch
- *The Social Dilemma*, dir. Orlowski, J. (USA, 2020)

Chapter 12: Be a Change Pioneer

Read
- Martin, G., *Be the Change: A Toolkit for the Activist in You* (Sphere, 2019)
- Agile Manifesto; https://agilemanifesto.org
- YESTEM resources and publications; http://yestem.org

Chapter 13: The Future of Work

Read

- Uviebinené, E., *The Reset: Ideas to Change How We Work and Live* (Hodder & Stoughton, 2021)
- The IFOW Good Work Charter: https://www.ifow.org/publications/the-ifow-good-work-charter
- IFOW Knowledge Hub; https://www.ifow.org/resources/knowledge-hub
- Tech Talent Charter Open Playbook; https://www.techtalentcharter.co.uk/open-playbook

References

Chapter 1: Be Curious

1   Egan, M., Matvos, G., and Seru, A., 'When Harry Fired Sally: The
    Double Standard in Punishing Misconduct', Working Paper
    19-047, Harvard Business School (August 2018). [Available from:
    https://www.hbs.edu/ris/Publication%20Files/19-047_be957781-
    c55c-4be0-994d-a29875374f32.pdf]
2   Sarsons, H., 'Interpreting Signals in the Labor Market: Evidence
    from Medical Referrals', Working Paper (November 2017).
    [Available from: https://scholar.harvard.edu/files/sarsons/files/
    sarsons_jmp_01.pdf]

Chapter 2: Choose to Engage

1   Liptak, A., 'Hawaii Residents Received False Emergency Alert
    About an Incoming Missile', The Verge, 13 January 2018.
    [Available from: https://www.theverge.com/2018/1/13/16888390/
    hawaii-missile-emergency-alert-false-alarm]
2   https://www.gov.uk/government/publications/essential-digital-
    skills-framework/essential-digital-skills-framework
3   Winter, D., 'Top 100 Global Brands 2019: The Full Ranking',
    Financial Times, 11 June 2019. [Available from: https://www.ft.com/
    content/3a3419f4-78b1-11e9-be7d-6d846537acab]
4   Marko M., '29+ Smartphone Usage Statistics: Around the World in
    2021', Leftronic, 7 February 2021. [Available from: https://leftronic.
    com/blog/smartphone-usage-statistics]
5   'The Scully Effect: I Want to Believe ... in STEM', Geena Davis
    Institute on Gender in Media, J. Walter Thompson Intelligence

and 21st Century Fox (2018). [Available from: https://seejane.org/wp-content/uploads/x-files-scully-effect-report-geena-davis-institute.pdf]

6   Buchholz, K., 'Card Over Cash?', *Statista*, 18 January 2018. [Available from: https://www.statista.com/chart/23950/preference-cashless-payment-selected-countries/]

Chapter 3: Whose Gate Is It Anyway?

1   https://www.invent.org/inductees/hedy-lamarr

2   Ash, S., Hinton, L., and Andrews, J., 'Women in Tech: Time to Close the Gender Gap', PwC report (2017). [Available from: https://www.pwc.co.uk/who-we-are/women-in-technology/time-to-close-the-gender-gap.html]

3   Fischer, F., Böttinger, K., Xiao, H., et al., 'Stack Overflow Considered Harmful: The Impact of Copy and Paste on Android Application Security', Fraunhofer Institute for Applied and Integrated Security (2017). [Available from: https://www.aisec.fraunhofer.de/en/stackoverflow.html]

4   Terrell, J., Kofink, A., Middleton, J., et al., 'Gender Differences and Bias in Open Source: Pull Request Acceptance of Women Versus Men', *PeerJ Computer Science* 3:e111 (2017). [Available from: https://doi.org/10.7717/peerj-cs.111]

5   Kelly, D., 'The Real Reason Behind Blue for Boys and Pink for Girls', *The List*, 5 January 2017. [Available from: https://www.thelist.com/32342/real-reasons-behind-blue-boys-pink-girls/]

Chapter 4: The Tech That's Shaping Our World

1   https://cphsolutionslab.dk/en/cases

2   https://www.youtube.com/watch?v=s9nrm8q5eGg

3   'Hackers Take Over Steering from Smart Car Driver', *USA Today* (video), 22 July 2015. [Available from: https://www.youtube.com/watch?v=AdZ8nx6nRfA&ab_channel=USATODAY]

4   https://cutecircuit.com/haute-couture/

5   Higgins, M., 'Geology of the Greek Islands' (University of California Press, 2009).

Chapter 5: A Woman's Work

1 'Mothers on the Lowest Incomes Are Eight Times More at Risk of Losing Their Job Due to School Closures in the UK', Women's Budget Group press release, 7 January 2021. [Available from: https://wbg.org.uk/media/press-releases/mothers-on-the-lowest-incomes-are-eight-times-more-at-risk-of-losing-their-job-due-to-school-closures-in-the-uk/]

2 Wood, Z., 'Richer Sounds Founder Hands Over Control of Hi-fi and TV Firm to Staff', *Guardian*, 14 May 2019. [Available from: https://www.theguardian.com/business/2019/may/14/richer-sounds-staff-julian-richer]

Chapter 6: The Herstory of Tech

1 https://10downingstreet.libsyn.com/international-womens-day-panel-discussion-with-the-prime-minister

2 Schiebinger, L., Davies Henderson, A., and Gilmartin, S. K., 'Dual-career Academic Couples: What Universities Need to Know', Stanford University research study (2008). [Available from: https://gender.stanford.edu/sites/g/files/sbiyhj5961/f/publications/dualcareerfinal_0.pdf]

3 Vincent-Lamarre, P., Sugimoto, C. R., and Larivière, V., 'The Decline of Women's Research Production During the Coronavirus Pandemic', *Nature Index*, 19 May 2020. [Available from: https://www.natureindex.com/news-blog/decline-women-scientist-research-publishing-production-coronavirus-pandemic]

4 https://www.media-diversity.org/additional-files/Who_Makes_the_News_-Global_Media_Monitoring_Project.pdf

5 Kassova, L., 'The Missing Perspectives of Women in Covid-19 News', International Women's Media Foundation Report (September 2020). [Available from: https://www.iwmf.org/wp-content/uploads/2020/09/2020.09.16-FULL-COVID-REPORT.pdf]

6   Kumar, S., 'New Study: Almost 70% of Professional Event Speakers are Male', *Bizzabo*, 1 November 2018. [Available from: https://blog.bizzabo.com/event-gender-diversity-study]

7   https://en.wikipedia.org/wiki/Gender_bias_on_Wikipedia

8   'The Gender Balance of Expert Sources Quoted by UK News Outlets Online', analysis carried out by the Centre for the Study of Media, Communication and Power, King's College London, on behalf of the Global Institute for Women's Leadership (July 2018). [Available from: https://kcl.ac.uk/news/men-nearly-four-times-more-likely-to-be-quoted-in-uk-media-as-an-expert-source]

9   https://en.wikipedia.org/wiki/User:Jesswade88

10 https://en.wikipedia.org/wiki/Special:Contributions/Jesswade88

11 https://en.wikipedia.org/wiki/Women_in_STEM_fields

12 https://en.wikipedia.org/wiki/Wikipedia:WikiProject_Women_in_Red

Chapter 7: The Value of Women

1   Extracted from World Bank President Robert Zoellick's speech at the MDG3 conference, Copenhagen, 25 March 2010.

2   Based on a speech by Jon Lomoy, Director of the OECD's Development Co-operation Directorate, at the Helsinki High-level Symposium, United Nations Development Co-operation Forum, 4 June 2010. [Available from: https://oecd.org/social/gender-development/45704694.pdf]

3   https://community.fitbit.com/t5/Feature-Suggestions/Extend-the-10-day-period-tracker/idi-p/2722339

4   'Buying Power', *Catalyst*, 27 April 2020. [Available from: https://www.catalyst.org/research/buying-power] Extracted from 'Women: Primed and Ready for Progress', Nielsen, 14 October 2019; and 'Beyond the VC Funding Gap: Why VCs Aren't Investing in Diverse Entrepreneurs, How It's Hurting Their Returns, and What to Do About It', Morgan Stanley (2019).

5   Deane, P., *Colonial Social Accounting* (Cambridge University Press, 1953).

6   Kikuchi, L., and Khurana, I., 'The Jobs at Risk Index (JARI)', Autonomy Data Unit, 24 March 2020. [Available from: https://autonomy.work/portfolio/jari/]

7   Ramirez, J., 'The Global Kitchen: A Speech on the Value of Housework Debate', delivered at the InterUniversity Consortium for International Social Development Conference, 23–31 July 1981, Chinese University, Hong Kong. [Edited text available from: https://caringlabor.wordpress.com/2010/10/06/judith-ramirez-the-global-kitchen-a-speech-on-the-value-of-housework-debate/]

8   Funk, C., and Parker, K., 'Women and Men in STEM Often at Odds Over Workplace Equity', Pew Research Center Report, 9 January 2018. [Available from: https://www.pewresearch.org/social-trends/2018/01/09/diversity-in-the-stem-workforce-varies-widely-across-jobs/]

Chapter 8: Holding Tech Accountable

1   Hern, A., 'Twitter Apologises for "Racist" Image-cropping Algorithm', *Guardian*, 21 September 2020. [Available from: https://www.theguardian.com/technology/2020/sep/21/twitter-apologises-for-racist-image-cropping-algorithm]

2   https://twitter.com/colinmadland/status/1307111816250748933

3   https://twitter.com/Abebab/status/1309387357595013120

4   Apostolides, Z., 'Want to Close the Gender Pay Gap? Start with More Women in Stem', *Guardian*, 10 November 2016. [Available from: https://www.theguardian.com/careers/2016/nov/10/want-to-close-the-gender-pay-gap-start-with-more-women-in-stem-careers]

5   https://www.oed.com/view/Entry/196680

6   https://gendershades.org/

7   https://www.sciencemuseumgroup.org.uk/blog/happy-
    birthday-mary-kenner/

8   https://irr.org.uk/research/statistics/criminal-justice/

9   Rahman, K., 'Black Teen Barred from Skating Rink After Facial
    Recognition Camera Misidentified Her', *Newsweek* (video), 15
    July 2021. [Available from: https://www.newsweek.com/black-
    teen-barred-skating-rink-after-facial-recognition-camera-
    misidentified-her-1610023]

10 https://www.ethnicity-facts-figures.service.gov.uk/crime-justice-
    and-the-law/policing/number-of-arrests/latest

Chapter 9: Who Gets to Choose?

1   https://www.ted.com/talks/timnit_gebru_how_can_we_
    stop_artificial_intelligence_from_marginalizing_communities

2   'Mind the Gap: How to Fill the Equality and AI Accountability
    Gap in an Automated World', Institute for the Future of Work
    Report, October 2020. [Available from: https://www.ifow.org/
    publications/mind-the-gap-the-final-report-of-the-equality-
    task-force]

3   https://sifted.eu/articles/uk-vc-sector-diversity-data/

4   'Report on Apple Card Investigation', New York State Department
    of Financial Services, March 2021. [Available from: https://cdn.
    vox-cdn.com/uploads/chorus_asset/file/22392556/rpt_202103_
    apple_card_investigation.pdf]

Chapter 10: Finding Your Voice

1   Allen, K., 'Technology Has Created More Jobs Than It Has
    Destroyed, Says 140 Years of Data', *Guardian*, 18 August 2015.
    [Available from: https://www.theguardian.com/business/2015/
    aug/17/technology-created-more-jobs-than-destroyed-140-
    years-data-census]

2   https://donotpay.com/
3   Ramsey, N., and McCorduck, P., 'Where Are the Women in
    Information Technology?', AnitaB.org, 5 February 2005.
    [Available from: https://www.alejandrobarros.com/wp-content/
    uploads/old_old/Where_are_the_Women_in_Information_
    Technology.pdf]

Chapter 11: Good Tech and Good Habits

1   https://www.statista.com/statistics/289201/household-internet-
    connection-in-the-uk/
2   https://citizenendo.org/
3   Wheaton, O., 'Gym's Computer Assumed This Woman Was a Man
    Because She Is a Doctor', *Metro*, 18 March 2015. [Available from:
    https://metro.co.uk/2015/03/18/gyms-computer-assumed-this-
    woman-was-a-man-because-she-is-a-doctor-5110391/]
4   Palmiter Bajorek, J., 'Voice Recognition Still Has Significant Race
    and Gender Biases', *Harvard Business Review*, 10 May 2019
    [Available from: https://hbr.org/2019/05/voice-recognition-still-
    has-significant-race-and-gender-biases]
5   'Silicon Valley Is Bad at Making Products That Suit Women. That
    Is a Missed Opportunity', *Economist*, 21 November 2019.
    [Available from: https://www.economist.com/leaders/2019/11/21/
    silicon-valley-is-bad-at-making-products-that-suit-women-that-
    is-a-missed-opportunity]
6   https://foundation.mozilla.org/en/privacynotincluded

Chapter 12: Be a Change Pioneer

1   https://www.simplypsychology.org/maslow.html
2   From Usher, D., *The Economics of Voting: Studies of Self-interest,
    Bargaining, Duty and Rights* (Routledge, 2016).

Chapter 13: The Future of Work

1   'Recession and Automation Changes Our Future of Work, But There Are Jobs Coming, Report Says', World Economic Forum Press Release, 20 October 2020. [Available from: https://www.weforum.org/press/2020/10/recession-and-automation-changes-our-future-of-work-but-there-are-jobs-coming-report-says-52c5162fce/]

2   Dizikes, P., 'How Many Jobs Do Robots Really Replace?', *MIT News*, 4 May 2020. [Available from: https://news.mit.edu/2020/how-many-jobs-robots-replace-0504]

3   Perez, C., 'Creepy Facebook Bots Talked to Each Other in a Secret Language', *New York Post*, 1 August 2017. [Available from: https://nypost.com/2017/08/01/creepy-facebook-bots-talked-to-each-other-in-a-secret-language/]

4   van Eerd, R., and Guo, J., 'Jobs Will Be Very Different in 10 Years. Here's How to Prepare', World Economic Forum, 17 January 2020. [Available from: https://www.weforum.org/agenda/2020/01/future-of-work/]

5   Schwab, K., 'The Fourth Industrial Revolution: What It Means, How to Respond', World Economic Forum, 14 January 2016. [Available from: https://www.weforum.org/agenda/2016/01/the-fourth-industrial-revolution-what-it-means-and-how-to-respond/]

6   https://www.youtube.com/watch?v=H6Z2n7BhMPY

7   'The Good Work Charter', Institute for the Future of Work Policy Brief, 18 October 2018. [Available from: https://www.ifow.org/publications/the-ifow-good-work-charter]

8   'Mind the Gap: How to Fill the Equality and AI Accountability Gap in an Automated World', Institute for the Future of Work Report, October 2020. [Available from: https://www.ifow.org/publications/mind-the-gap-the-final-report-of-the-equality-task-force]

9   'Machine Learning Case Studies', Institute for the Future of
    Work, February 2020. [Available from: https://uploads-ssl.webflow.
    com/5f57d40eb1c2ef22d8a8ca7e/5f71c9db66c3a40e386010b3_
    IFOW-Machine%2Blearning%2Bcase%2Bstudies.pdf]

10 'Terror on Flight QF72: "I'm Not in Control of This Plane"', *New
    Zealand Herald*, 18 June 2018. [Available from: https://www.
    nzherald.co.nz/world/terror-on-flight-qf72-im-not-in-control-of-
    this-plane/PT5BYNBOHMDZC26STD4DJOXA7E/]

11 Taddonio, P., 'In 737 Max Crashes, Boeing Pointed to Pilot
    Error – Despite a Fatal Design Flaw', *Frontline*, 14 September
    2021. [Available from: https://www.pbs.org/wgbh/frontline/article/
    video-clip-boeing-737-max-crashes-fatal-design-flaw-
    documentary/]

12 Condliffe, J., 'US Pilots Forget How to Fly Manually, Says
    Department of Transportation', *Gizmodo*, 13 January 2016.
    [Available from: https://gizmodo.com/u-s-pilots-forget-how-to-
    fly-manually-says-department-1752668219]. 'Enhanced FAA
    Oversight Could Reduce Hazards Associated with Increased Use
    of Flight Deck Automation', Federal Aviation Administration
    Report AV-2016-013, 7 January 2016. [Available from: https://www.
    oig.dot.gov/sites/default/files/FAA%20Flight%20Decek%20
    Automation_Final%20Report%5E1-7-16.pdf] See also Doran, M.,
    'Qantas Flight 72: Captain Kevin Sullivan Saves 315 People on
    Board', 7news.com.au, 2 June 2016 [Available from: https://7news.
    com.au/spotlight/captain-kevin-sullivan-saves-315-people-on-
    board-qf72-c-138996] and 'Former Pilot Warns Against
    Increasing Aeroplane Automation', RN Breakfast with Patricia
    Karvelas, 24 May 2019 [Available from: https://www.abc.net.au/
    radionational/programs/breakfast/former-pilot-warns-against-
    increasing-aeroplane-automation/11145262]

13 https://www.historyofinformation.com/detail.php?entryid=4108

14 Hunt, E., 'Tay, Microsoft's AI Chatbot, Gets a Crash Course in
    Racism from Twitter', *Guardian*, 24 March 2016. [Available from:
    https://www.theguardian.com/technology/2016/mar/24/tay-
    microsofts-ai-chatbot-gets-a-crash-course-in-racism-from-
    twitter]

15 Gaucher, D., Friesen, J., and Kay, A. C., 'Evidence that Gendered
    Wording in Job Advertisements Exists and Sustains Gender
    Inequality', *Journal of Personality and Social Psychology*, 101:1
    (2011), 109–28. [Available from: https://gap.hks.harvard.edu/
    evidence-gendered-wording-job-advertisements-exists-and-
    sustains-gender-inequality]

Conclusion

1   https://specopssoft.com/blog/women-in-tech-reveal-biggest-
    challenges-they-face/

Acknowledgements

This book, my first one for an adult audience, has been a roller-coaster. I'd like to thank Claire Conrad, who kickstarted this chapter in my life; Sam Bailey and Michael Levey, who kicked it round for me; and Omotola Haskell and Carl Hazeley, who were instrumental in the early stages. Thanks, of course, to my publishers at Transworld – Andrea Henry, Helena Gonda and Susanna Wadeson – who were all incredibly patient with me. Shoutout to the remaining members of Team AMI – Zelica Jones, Angela Sheehan and Ronke Lawal, who keep things tickety-boo in my life, and did so even when I had to disappear for months to get this done.

Huge thanks go to Timandra Harkness and Arzu Tahsin, who held my hands tightly when I needed it, and to the editors at Transworld who completely rejigged my disparate thoughts on paper. Big thanks to my top researcher, Nyasha Duri, who was assisted by Paula Imafidon, and to cheerleaders Sharmadean Reid, Emma-Ashley Liles and Vanessa Vallely. And to designer Michaela Hope, who designed an elite cover, as I'd asked for.

Of course, Team Stemettes were incredibly excited and posi-tive throughout the time I spent writing – my two fellow execs, Charlotte Pascual and Yasmin Lodhi, and team managers Julia Piekarczyk and Lucy Cox. To the partners, supporters and vol-unteers at Stemettes over the years – thanks for believing in this message. To the young people who have trusted Stemettes with time in their formative years, and who inspire me on a daily basis to continue with this mission and on this journey.

My interviewees across the book and the podcast – thank you – for your time and for your insight: Alice Bentinck, Ghislaine Boddington, Eugenia Cheng, Noémie Elhadad, Jenny Griffiths, Sunita Grote, Mar Hicks, Emma Lawton, Deborah Okenla, Tobi Oredein, Anisah Osman Britton, Abadesi Osunsade, Billie Quinlan, Savinay Sood, Sharmadean Reid and Check Warner. Thanks also to the team at the *Evening Standard*, who have backed the three seasons (and counting) of *Women Tech Charge*, which inspired so much of the content in this book, and to our listeners, who showed it was info worth sharing.

To the chorus of herstorical women who took the steps before we did and who inspire me every day with what they achieved in less-than-stellar circumstances. To those women who did their bit for the tech world of today and who created the space that allows me to thrive to this day. Thank you, Hedy, Stephanie, Gladys and Marie-Sophie.

Finally, to my family and friends, who I love and who applied pressure where needed in this process. To my siblings – I'm excited to see your writing debuts. To my dad – I'm sorry my face isn't on the cover. To my husband, Welshy – you're the best.

Index

About the Author

Dr Anne-Marie Imafidon is a keynote speaker, leader and creator of the award-winning social enterprise Stemettes, which engages, inspires and connects the next generation of women and non-binary people into the science, technology, engineering and maths field. A recognized and respected thought-leader in the tech space, in 2017 she was awarded an MBE for services to young women and STEM sectors. In 2020 she was voted the most influential woman in tech in the UK by *Computer Weekly*.